PRAISE FOR *DEVELOPING EMPLOYABILITY AND ENTERPRISE*

'It's great to read a book that tackles the big employability skills issue. Being able to get hints, tips and techniques from mentors and business people will help the next generation to become more employable.'
Ben Dyer, MD and Co-Founder, National Enterprise CIC

'In my experience, across education and training, an individual's mental toughness is the differentiator between success and failure in their development, but more importantly their access to and success in future opportunities and career development. Charlotte and Doug are spot on with their articulation of the importance of mental toughness in employability.'
Mark Dawe, CEO, AELP

'There are already a lot of really good books on the market that aim to offer their readers some sound advice about developing employability skills – what makes this one any different? It tackles the underpinning issues, from individuals lacking motivation or focus to really understanding what skills employers want. Written in a concise, conversational, and persuasive way, it's like having a toolkit to employability success at your fingertips.'
Shane Mann, Managing Director, Lsect Ltd – publisher of *Schools Week* and *FE Week*

'Success is all about people and a little luck! This book gives a superb insight into employability within education and how, with the right coaching strategies, you can enrich both the next generation and your enterprise.'
Christopher Nieper, MD, David Nieper Ltd and founder, David Nieper Educational Trust

'Developing students' behaviours and the attributes needed to thrive in a 21st-century workplace is an essential part of the education experience. This book goes beyond the traditional employability of CVs and job applications, giving practical guidance in mentoring individuals to be confident, motivated and develop mental resilience.'
Jatinder Sharma OBE, Principal and Chief Executive, Walsall College

'The transition from school to work is one of the toughest challenges facing most young people. Understanding how to develop the skills and mindset needed to improve success is key. Charlotte and Doug are experts in their field and have really got to the heart of the subject in this book.'
Laura-Jane Rawlings, Founder, Youth Employment UK

Developing Employability and Enterprise

Coaching strategies for success in the workplace

Doug Strycharczyk and
Charlotte Bosworth

Publisher's note

Every possible effort has been made to ensure that the information contained in this book is accurate at the time of going to press, and the publishers and authors cannot accept responsibility for any errors or omissions, however caused. No responsibility for loss or damage occasioned to any person acting, or refraining from action, as a result of the material in this publication can be accepted by the editors, the publisher or any of the authors.

First published in Great Britain in 2016 by Kogan Page Limited

Apart from any fair dealing for the purposes of research or private study, or criticism or review, as permitted under the Copyright, Designs and Patents Act 1988, this publication may only be reproduced, stored or transmitted, in any form or by any means, with the prior permission in writing of the publishers, or in the case of reprographic reproduction in accordance with the terms and licences issued by the CLA. Enquiries concerning reproduction outside these terms should be sent to the publishers at the undermentioned addresses:

2nd Floor, 45 Gee Street	1518 Walnut Street, Suite 1100	4737/23 Ansari Road
London	Philadelphia PA 19102	Daryaganj
EC1V 3RS	USA	New Delhi 110002
United Kingdom		India

© Doug Strycharczyk and Charlotte Bosworth 2016

The right of Doug Strycharczyk and Charlotte Bosworth to be identified as the authors of this work has been asserted by them in accordance with the Copyright, Designs and Patents Act 1988.

ISBN   978 0 7494 7847 6
E-ISBN 978 0 7494 7848 3

British Library Cataloguing-in-Publication Data

A CIP record for this book is available from the British Library.

Library of Congress Control Number

2016953529

Typeset by Graphicraft Limited, Hong Kong
Print production managed by Jellyfish
Printed and bound by CPI Group (UK) Ltd, Croydon CR0 4YY

CONTENTS

List of Figures ix
List of Tables xi
Editors, Authors and Contributors xiii
Acknowledgements xix

01 Why employability? i
Why is employability so important 1

02 The growing importance of employability 17
Schools 17
Offenders 25
Enterprise and entrepreneurship 28

03 Models of employability 31
CARRUS – essential behaviour-orientated attributes 33
Mental Toughness 43
Control 46
Commitment 47
Challenge 49
Confidence 51
Mental Toughness – its relationship with enterprise and employability 52
Case Study – Manchester Metropolitan University 56
The CareerEDGE model of graduate employability 57
Measuring graduate employability 61
Case Study 1 – University of Lancaster 63
Case Study 2 – University of Central Lancashire 64

04 Developing employability and enterprise 67
More than qualifications 68
Changes in labour market and workplace 69
More resilient and self-confident 72
Positive impact 76

Contents

05 Developing mental readiness for the world of work 81
Preparation 82
Careers Lab 84
Barclays Bank 84
Bradford Pathways 85
Career WorkOut 87

06 A clear line of sight to work 93
A wonderful learning environment 94
Conversations make a difference 95
Demystifying soft skills 95
Five lessons that we have learned 98

07 Self-confidence and inter-personal skills 101
OCR's project approach 102
Volkswagen Group UK and the Outward Bound Trust 103
BAE Systems and the Outward Bound Trust 103
The Luminary Bakery project 104

08 The best choices for jobs, careers and study 109
Why is this important? 109
RACPAC 110
Analyse to consider Alternatives 114

09 Presenting personal information for employers 119
The start of the journey 119
Second chance education 125
Working with people who are seeking a career change 127

10 Selection: interviews and assessments centres/tests 131
Assessment centres and psychometric measurement 131
The interview 133
After the interview: what's next? 139

11 Work placements and internships 141
The apprenticeship route 141
University work placements 142
Internships 143

Contents

12 Delivering effective work experience 147
When to do it 148
What to do 149
Who does it? 149
How to do it 151

13 Enterprise: more than being Richard Branson 155
NACUE (National Association of College and University Entrepreneurs 156
Case Study 1: Northbrook College 158
Case Study 2: Westminster Kingsway College 159
Case Study 3: Uxbridge College 160
Case Study 4: Chichester College 160
Case Study 5: Newcastle under Lyme College 163
Case Study 6: Student Engine 165

14 Coaching for employability and enterprise 167
The GROW coaching model 169
A case study in coaching using MTQ48 176

15 Developing mindset and mental toughness 181
What can we do about it? 181
Reflection 184
Positive thinking 185
Visualization 188
Anxiety control 189
Goal setting 189
Attentional control 190

16 Global perspectives: China and the Far East 193
Background to Entrepreneurship Education issues 193
Development of Entrepreneurship Education in China 194
Employability Education 197
Education models and methods 198
Likely future trends 200

17   Lifelong learning: responses in the USA   203
More deeply integrated   204
Preparing an increasingly diverse workforce   205
Costly coursework and attendance   208
Initiatives to redesign the community college   208
Four most in-demand competencies   212
Competency-based education   213
A changing outlook   217

18   Employability and enterprise   219
Building the right mindset and unearthing talent   220
Building mental toughness or resilience   221
Case study: Project New Horizons   222
Building strong relationships and networks   223
Case study: Entourage   224
Case study: Launch22   227
Appropriate routes into work: apprenticeships   228
Case study: Care2Work   230

19   Clients with mental health problems   235
Barriers to employability   236
Employability, illness and mental toughness   238
Assessing mental toughness through the MTQ48   243

20   The role of sport   251
A metaphor for life   251
Case study: Manchester United Foundation   255
Case study: London Youth Rowing   260
Looking forward   266

Index   269

LIST OF FIGURES

FIGURE 3.1	Active problem solving	35
FIGURE 3.2	Organization and continuous improvement	35
FIGURE 3.3	Conscientiousness and standards	36
FIGURE 3.4	Growing capability and achieving potential	36
FIGURE 3.5	Abilities, motivation, skills, problems	40
FIGURE 3.6	Your Carrus Profile	41
FIGURE 3.7	Assertiveness	42
FIGURE 3.8	Mental Toughness: sample scores	54
FIGURE 3.9	Coaching and assesser report sample	55
FIGURE 3.9(2)	Suggested questions	55
FIGURE 3.10	CareerEDGE graduate employability	58
FIGURE 4.1	New Horizons, social ROI	77
FIGURE 6.1	The STEPS framework	97
FIGURE 8.1	Force Field Analysis	115
FIGURE 14.1	GROW coaching model	169
FIGURE 15.1	Kolb learning styles model	183
FIGURE 17.1	Job openings by 2020	205
FIGURE 17.2	The need for post-secondary education	207
FIGURE 17.3	Earnings and unemployment rates	210
FIGURE 17.4	Student expenses	211
FIGURE 19.1	Barriers to employment	237
FIGURE 19.2	Wanting to work	240
FIGURE 19.3	Is your health conditioned managed?	240
FIGURE 19.4	STEN score distribution	244
FIGURE 19.5	Declared health conditions	245
FIGURE 19.6	Gender	246
FIGURE 19.7	Jobseeking behaviour and well-being	246
FIGURE 19.8	Self-assessment scores	247
FIGURE 19.9	Out of a black hole	248

FIGURE 19.10	Low STEN score	249
FIGURE 19.11	Before and after	249
FIGURE 20.1	Engage, inspire, unite	256
FIGURE 20.2	Breaking barriers	261
FIGURE 20.3	4Cs mental toughness model	262
FIGURE 20.4	Monitoring and measurement	264

LIST OF TABLES

TABLE 1.1	Attributes managers look for	9
TABLE 1.2	Problem areas managers face	10
TABLE 1.3	Skills managers want most	10
TABLE 2.1	Behaviours and attitudes	23
TABLE 3.1	Mental Toughness and MTQ48	45
TABLE 3.2	Key employability competencies	53
QUESTIONNAIRE CH 3	The CareerEDGE questionnaire	62
TABLE 4.1	Skills to improve resilience and well-being	71
TABLE 4.2	Education, Employment and Training rates	78
TABLE 4.3	Achievement of Qualifications	78
TABLE 4.4	Rate of churn between NEET and EET	79
TABLE 12.1	When work experience was done	148
TABLE 12.2	Relevant experience	150
TABLE 16.1	Development of Chinese Entrepreneurship Education	196

EDITORS, AUTHORS AND CONTRIBUTORS

Doug Strycharczyk

Doug is the CEO of AQR International Ltd which he founded in 1989 – now recognized as one of the most innovative test publishers in the world.

Doug's expertise includes development of Psychometric Tests and Programmes – playing a key role in developing the MTQ48, CARRUS and ILM72. The first two have emerged as important models and measures within employability and enterprise. Directly and indirectly AQR is now involved in major employability projects around the world.

Doug has pioneered the application of the mental toughness concept to any sector where individuals face challenge or stressors. He is now recognized as one of the leading authorities worldwide on the application of the model. Doug works in the Occupational World, Education, Social Work, Sports and Health.

Doug co-authored, *Developing Resilient Organizations* (Kogan Page 2014) with Charles Elvin, CEO ILM. He also co-authored *Developing Mental Toughness – Coaching Strategies to Improve Performance, Resilience and Wellbeing* (Kogan Page 2015) with Professor Peter Clough.

Doug has co-authored with Peter Clough chapters in the following leading books:

- *Psychometrics in Coaching* (2009) (Kogan Page & Association for Coaching)
- *Leadership Coaching* (2010) (Kogan Page & Association for Coaching)
- *Coaching in Education* (2011)

Doug holds a first class honours degree in Economics. Email Doug at doug@aqr.co.uk

Doug has established the AQR Foundation which supports individuals during their development, who would otherwise be held back for economic, social or family reasons. All Doug's royalties go to the Foundation.

Charlotte Bosworth

Charlotte Bosworth is a Director of OCR (Oxford, Cambridge and RSA) and has responsibility for vocational provision focused on qualifications to prepare young people, the unemployed, offenders and disadvantaged adults for the world of work and employment.

She is also a Commissioner for The Skills Commission Cross Parliamentary Group which feeds into the manifestos for all political parties. Charlotte is also an adviser for the All Parliamentary Group for Apprenticeships and the All Parliamentary Group for Youth Employment.

In addition, Charlotte is an FE College Governor and works with a number of employers to ensure they can have input into improving education delivered within schools, thereby making sure as many young people as possible are 'work ready'.

Charlotte is passionate about ensuring everyone has the opportunity to gain recognition for their achievements and to become an active member of our society.

The following have contributed their expertise and their experience in developing employability and enterprise

Kieran Gordon

Kieran Gordon is the Chief Executive of Career Connect. He has 30 years' experience of working with people of all ages as a professionally trained Careers Adviser. Kieran is also a Past President of the Institute of Career Guidance (ICG), and was a member of the UK Career Council.

Dr John Perry

Dr John Perry is a Senior Lecturer in Sport Performance and Coaching at University of Hull. John is a Chartered Psychologist and an accredited Sport and Exercise Scientist. He has a particular interest in the application of sport in the development of life skills for people of all ages.

Professor Peter Clough

Professor Peter Clough is the Chair in Applied Psychology at the Manchester Metropolitan University. Peter is both a Chartered Sport Psychologist and a Chartered Occupational Psychologist. He is mainly focused on the application of psychology to performance enhancement.

More specifically, he researches the area of Mental Toughness. This work started in the sports domain but is now used extensively in both business and education.

Philippa Harrison

Philippa Harrison is the Quality Assurance Manager at the Manchester United Foundation and has worked across the Education and Employability divisions of the Foundation for the past six years. She has a BPS-accredited degree in Psychology and is currently completing an MSc in Sport Psychology with her research focused on critical moments in professional football.

Stacey Güney

Stacey Güney is director of the Highland Campus ACCelerator at Austin Community College and an adjunct professor in Mathematics and Student Development. The ACCelerator is a large-scale technology-rich learning environment that is a modern reimagining of the one-room school house.

Dr Jin Quan

Dr Jin Quan is the Deputy Dean of the School of Business at Shanghai University of International Business and Economics (SUIBE) and an Associate Professor of International Business. She is mainly focused on the application of entrepreneurial education to undergraduate students and researches the area of entrepreneurial team and venture performance. She currently teaches Organization Theory, Strategic Management, Entrepreneurship Management and Global Marketing Consulting courses to junior or senior undergraduate students or graduate students.

Serena Bradshaw

Serena Bradshaw is a Performance Coach and Teacher. She is a founding Director of Goddards and specializes in helping people to find work. A significant majority of Goddards' programmes are designed for customers with long-term health conditions, including mental health problems, and the Company uses Mental Toughness as the foundation for this work.

Layal Marten

Layal Marten is currently working at the University of London. Prior to this, she was the Head of Development at London Youth Rowing where she worked on the launch of the *Breaking Barriers* programme from late 2014. Her areas of interest are in developing ways for the non-cognitive attributes gleaned through sport to be used as a signpost to further education, employment and training.

Dr Peter Sewell, CPsychol AFBPsS, FHEA

Peter has wide experience of working with students and graduates, executives, managers, entrepreneurs and creative professionals. He is known for his work on the internationally acclaimed *CareerEDGE* model of graduate employability and the *Employability Development Profile* (EDP) assessment tool, which has been used in many universities in the UK and elsewhere around the world. In 2010 he established LanHai Career Management Ltd, an award-winning career management company which provides business and higher education training, and consultancy services in the UK and China.

Chris Wright

Chris Wright is Chief Executive of social business and charity, Catch22. After training as a probation officer Chris moved into senior roles in the youth justice sector, establishing Nottingham's first multi-agency YOT and then joining the YJB. Chris is a long-standing advocate for the VCSE sector playing a greater role in the delivery of public services. Since joining Catch22 in 2006, he has built the organization's reputation for innovative and collaborative approaches to justice, education, employability and social care.

Millie Shuter

Millie Shuter joined Catch22 from a communications and public affairs consultancy where she specialized in housing, technology and voluntary sector clients. As External Affairs Manager at Catch22, she works closely with senior leaders to build and manage the organization's public profile and reputation. Millie has previously worked in secondary schools as a teaching assistant and for the youth service as a mentor and personal adviser.

Dr Anthony Mann

Dr Anthony Mann is Director of Policy and Research at the Education and Employers Taskforce (www.educationandemployers.org). He is the author of numerous works on employer engagement in education and regularly advises government on the policy area.

Stephen Carrick-Davies

Stephen Carrick-Davies is a social entrepreneur, community leader and is the CEO of the Inclusion Trust. Working directly with 'pushed-out' young people he co-designed the Facework project which focuses on helping those excluded from mainstream school to understand and develop the 'soft' skills needed in the changing world of work.

Tom Bulman

Formerly an English teacher, Tom Bulman has worked for Worktree (formerly Countec EBP) since 1997. He has worked in the Netherlands, USA and Australia, to observe and advise on employer engagement in education. In recent times, he has travelled to Uganda, China and India to deliver employability training and train-the-trainer workshops, and published *Employability Now – a guidebook for teachers and trainers*.

Alice Williams

Alice Williams is the founder of East London's Luminary Bakery. This social enterprise is designed to offer opportunities for disadvantaged women to build a future for themselves and their families. Baking is used as a tool to take women on a journey to employability and entrepreneurship, equipping them with practical and transferable skills for the working world. The aim is to break the generational cycles of abuse, prostitution, criminal activity and poverty, which hold these women back from reaching their potential. The Bakery is now opening its own shopfront premises in Hackney, London. Alice's experience embraces youth work, marketing, café management and supporting women to exit prostitution in Bangkok, Thailand.

Ros Kaijaks

Ros Kaijaks is a Sector Manager for Employability, Enterprise and Entrepreneurship and Traineeship provision at OCR. Ros has been with OCR since 1997, and has been involved in a variety of qualifications including CLAiT, Key and Functional Skills and Higher Apprenticeships. She is also a governor of a local primary school.

Ruth Carter

Ruth Carter is Sector Specialist for Employability, Enterprise and Entrepreneurship at OCR. Ruth works closely with employers, organizations and education providers to support and guide curriculum and programme delivery and development. Much of Ruth's work involves building relationships and interpreting the needs of employers in relation to supporting young people to gain the necessary skills and attitudes for work and life. Ruth also volunteers as an employer guest for Worktree and Inspiring the Future and mentors young people through the RSA Academies Broadening Horizons programme. She is a Fellow of The Royal Society of Arts.

David Summers

David Summers is a Sector Manager at OCR managing a vocational portfolio. He has worked in the education and skills sector for the best part of thirty years in the UK Department of Education & Employment, the Learning & Skills Council and two Sector Skills Councils. David is Chair of the Coventry & Warwickshire Business Class Cluster, part of Business in the Community.

Heather Akehurst

Heather Akehurst is the CEO for Open Awards. Open Awards is a qualification – awarding body whose vision is to change lives through learning by supporting educational achievement for all learners. A highly innovative organization, Open Awards has in 2016 launched a range of Life Skills/Employability Qualifications to support its broader work around the development of young people. Heather's experience embraces being a director of Local Solutions, the Liverpool Welfare to Work programme and the Greater Merseyside Learning and Skills Council. She is also a Career Enterprise Adviser for Liverpool schools.

ACKNOWLEDGEMENTS

Writing this book on Employability and Entrepreneurship has proved to be an epiphany for both of us. We started, as many authors do, through discussion and conversation where we began to identify the extent of change that was happening in this area... and its growing importance. With that came an observation that not everyone who had a role to play in this area was keeping up to date. Hence the book.

Both of us are fortunate to be networked and connected with some remarkable people who are all innovators and experts in some aspect of employability and enterprise development. They are also extremely effective at what they do.

All the contributors to this book come from this cohort.

The upshot is that, while we sought to share our thoughts and observations with the reader, in fact we have both found the process to be a learning journey for us too. Particularly when considering the global picture.

So we give our very grateful thanks to all the contributing authors – they are all stars.

Internally at AQR, we are especially grateful to Doug's colleague Toni Molyneux who worked tirelessly to bring the book to a conclusion.

Finally, Charlotte offers her dedication to her son Brandon who proved that through motivation, hard work and dedication you can achieve your dreams.

Doug offers his to his grandchildren Jay, Charlie, Bella and Axel. This book is very much about their future.

Why employability?   01

**DOUG STRYCHARCZYK AND
CHARLOTTE BOSWORTH**

Why is employability so important and how does it differ from what has gone before?

Providing career guidance to people of all ages, especially for the young person, has always been recognized as important. For much of the 20th century this has focused on supporting people to acquire skills, techniques and approaches that help them to get a job.

This was and remains valuable. People, whether in the world of education or already in the world of work, are often ill-equipped with the skills and experience to write good CVs, to pen letters of application, to prepare for and attend interviews and, increasingly, to cope with the variety of selection approaches adopted by employers – particularly the use of psychometric testing and assessment centres.

However, the advent of the 21st century has seen the emergence of significant structural changes for both individuals and employers. This is particularly the case since the 2008 global financial crisis, although in reality the changes were beginning to be evident before that. They have since accelerated. It is these changes that affect the way that people look at their life and their work opportunities and have changed permanently the way that employers and society see employment.

One of the most fundamental changes has been that individuals in all societies are very different to individuals from previous generations. Observers and social scientists have noted this and it has come to be described as the Generation Y and Generation Z phenomena. Now these are more generally described as the Millennials – including young people who were born immediately before and since the turn of the 21st century and who are now poised to enter the next phase of their lives – either higher education, an apprenticeship programme or seeking some form of employment. Even this more recent generation is different from its immediate predecessors. We also have much more of a focus on ensuring that we are all better members of society and have the ability to adapt to changing communities and to be more globally aware.

Although many employers and educators are now well aware of these differences, a great many are still not clear about what these changes are, what they represent and particularly what they mean for the way they need to deal with the newly emerging employee or student.

So what do these changes look like?

In the first place, generally young people are better educated in the sense that many more go on to further and higher education than ever before. In the UK, the Department for Business, Innovation and Skills showed the proportion of people aged between 17 and 30 who entered the UK Higher Education system in the autumn of 2014 came to 47 per cent of all young people aged 18/19. In 1968, almost 50 years earlier, that figure was around 5 per cent. This trend can be expected to continue.

Digging more deeply into the statistics revealed that by 2014 more than half (51 per cent) of all young women were entering higher education (having overtaken males of whom comparatively fewer, 42 per cent, were entering education). This represents a trend within a trend and will have ramifications into the future. The nature of the gender difference debate may well change.

These trends are also true internationally. OECD reports show an upward trend virtually everywhere. What is observed in the UK is true globally. The picture is one of increasing participation rates and improving education standards – indeed in South Korea participation rates according to the OECD are in the order of 68 per cent (2104), in Canada 58 per cent, Russia also 58 per cent and in the USA 46 per cent.

This matters because, as we will shortly see, well-qualified people are immeasurably more mobile than ever before. Where at one time people would prefer to work close to family and where they were brought up, they are now more likely to work anywhere – including internationally, with its consequences for such things as 'brain drains'. They will go to wherever the opportunity is.

There is also a parallel development – the less well-educated may often be economically and socially immobile for a variety of environmental and socio-economic reasons. Often the target of easy criticism, labelled as 'work shy' or worse, close examination reveals that they can be trapped for reasons not of their making or choosing. In many situations we observe generations of families that have never been actively in employment and where sources of income are provided through the benefit system or through crime. The challenge of employability is different here. It is often about developing aspirations, opening people's minds to opportunities and their own capabilities, and building confidence to do something about that.

Later chapters in the book describe some proactive and highly effective approaches to dealing with many of these challenges. The solutions do need to embrace new thinking. Otherwise, we resign ourselves to creating an underclass with all that this implies and ignoring a potentially valuable and important resource. It is an issue which needs to be addressed for social and economic reasons.

Interesting as they are, these overall figures can mask another set of differences. In the UK, participation rates in further and higher education also varied according to where the young person lived. In some areas, participation rates could reach 80 per cent! In other areas, they could be extremely low – less than 5 per cent.

By far the biggest explanation lies in the environmental and socio-economic factors leading to disadvantage for many, which represents a waste of resources in society as well as unwanted difficulties for the individual. Again, the phenomenon of social mobility and dealing with disadvantage is rising in the political agenda everywhere and is a major consideration when we examine employability.

We still have a hurdle to overcome when reviewing post-16 vocational learning. The introduction of study programmes has encouraged more socio-emotional components but this tends to be in an ad hoc manner, based on qualitative elements; also, it does not focus much on measuring these skills or the results of delivering training with regard to improving them, along with the impact on improving overall academic achievement. Recent evidence on the importance of non-cognitive skills both from econometric and qualitative analyses of determinants of success in the labour market have demonstrated that.

Employers value certain behaviours that are linked to high-productivity workers. While conceptually socio-emotional skills are well defined, it has previously been difficult to measure and analyse them.

When reviewing the employability of people, the focus tends to be almost exclusively on the labour-market impacts such as employment rates, earnings and quality of employment. Often lacking in such reporting are the mechanisms that are supposed to improve an individual's labour-market performance, specifically by increasing the non-cognitive and socio-emotional skills with which they gain employment.

To some extent, these emerging patterns are indicative of the predictions made by Joseph Schumpeter in the early part of the 20th century. Writing in the 1920s he predicted a good deal of what we now see, including that people would become better educated. He theorized that this might create problems because there would not be enough interesting work to satisfy the need of this more able workforce.

What we actually see now is a change in the type of work available to people. The trend is to what is called 'white-collar' work and the shrinkage in manufacturing has been more than compensated for by the growth in service industries.

Despite the increase in the numbers of educated and qualified persons, we still see the paradox of governments and employers talking about skill shortages – particularly in some sectors of the economy.

Digital and better informed

Secondly, the current and most recent generation entering the workforce is usefully described as consisting of 'digital natives' as opposed to 'digital visitors'. They are very different to preceding generations. Just as a young person learns a language naturally because they are brought up in an environment where speaking that language is the norm, so they become familiar and comfortable with new and developing technology in the same way. They are completely at home with technology and technological change.

This brings two immediate and major benefits – their access to knowledge and expertise is in a totally different league from graduates and people of their parents' generation. And they also know how to use technology to do and make things. And given that technological change is a significant factor in determining both the type and pace of change in all economies, this ability to handle technological change is important and valuable.

A digital visitor is like a person who moves to another country and must learn a new language to be able to engage in that society. That language will almost always be a second language for them, involving some loss of fluency. The native speaker will always have the edge over a visitor.

Thirdly, arguably, the millennial generation is better informed about what is happening in the world and the quality of that information is much, much better. Whether this translates into understanding the opportunities that go with better information is perhaps debatable.

Leading up to the end of the 20th century, most people, if they had access to television, would watch news programmes about world events. the news was often several days old and may have been censored and edited. It was difficult to know what was truly happening in the world at any point in time. Now, if something happens on the other side of the globe, someone is there with a camera phone recording it and posting on the world wide web in minutes.

It is dangerous to generalize and it is certainly true that there are many different descriptions of the new 'millennials'. Not only do the definitions vary according to the observer but they differ according to locality. The behaviour of young people in the West appears to be quite different in many ways to that of those in the East although there are indications that these are converging.

Characteristics of the millennial generation

Some interesting patterns are emerging, which had their roots in the development of Gen Z/Y. Today's millennial generation:

- Are much less likely to believe in a 'job for life'. Many don't even want this. They want to do different things at different times.
- Are less likely to be 'loyal' to a company and more likely to be loyal to a person. They will be more inclined to support a good boss who understands their needs. They do not have a belief that any employer can give them 'a job for life'.
- Will look for a job with a purpose that provides intrinsic motivation. Arguably, this is a result of exposure to global news. They seem to have a greater sense of social responsibility than previous generations – and trust politicians much less.
- Are flexible in the way they work and are more adept at multi-tasking. Technology enables them to deal with several things at a time. They will expect equivalent flexibility in the workplace.
- Are often more questioning and less likely to accept what they are told. This is not necessarily a negative. It can be very positive – they are often more likely to question inefficient or ineffective practice that in the past might have gone unchecked.

- Are able to deal with large amounts of data and work quickly. They are generally brighter than previous generations. Arguably they make more errors because of this but they also deal with them better.
- Routinely use social media and expect quick responses when they do so. Waiting for responses to e-mails is not acceptable.
- Learn in a different way. They are less keen on classroom-based learning. They are keener on digital technologies especially those that use visual approaches.
- Prefer to learn by doing. They prefer interactive media rather than passive media (eg watching a TV programme or film). This openness to experiential learning is a big plus but represents a challenge for traditional employers and educators.
- Know how to access global knowledge quickly. Finding out things is rarely a challenge. It's sometimes just a couple of clicks on Google.
- Are used to collaborating with others. They network freely. They don't expect to solve problems on their own.
- Have high expectations – some of which might not be realistic.
- May be very flexible in their thinking and the way they work – and they expect employers to be flexible too.
- Are much more likely to accept diversity wherever they find it.
- Their interest and motivations can be different. One study in 2015 indicated that up to 25 per cent of graduates in the UK consider self-employment and enterprise as an alternative to seeking a job or a career with an employer. Some may choose to build work experience through a short period of employment although self-employment is their goal.
- Are less interested in home ownership – preferring the flexibility that goes with renting (or even living with Mum and Dad for longer).

These are features that are generally positive. At least they are from the young person's perspective (although some have a downside). Many of these features are driven by developments in IT. There are also negative features that some are beginning to identify.

- They are generally less healthy because they spend more time at a desk and on a PC, iPad, etc.
- Their involvement in gaming teaches them when something goes wrong they can put it right by pressing a reset button. Real life doesn't have a reset button.

- Their ability to work quickly can mean they also make more mistakes.
- They will, on average, probably earn less (in real terms) than their parents did over a lifetime.
- Career opportunities will be different. Careers will emerge and others will disappear as society and technology change.

There are other features that others may bring into the picture and some may argue about the features listed above. But the probability is that the new entrants to the workforce are different in knowledge skills and especially mindset to previous generations. And the most important of these is mindset.

Consequently, in fast-changing complex global marketplaces for skills and qualities, the challenge is much greater than just writing a good CV or presenting oneself effectively at interview. It is now much more about a wider understanding of employability. Are there qualities that need to be developed which would ensure my employability now, in the near future and probably in the distant future? The short answer is 'there are' – these are examined more closely next and in some detail in Chapter 3.

Employability defined

Now is a good point to introduce a definition of employability that works from the perspective of the individual.

One of the most widely used definitions is the one developed by Professor Mantz Yorke:

> 'a set of achievements – skills, understandings and personal attributes – that make [a person] more likely to gain employment and be successful in their chosen occupations, which benefits themselves, the workforce, the community and the economy'.

He adds:

> 'Employability is not the same as *gaining* a... job, rather it implies something about the capacity of the individual to *function* in a job and be able to *move between* jobs, thus remaining employable throughout their life'.

And this is the key. Employability is about both securing a role as well as demonstrating within that role that you were worth hiring or recruiting into a role, course of study or for the provision of a service or product. The ultimate transferable skill.

Before we leave the individual's perspective, this lifetime notion is increasingly important. Employability is for people of all ages to consider.

In discussions with Stacey Guney, author of the North American perspective elsewhere in the book she drew our attention to an interesting fact. Of students enrolling on vocational programmes with community colleges in the USA, 25 per cent were aged 50 and over. These were very often individuals who had not only lost their jobs through the 2008 recession but were individuals whose jobs may no longer exist – either because they had been exported or they had disappeared through technological change.

They may possess an advantage as they have work experience. But they still need to demonstrate employability.

Turning now to look at the topic from the employer's perspective, we can see change and development there also. Although we focus for the moment on employers, what emerges is just as true for the person wishing to go on to higher education or to the person wishing to be self-employed and to develop a living from meeting the needs of the customer.

In the world of work we have seen a massive growth in the 'customer service' movement where businesses and individuals learn that they need to recognize and meet the needs of their customers in all respects. Not just in providing goods or services that work. It's a useful way to consider employability. The proactive employee of an enterprise owner might ask, 'What must I do to ensure that the employer/educator/customer is perfectly satisfied with what I am offering including the way I do my work or provide my service'.

In 2011, the Chartered Management Institute in the UK carried out a survey which sought to examine managers' perceptions about young people and the education system.

In some way, this is examining an old issue. Employers have long complained about educators not providing what employers need – work-ready young people who have some degree of life skills in addition to qualifications and knowledge. The educators' response has often been to be equally critical about the lack of engagement on the part of the employers by providing work experience, opportunities, etc.

The answer as ever, lies somewhere in the middle. The survey is extremely thorough and addresses a wide range of issues including many which are central to our understanding of employability. One question posed is, 'What do managers look for when recruiting young people?'

Table 1.1 Attributes managers look

Factor	% of managers responding
Personal presentation	66%
Academic qualifications	61%
Ambition	50%
Wider 'non-professional' experience	36%
Vocational qualifications	32%
Knowledge of industry or sector	29%
References	13%
Knowledge of the organization	11%

This is in line with expectations. By far the two biggest factors are personal presentation and academic qualifications, essentially the cornerstone of traditional career guidance. Ambition is a factor along with experience and vocational qualifications.

However when the survey asks 'what problems do managers associate with young people?' we get an interestingly different response. This time attitude and ambition are the main concerns. As we will see in Chapter 3, employers and educators will often talk about attitude as a critically important factor but it doesn't appear to be something that employers examine when recruiting people.

Other factors that emerge as important are workplace skills (eg communications), discipline and punctuality, literacy and numeracy, commercial awareness and decision-making abilities. Again, these are fairly specific issues – which help to build a picture of what employability means to employers or educators. These are qualities which it is possible to assess reliably in the recruitment process – and again this is rarely done except perhaps in the assessment of literacy and numeracy skills.

It's the so-called 'soft skills' which emerge as important and valuable.

All of this is perfectly consistent with the research carried out by AQR International and Career Connect in developing the CARRUS employability framework described in the first part of Chapter 3. When we talk about attitude we are again also describing aspects of mindset – the personality traits that are determined by the way 'we think'. This is described in detail in Chapter 3 where we examine the mental toughness personality trait and framework.

Table 1.2 Problem areas managers face

Factor	% of managers responding
Attitude and ambition	66%
Workplace skills	63%
Discipline and punctuality	61%
Literacy	58%
Numeracy	48%
Commercial awareness	38%
Decision making abilities	33%
Technical skills	30%
Turnover (retention)	15%

The survey then examined issues such as 'What initiatives will improve the employability of young people?', and 'What differences would a management qualification make?' with predictable results. These include a call for involving employers in the education process, provision of work experience and, interestingly, improved careers guidance.

Perhaps most revealing was the response to the question 'What skills should young people have when they start work?' This is another way of asking the respondents 'What, in your view, defines employability?'

Table 1.3 Skills managers want most

Factor	% of managers responding
Communication	92%
Planning and organizing	62%
Customer service	56%
Decision making	29%
Quality control	17%
Team leading	15%
Performance monitoring	13%
Resource management	11%

The upshot is that employers do understand what employability is. Whereas it might seem reasonable that the 'system' should provide potential employees who are already fully equipped with these important attributes (some are broader ideas than skills) it is important that employers engage with educators to ensure that these skills are developed.

Nevertheless, quite apart from that, there are two activities that emerge as important and, given the way the world of work is developing globally, emerge as essential:

Those engaged in supporting people (of all ages) to be employable in the full sense of the word must embrace this wider understanding of employability. In preparing this chapter, the authors visited one middle ranking university, which had re-titled its Career Guidance Services as Employability Services. Unfortunately, the name had changed but the content of what is on offer hadn't.

We are now seeing the emergence of curricula, which embrace this wider notion and draw attention to a more complete picture of employability. In the UK there has been a concerted attempt to create this curriculum which in addition to looking at attitude examines skills such as problem solving, team working, planning and organization, interpersonal skills, etc.

The middle sections of this book focus on much of this agenda and seek to provide insights and ideas for enabling this.

A good example of this being applied in practice can be found in the London Youth Rowing case study in Chapter 24. The content of their *Breaking Barriers* programme goes way beyond traditional career guidance. The Career Connect programme described in Chapter 4 does this too. Both are hugely successful.

Employers too need to be more proactive in their recruitment methods. Most of what is on their wish list can be assessed. A new generation of evaluation measures, including psychometrics, enable an appraisal of most of these attributes. These can be woven into other recruitment methods such as structured interviews, assessment centres, trial work placements, etc, to improve the quality of decision making about prospective employees.

This is explored further in Chapter 3 where two psychometric measures are discussed. One assesses mindset, the other examines core behaviour-based attributes.

As any employer will know, recruitment decisions are extremely difficult to get right. A proactive employer will use this assessment of the prospective employee to understand not only their strengths but also their development needs... and do something about them.

We are beginning to see employers and educators do this. This includes assessing the newcomer *after* they have joined the organization – to evaluate their mindset and their development needs – and attend to these quickly.

The Hult International Business School has for several years assessed its MBA intake in its first week and directed pastoral care where it is needed *before* any shortcomings become an issue.

As with many things, prevention is more effective than the cure. In the UK we are seeing a switch in emphasis in the prison and youth offending services from custodial sentences being mostly about punishment to using this time for education and development so that the individual at the end of their sentence is less likely to re-offend and more likely to become a contributor to society. The Luminary Bakery perspective detailed in Chapter 7 shows how this new way of thinking is working in practice.

Early and more comprehensive intervention is an emerging theme in employability and especially in preparing people for enterprise. It's difficult to be aspirational unless you understand what there is to aspire to. We'll revisit this theme throughout the book.

Challenges to overcome

So what are the potential hurdles for delivering effective solutions to the challenge of employability?

The first is understanding employability and what is its content. The first part of this chapter has touched upon that. Chapter 3 examines this much more closely and much of the book responds to that.

In 2015, the UK Government established the Careers and Enterprise Company for schools, to transform the provision of careers education and advice for young people and inspire them about the opportunities offered by the world of work.

The company is designed to support the Government's long-term economic plan by helping young people consider **all** the options available to them when they leave school and ensure they leave school **fully prepared for life** in modern Britain. A key element of this initiative is that schools, colleges and employers should work in partnership to spread effective careers advice, guidance and inspiration to every young person across the country, **regardless of their background or location**.

It's a bold and welcome initiative.

Particularly interesting is the phrase 'regardless of their background or location'.

The opportunity to aspire to develop and enhance employability and life skills is not available equally to all.

Some have little opportunity where some have it in abundance.

Some by virtue of their family background, education, perhaps social background, may have a comparatively easy journey to make. Others without these factors may not even know where to start and if they do they start from a different point.

This too is explored throughout the book. Employability as a concept is applicable to everyone. Even those who appear better prepared are often not fully prepared. Others at the other end of the spectrum need to start from a different place.

The foundation may need to be built and this is where developing mindset is even more important. Attending to low aspirations, low self-belief and low self-efficacy is important as a prerequisite before adding skills and knowledge.

This is illustrated very clearly in the work of organizations such as Career Connect, Catch 22, Manchester United Foundation, Luminary Bakery and London Youth Rowing that are described in this book. They are all pioneers in adopting a much more holistic view towards career guidance and employability – and it works.

The key questions as they appear to the authors in this book are:

1 What does good content for employability or an entrepreneurship programme look like? What does the individual need to know, do and think?

2 How can this best be delivered and how can it be delivered to different groups whose needs will vary.

3 Who are these different groups?

4 What resources are needed and from where do they come?

5 How do we encourage the capability of those who play a key role in developing and guiding people in this area? It's a growing area and Continuous Professional Development is essential as well as having a mind open to new thinking.

And finally

6 Can we stop reinventing the wheel? Can we ensure that what happens is sustainable and can we be certain that what is introduced does make a real difference?

We can respond to these questions at two levels: a big picture perspective and a more detailed perspective which allows us to look at specific challenges under each heading.

One useful approach, which is reflected in the position of the Careers and Enterprise Company in the UK, is that early intervention is important and is likely to be more productive in the long run. Their focus is to work with those aged 12–18 and ensure that all are developed in this area.

Usefully they have picked up the research carried out by the Gatsby Foundation that is summarized below. This provides a valuable overview of what good career guidance embraces – and which is very consistent with the notion of employability.

It is an effective overview of content. Although directed towards those in secondary education, it is not difficult to translate this into a template for any age group or cohort.

This is supported with a complementary description of the journey that young persons will make and what might be expected of them in terms of goals and drivers – and what should be encouraged and developed. This is summarized below. Several of these – motivation, awareness, acquisition of skills and attainment are crucially dependent upon mindset.

Both overviews are supported in turn by checklists, sources of information and examples of good practice. These can be found in the toolkit available by going to www.careersandenterprise.co.uk/resources.

For good reason, the focus of attention for this and many initiatives is on young people aged 12–18. It is also important to notice detail. Not everyone has equal access to good guidance. It's a clear goal but there are likely to be differences. A young person's guidance comes from a variety of sources, family, friends, school, peers, etc, and there are other important players such as government, which is setting policy, employers with a vested interest in the outputs from policy and specialist organizations (many of them charities, trusts and foundations) who provide products and services into this market.

Some will always to be positive, others less so.

So the question is – can we level the playing field for all? Or if not for all, for the vast majority – although 'for all' has to be the goal.

One factor is funding. This is out of the scope of this book but does warrant more than a mention. Providing high quality employability development is not and cannot be cheap.

One interesting development in the UK is the Social Impact Bond where the Government funds activity based on a formula that pays the provider of services according to distinct, measurable and valuable outcomes which are reliably and objectively measured. Gone is the day of the 'happy sheet'.

One of the pioneering organizations in this regard is Career Connect who write in Chapter 4 about their early involvement with Social Investors such

Why Employability?

as Bridges Ventures in the UK and Triodos Ethical Bank, based in the Netherlands, using Social Impact Bonds to fund employability programmes.

Doug's work in AQR sees a significant growth in this activity around the UK.

A useful guide to Social Impact Bonds can be found at http://bridgesventures.com/social-sector-funds/social-impact-bond-fund/. In 2016 Bridges Ventures won the UK Cabinet Office Public Service Transformation Award for the Career Connect programme.

It does sharpen thinking. As a provider you have to be certain of what you are doing and of your ability to make a sustainable difference. Just as importantly, you need to really embrace performance management and be prepared to show evidence for your claimed achievements.

What about the rest of the workforce?

As Kieran Gordon notes in Chapter 4, people are working for longer, commonly into their late 60s and 70s. As Stacey Gunney notes, in the USA, 15 per cent of people entering Community College for vocational education are aged 40 or over (the average age of a student is 29).

Aviva, the Insurance company, published a research study (Voice of New Retirement) in May 2016 which showed that, of people approaching 65 (traditionally the retirement age in the UK), 40per cent intended to carry on working beyond that age. Furthermore, 20per cent of those intended to do so by setting up their own businesses.

The reality is that employability is an issue for everyone at every age.

The principles described in this book apply in fact to everyone. Individuals may have different needs according to their knowledge, skills and experience but the 'employability checklist' applies to all.

In 2015, AQR provided the assessment tools and some of the framework for a significant project delivered by Capita which worked with mature individuals (mostly over 50) who had been out of work for 12 or more months. Sponsored by Barclays Bank, the programme was a huge success with 50per cent getting employment at the end of the programme and most of the remainder finding an opportunity in the months that followed.

One consistent observation, recognizable to many who work in this area, was the general lack of confidence, aspirations and self-belief amongst this group once they had been out of work for some time. These issues are the same everywhere.

Delivery sources

Finally, who delivers employability development, whether it be training programmes, coaching or facilitated experiential learning?

It depends. It can be teachers, lecturers, pastoral care staff, specialist mentors and coaches, carer's adviser, development trainers. Ideally, it's a collaboration which includes parents where it can.

Their challenge is to do what they do well and ensure it is fresh and up to date. This book is largely for them.

And, few of these people work in a vacuum. They work in organizations that also need to understand and direct strategy, activities and resources to this most important of activities. We hope this book is useful for them too.

The growing importance of employability

02

CHARLOTTE BOSWORTH

Schools

When we talk about education in the UK, our first thoughts often turn exclusively to exam results and academic achievement. However, we do know that where we also focus on developing so-called 'soft skills', young people leave school and university much better equipped to face life and its challenges. Indeed, even talking about 'soft skills' is something of a misnomer because these aren't fluffy or superficial skills we're talking about – this is about having the fundamental drive, tenacity and perseverance needed to make the most of opportunities and to succeed whatever obstacles life puts in your way.

There is a growing body of research linking social mobility to social and emotional skills, which range from empathy and the ability to make and maintain relationships to application, mental toughness, delayed gratification and self-control. People who overcome adversity and realize their full potential tend to exhibit many of these traits. In simple terms, these traits can be thought of as a belief in one's ability to achieve, an understanding of the relationship between effort and reward, the patience to pursue long-term goals, the perseverance to stick with the task in hand and the ability to bounce back from life's inevitable setbacks. We can debate whether this should be termed as employability, character or whichever is the current 'buzz word', but ultimately we want to ensure that people are good members of society and have the traits to be employable and to succeed.

I also feel that as good citizens ourselves, we have a responsibility. We know that by focusing on growing these traits, we can improve achievement in other areas such as literacy and numeracy. So these so-called 'soft skills' can lead to hard results and should not be underestimated. For employers, these more intangible skills of sticking at it, not accepting second best, empathy and teamwork are precisely what they are looking for in potential recruits. Having been in many discussions with academics, head teachers, employers and charity leaders alike, 'whatever qualifications you might have, where you are on the soft skills scale will have a big impact on what you can achieve in life'.

It is also interesting to have observed many debates about whether people are born with or without these traits. Rather, a person learns to develop and use these abilities throughout their life. They can be taught and learned at all stages of life but ideally need to begin at primary age and be a continual investment throughout.

We are still in a position where we have an unacceptably wide gap in life chances between children from different backgrounds. We know that permanently closing the opportunity gap between the affluent and the disadvantaged will require more than raising test scores, important though that undeniably is. Rather, it will require inspiring people from all backgrounds to change their perceptions of themselves, what they can achieve and their relationship to society at large.

Bringing about such significant change is not an easy task and many attempts have gone before to address this but it still feels as if this is a nut we have not yet cracked. It is fair to say that 'improving productivity' in our country is high on the agenda and we need to ensure that the link between improved productivity and investment in our young people is made.

Funding aims

In January 2015, a £5 million innovation fund was launched by the UK Government to support the funding character in schools with an aim to:

- build a school's or college's capacity to improve character education by developing the knowledge and skills of staff;
- achieve integration into the curriculum and wider aspects of a school;
- initiate investment in extra-curricular activities, such as sport and music;
- introduce outward-facing activities, such as community work and volunteering.

Overall, this programme was welcomed as a way of ensuring that young people can emerge from school more rounded and better equipped to meet the challenges of employment and future life. The challenge has been providing evidence that proves the programmes have had an impact on engagement, attainment or employment outcomes.

In addition, the current focus within a school still tends to concentrate on academic examination achievement, so however much these skills are being encouraged, until they have parity they will drop off the curriculum timetable.

£5 million may seem like a sizeable investment, particularly at a time when we know money is tight but if we just take secondary schools within the UK (3,268 mainstream secondary schools in the UK in August 2012), then the investment per school is less than £1,500.

Can £1,500 successfully fund:

- Providing extra-curricular activities after school or college – this could include competitive sports, music, debating, outdoor activities or survival weekends?
- Providing community volunteering activities/projects and work experience by making links with the local charities, employers and major industries?
- Peer-to-peer support and mentoring through dialogue and role modelling with successful students or professionals in the community?
- Developing a practical suite of tools and/or accessible educational materials and techniques that support schools in developing character?
- Establishing effective ways to track the progress of pupils throughout their educational journey through to employment?
- Establishing innovative ways to build character in children with high-risk factors, such as special educational needs or a disability, poor family-functioning, maltreatment and poverty?

The other challenge for schools is measuring the impact of the delivery of this agenda. With so many school measures relating to exam-result achievement, a hurdle to overcome will be finding ways of measuring these wider outcomes.

Change in focus

In September 2015, The Ofsted common inspection framework was revised and one of the most notable changes was the focus on personal development, behaviour and welfare. To achieve an outstanding grade, a number of features must be demonstrated which include:

- Pupils being confident, self-assured learners where their excellent attitudes to learning have a strong, positive impact on their progress. They are proud of their achievements and of their school.
- Pupils understand how their education equips them with the behaviours and attitudes necessary for success in their next stage of education, training or employment and for their adult life.
- Pupils' impeccable conduct reflects the school's effective strategies to promote high standards of behaviour. Pupils are self-disciplined. Incidences of low-level disruption are extremely rare.
- The school's open culture actively promotes all aspects of pupils' welfare. Pupils are safe and feel safe at all times. They understand how to keep themselves and others safe in different situations and settings. They trust leaders to take rapid and appropriate action to resolve any concerns they have.
- Pupils can explain accurately and confidently how to keep themselves healthy. They make informed choices about healthy eating, fitness and their emotional and mental well-being. They have an age-appropriate understanding of healthy relationships and are confident in staying safe from abuse and exploitation.
- Pupils' spiritual, moral, social and cultural development equips them to be thoughtful, caring and active citizens in school and in wider society.

We are all aware that each one of these outcomes provide the basis for the skills needed to become more employable in the future, but for many schools that have focused on exam results as the main tangible outcome we do need to ensure that we provide them with the tools to measure this progress accurately. Many of the contributors cited within this book have successfully developed such tools and I am sure will provide ideas of how you may best use these to measure the progress you wish to measure.

The most telling difference between successful and less successful schools and systems lies in how they articulate what their schools should achieve, and the willingness of the system to align three key enablers with this – parental and community engagement, decentralization of responsibility for the delivery of the outcomes and an ethos and culture of stretch in everything a school does, including the curriculum.

This avoids each change to the system being its own stand-alone debate, and the creation of confusion in the system sown by inappropriate incentives. In effect, it forms a guardrail around the system that ensures all actions are aligned with supporting every child's development towards a clearly articulated set of goals; also that it sets out aspirational goals, whether about the percentage of children who go to university or the number of a certain type of school we want to encourage.

Another challenge for schools is having time to plan, prepare and embed activities that will support the growth of these traits. Again, I am sure some of the examples suggested in the next chapter will provide some ideas.

Another area that is core to success is the up-skilling of teachers. Continued Professional Development (CPD) needs to be part of the investment plan. Such development should not just be focused on providing tools and techniques that can be used within the school day but also on enhancing the teachers' professional and employability knowledge and skills. The wider programme needs to ensure that teachers can reflect critically their own skills and employability prospects, that they can reflect critically on the importance of teamwork and leadership skills and can also synthesize complex information. This progression should provide a sense of personal ownership of development and a hunger to grow personal expertise and to push boundaries.

In England, the Government has defined its approach as being based on curriculum rigour. And it is clear from looking at high-performing systems globally and the best schools here that this is a vital part of any successful definition of achievement – but it is not enough on its own.

Exam and curriculum rigour must be part of a wider system that also addresses social and behavioural aspects of education. In Singapore, the definition of achievement goes far beyond exam scores.

The agenda of localizing decision-making and increasing rigour that the Secretary of State for Education has set out for England offers the potential to deliver change that accords with the best systems that have been observed globally.

But this change is currently partial; it must extend to all aspects of how schools in England are run – not just curriculum and exams – to be truly successful. For real transformation in our education system to be possible, a national consensus needs to be reached on a clear and stable statement on what schools should deliver.

This is needed at the centre so that an important guardrail is in place for all schools. It should be able to survive changes of government and provide the test against which policy-changes and school-actions are judged. It should also help to shine the light on whether the system is truly addressing the needs of all pupils.

From discussion with companies across the UK, businesses believe the school system should:

- Focus on raising the ambition and attainment for every child as far as their abilities permit.
- Start from the principle of ensuring everyone leaves school with the basics of literacy and numeracy required for success in every walk of life.
- Embed wider core subjects (like the sciences and computer science) and guide young people effectively on their choice of enabling subjects.
- Expect schools to create the ethos and culture that build the social skills also essential to progress in life and work, and allow them time to focus on this.

Development across three areas

In the view of businesses, this kind of outcome can be delivered through development and measurement of school achievement across three areas. First, every young person must master a range of core subjects to an adequate level – including, critically, maths, English, the sciences and – increasingly – effective use and understanding of computer science.

These are core because only when young people have reached a sufficient standard in these subjects can they make substantial progress in their studies and wider life. They furnish the essential scaffolding for gaining other knowledge and skills, whether in the classroom or a workplace.

Secondly, there are what businesses call 'enabling subjects' – those that expand and enhance the core subjects – including humanities, languages, arts, technical and practical subjects. The range of these and the extent of specialization in their study will vary according to interest and design, particularly from the secondary phase of schooling onwards.

These are the subjects that equip a young person to move on – either to university, or to an apprenticeship or vocational pathway.

Finally, there is a set of behaviours and attitude that we must foster.

These personal behaviours and attributes play a critical role in determining personal effectiveness in a young person's future life. The CBI consulted with a number of businesses to determine what these elements should be and in their view the key ones are as follows.

Table 2.1 Behaviours and attitudes

Instil the Following Attributes	Examples
Grit, resilience, tenacity	• Finish tasks and understand the value of work • Learn to take positives from failure experienced • Work independently and be solutions-focused
Self-Control	• Pay attention and resist distractions • Remember and follow directions • Get to work right away rather than procrastinating • Remain calm, even when criticized • Allow others to speak without interruption
Curiosity	• Be eager to learn new things • Ask and answer questions to deepen understanding
Enthusiasm	• Actively participate • Show enthusiasm • Invigorate others
Confidence and ambition	• Recognize and show appreciation for others • Recognize and show appreciation for their own opportunities
Creativity	• Be willing to try new experiences and meet new people • Pursue dreams and goals
Humility	• Find solutions during conflict with others
Respect and good manners	• Demonstrate respect for feelings of others • Know when and how to include others • Be polite
Sensitivity to global concerns	• Be aware of pressing global issues and contribute to leading society internationally

Developing a pattern of behaviour, thinking and feeling based on sound principles, integrity and resilience involves broadening our traditional expectations, using curricular and non-curricular activities to help bring out those qualities in young people.

In the past within schools we have termed these as employability skills or soft skills. Businesses felt this terminology was misleading, giving the impression that they could be taught separately in the curriculum. That is not the case – the curriculum is the space in which we deliver core knowledge and enabling subjects.

Behaviours can only be developed over time, through the entire path of a young person's life and their progress through the school system and beyond. Everything that happens in a school should embed the key behaviours and attitudes.

None of this can happen without the right context at school and in the lead-up to formal schooling. A supportive culture, pastoral care and the right ethos are all needed to make the difference. Greater use of role modelling, exposure of young people to teachers and others from a wide variety of backgrounds, use of new techniques and tools and stronger linkages between school, home and other non-school environments all have a part to play, alongside a culture and ethos of expectation and rigour.

An essential feature of this approach is that a long line of pupils failing to achieve the desired outcomes can no longer be accepted. Different and innovative methods are needed and we provide some examples of these different approaches within the following chapters. The aim must be to enable all of our young citizens to reach the desired standards.

For reform to be a coherent whole, all the incentives acting on schools need to be addressed. This includes the essential role of the accountability system and the many conflicting expectations placed on schools.

Judging real outcomes for every child is complex and not easily reducible to a league table or test, but this is the key point and a mechanism to allow the judgement of performance against the goals can be found within the AQR *Mental Toughness* programme.

Education is the bedrock of sustainable growth

In summary, ensuring that our education system equips young people, our future talent, with attitudes and attributes to be contributing participants of our workforce, underpinned by their skills, is the most critical factor in determining the UK's ability to grow the economy and strengthen its society over the years ahead. In other words to achieve a step change in the UK's global competitiveness.

There is solid evidence to support the view that education lies at the heart of a sustainable growth strategy.

Over the past half century, those countries that have most successfully driven up their educational standards have enjoyed faster growth than those lagging behind in improving education.

If we apply the conclusion of a key World Bank paper that a move of just 0.5 stens of a standard deviation in the final results of school leavers can raise GDP by 30 per cent over 75 years, the results are startling. At current GDP levels, 30 per cent of the UK's GDP is over £450bn, equivalent to over £7,000 per person. Since this result was published, the authors have done further work looking specifically at EU member countries.

For the UK, they estimate that raising the performance of UK schools to match that of Finland on core subjects could have a value of more than £8trn over the lifetime of a child born today. No other change would have such a significant and sustained impact on long-term economic growth. It could boost growth in the UK by more than one percentage point every year (1.08pp).

Inspiring ambition and aspiration in young people drives economic performance but it also encourages wider engagement and an ability to cope with modern life.

There is plenty of evidence in the UK, too, of the wide-ranging positive social benefits of good schooling that focuses on developing the wider attributes mentioned earlier. On every measure of social exclusion and well-being from dependence on benefits to early parenthood, from unemployment to smoking, those with poor levels of education fare worse than those who are better educated.

Achieving educational success is associated with greater happiness, life satisfaction, self-esteem and a reduced risk of depression. It is also linked to better health and less likelihood of criminal activity. Of course, firms look to schools to foster young people with the competencies they need to function effectively at work. But they also fully recognize broader individual and social concerns as major reasons for pushing up standards of educational attainment.

Enabling young people to lead fulfilling lives and minimizing the risk of educational underachievement contributing to social breakdown both feature among the most important reasons given by employers to raise standards in schools.

The importance of employability – Offenders

Prison populations are diverse communities and currently have one approach to engaging and encouraging offenders to participate in education and training. Engagement with this audience is challenging. The adult prison system contains a specific set of educational challenges. Some 24 per cent of prisoners report having been in care at some point in their lives compared to an estimated 2 per cent in the UK population; 42 per cent report having been permanently excluded from school, with 47 per cent having no formal qualifications and 13 per cent never having a job before prison.

As the facts suggest many offenders have had negative experiences with education in their formative years. With education or training not being a mandatory part of prison life or a rehabilitation programme, different approaches from the traditional classroom approach are required to even encourage participation. Ultimately we need to reduce the percentage that reoffend upon release and support the growth of skills to ensure employability is a feasible option.

The main thrust of education in prisons is to provide opportunities for offenders to attain a range of nationally recognized qualifications up to level 2, and in some cases beyond, which will enhance their employability on release. All prisons must provide a core curriculum, which includes:

- Initial assessment
- National Record of Achievement
- Basic skills
- Key skills
- English for speakers of other languages
- Information and communications technology
- Social and life skills
- Generic preparation for work.

To overcome the barrier to engagement with education within prisons, most of this provision is focused on providing courses that are based around the function that the offender is carrying out. This is particularly true within local prisons where the stay tends to be short-term. Programmes within life/long-term prisons tend to be focused on keeping offenders occupied while open prisons have much more of an emphasis on preparing for employment.

At the other end of the scale, there are highly qualified offenders who both enjoyed and did well at school, many of whom would like to continue their education. There are offenders who seize the opportunity for what they see as a second chance at education and who excel. The massive range of ability, motivation, prior learning experience and attainment presented by offenders, together with the prison regime within which prison education takes place, make for a unique education environment.

These differences coupled with different ages, backgrounds and cultures make it difficult for a one size fits all approach to work. In order for offenders to develop the skills, knowledge and personal qualities necessary to manage effectively both inside prison and on release, a wide range of different opportunities that reflect the diverse needs of the prison population is fundamental. Simply offering a relatively inflexible, academically inclined, school-based curriculum will not work. And that has implications for education staff, too. The need to recruit and retain high-quality education staff, supported by a structured programme of continuing professional development and a rigorous inspection framework would seem to be integral to ensuring progress.

Wider benefits of learning

The purpose of education and training in prisons should be to play a key role in improving the employability of prisoners and therefore contribute to reducing reoffending. However, the purpose of prison education should be more than just improving the employability of an offender. Education programmes should also be about doing what is right to ensure we have a civilized society. Education has a value in itself and it is important to develop the person as a whole, not just in terms of the qualifications they hold for employment. The breadth of the education curriculum is important and employability skills should not be emphasized to such an extent that the wider benefits of learning are excluded.

The provision of more extensive projects such as art and music courses, the engagement in sport or broader programmes to encourage personal and social development is not currently part of the Offenders' Learning and Skills Service (OLASS)-funded contract and creates a barrier to ensuring that programmes are shaped to the needs of the offender and the traits we need to encourage. Prison education is, for many, a second chance to learn the skills and social competences they will need in order to be reintegrated. But there is a catch: that education is offered in an institution which by its very nature isolates still further many who are already excluded from society. Imprisonment widens the gap between those people and mainstream society and brands them in a manner that compounds their social exclusion.

When considering the attributes we need to encourage they do not differ from those referred to in the school section of this chapter but we need to ensure we have relevant programmes for this audience to encourage the growth of these skills.

In addition to the education programme detailed, OLASS also currently delivers support and training for enterprise and self-employment. The programme is specifically aimed at being an alternative route for offenders where the nature of the convicted offence may be deemed as unsuitable or unlikely to allow them to successfully get a job with an employer upon release.

The importance of employability – enterprise and entrepreneurship

So what do we mean when we talk about enterprise and entrepreneurship and how does this link to employability?

Learning often takes place without bearing the label of 'enterprise'. More important than labels are the approaches taken and the behaviours, attributes and skills developed: those that are referred to throughout many chapters.

Enterprise

Enterprise is the application of creative ideas and innovations to practical situations. This is a generic concept that can be applied across all areas of education.

It combines creativity, ideas-development and problem solving with expression, communication and practical action. This definition is distinct from the generic use of the word in reference to a project or business venture.

Enterprise education aims to produce a mindset and skills to come up with original ideas in response to identified needs and shortfalls – and the ability to act on them. In short, having an idea and making it happen. Enterprise skills include taking the initiative, intuitive decision-making, making things happen, networking, identifying opportunities, creative problem solving, innovating, strategic thinking and personal effectiveness. Enterprise education extends beyond knowledge acquisition to a wide range of emotional, intellectual, social and practical skills.

Entrepreneurship

Entrepreneurship is the application of enterprise skills specifically to creating and growing organizations in order to identify and build on opportunities.

Entrepreneurship education focuses on the development and application of an enterprising mindset and skills in the specific contexts of setting up a new venture, developing and growing an existing business or designing an entrepreneurial organization.

Entrepreneurship education aims to produce individuals who are capable of identifying opportunities and developing ventures, through setting up new businesses or developing and growing part of an existing venture. Many would argue that entrepreneurship is nature rather than nurture, which is a debate for another time, but entrepreneurs do still require enterprise skills and behaviours as well as business knowledge, actions and skills that are specific to the particular context.

The link between employability and enterprise

As many of the sections in this book show, employability is high on the education agenda but the relationship with enterprise and entrepreneurship is frequently discussed. There is unquestionably an overlap between the broad set of skills which contribute to employability and the characteristics of enterprise, but they are not identical. Enterprise education can enhance careers education and student employability by enabling students to be more opportunity-focused, self-aware and attuned to the business environment, for example. Entrepreneurship is part of a wide range of career options which include freelancing, portfolio careers and running a part-time business.

Who is an entrepreneur and who is a business owner?

It is helpful to make an additional distinction between entrepreneurs and owners (or managers) of small businesses. These categories are not mutually exclusive – many business owners are also entrepreneurs – but the concepts are distinctive. An individual running his or her own business may wish to retain strong control and be resistant to changing structures and approaches. An entrepreneur demonstrates enterprising approaches and attributes, such as creativity, vision, responsiveness to opportunity and ambition for business growth, which are distinct from business skills and knowledge.

Both enterprise and entrepreneurship education should focus on equipping individuals to develop their overall effectiveness beyond the educational setting. Entrepreneurial effectiveness is developed through a combination of enterprise awareness, entrepreneurial mindset and entrepreneurial capability.

Entrepreneurial effectiveness can be defined as the ability to behave in an enterprising and entrepreneurial way. This is achieved through the development of enhanced awareness, mindset and capabilities to enable learners to perform effectively in taking up opportunities and achieving desired results. Effective performance means adapting and applying the mindset and capabilities to the relevant context, and exercising judgements about the optimal actions to take within set environments.

Within the next chapter, some frameworks are provided not just to support the growth of employability skills but also to develop enterprise characteristics. Case studies of how various organizations in schools, prisons and community environments have adopted the framework to suit their needs, provide useful contexts to allow you to adapt to your own situation.

Models of employability

03

DOUG STRYCHARCZYK, PROF PETER CLOUGH AND DR PETER SEWELL

To begin this section of the book we need first to clarify what we mean by employability and to examine where there are common and consistent elements, which make up a widely accepted understanding of what generates employability.

A number of definitions of 'employability' have been proposed, applied and researched since the term established currency in the late 1990s. For example, Hillage and Pollard (1998, p. 2) described employability as: '... *being capable of getting and keeping fulfilling work. More comprehensively employability is the capability to move self-sufficiently within the labour market to realize potential through sustainable employment.*'

Since that time the most widely cited definition of employability is provided by Professor Mantz Yorke (2006), '*a set of achievements – skills, understandings and personal attributes – that makes graduates more likely to gain employment and be successful in their chosen occupations, which benefits themselves, the workforce, the community and the economy*' (p 8).

He goes on to add that:

> 'Employability is not the same as *gaining* a (graduate) job, rather it implies something about the capacity of the individual (graduate) to function in a job and be able to move between jobs, thus remaining employable throughout their life.'

Although developed for use with a graduate population, the principles hold good for all, whether non-graduates, career changers, the mature employee, etc.

This description can be considered accurate, although it is offered from the perspective of the individual who seeks to be employed or to be enterprising. It works if it matches the expectations and wishes of employers and other users of the individual's services with the expectations of the applicant. There is a need to drill down to another level to give this work some more meaning – particularly at an operational level.

This definition arose from the USEM employability model (Yorke and Knight, 2002; Yorke and Knight, 2004). USEM is an acronym for four interrelated components of employability:

- understanding;
- skills (including deployment of skills);
- efficacy beliefs (including an individual's self-awareness). Fundamentally important is the extent to which individuals feel that they are able 'to make a difference';
- meta-cognition (the individual's awareness of their own learning, their capacity to reflect and to plan what to do).

Can we be more specific about understandings and personal attributes? Skills and knowledge can be closely defined and can be comparatively simple to assess (although that too has its limitations). A common observation when asked about unsatisfactory employees or unsatisfactory service from employers (and clients) is that knowledge and skills may be there but it is 'attitude' that is the issue. Often 'attitude' remains ill-defined and rather vague.

Employability can, to some extent be considered the equivalent of client satisfaction in the sales or commercial process. It's not a bad comparator. In many ways engaging with an employer to hire you or a client to buy you or your offering is one thing. It's very like persuading someone to buy what you are offering. You may be confident that your offering meets the needs of the client. The problem might be that your offering may be very similar and perhaps indistinguishable from the offerings of others. It's quite another to delight the customer and this can usually only be achieved by identifying what exactly will delight the customer and then proceeding purposefully to deliver to that specification.

We are leaving aside for the moment the circumstance where the client sometimes doesn't know what they want until after the event (and doesn't appreciate what it is that you are offering). This is another perspective, which applies equally to both situations and it is equally important that the employer or institution understands what employability is.

In the remainder of this chapter, we examine three approaches to defining and developing employability in its widest sense – similar principles apply to enterprise and entrepreneurship. All require being able to work with others' expectations as well as being able to cope (or preferably perhaps) deal with all that life can throw at you – good, bad, challenging and with opportunity.

What is striking about all three approaches is how complementary they are even though they have all come from different origins – sometimes the theoretical and academic and sometimes from experience and practice.

The first approach is a description of CARRUS, which is a very specific attempt to approach employability from the perspective of the employer, the educator, or the client to identify what might be the essential behavioural qualities sought by these parties.

The second, the 4Cs model of Mental Toughness, looks at the impact of mindset in employability.

Finally, we look at Career Edge, which is a direct descendant of the USEM model developed by Professor Yorke (see above).

Employability – CARRUS – a picture of essential behaviour-orientated attributes

In 2012, AQR Ltd in partnership with Career Connect (then Greater Merseyside Connexions Partnership) initiated a project in the United Kingdom to dig more deeply into the notion of employability starting with a process of consultation with employers. This led to the development of the CARRUS model and accompanying psychometric measure described below and to a further application for the mental toughness model. Together these appear to provide a comprehensive picture of employability – certainly from the employer's perspective.

The first stage was to approach around 700 employers from over 30 industrial classifications and ask them – without any steer – what, in their view made a highly effective and contributing employee.

The responses which came back were, predictably, often woolly or vague – featuring terminology such as 'good attitude', 'enthusiasm', 'hard-working'. However, there was sufficient specificity in a good number of the comments to identify clusters of thought around 24 themes.

A by-product of the research at this stage confirmed that, although many employers paid attention to qualifications (and knowledge) in the recruitment process, markedly fewer considered this as significant when considering the effectiveness of an employee after say 12 months.

Essentially, they were confirming that qualifications and knowledge could get a person into the recruitment process and perhaps, with newly qualified individuals, this was one of the few factors that employers had to go on. However, once in employment or in further/higher education, these counted for less than what the individual did and what they brought to the role in terms of their behaviour and 'attitude'.

The next stage was to take this list of qualities back to employers and ask them to identify which were:

- essential – must-have qualities which defined all highly effective employees;
- useful – qualities which, when available, were indeed valuable but could not be defined as essential;
- nice to have – they added something but were by no means essential.

Of the 24 themes, 16 emerged as 'essential'.

When examined more closely, four of the themes were about control, commitment, challenge and confidence. They differed from the other 12 themes in that they represented aspects of mindset – how people think. The other 12 were more behavioural – representing how people acted.

The 4Cs – control, commitment, challenge and confidence – are the four components of mental toughness described later in the chapter. A means of reliably assessing these already exists in the MTQ48 measure also described later.

The 12 remaining scales clustered around three themes – all to do with behaviour – which we developed into the CARRUS employability model – with an accompanying measure.

The resulting framework looked like this:

Dealing with problems

Whatever one does, one hits problems, changes and setbacks – often for reasons outside of one's control. In the workplace it might be a difficult customer, or being late for work because your transport arrangements are unreliable or being let down by a colleague or being provided with the wrong components to do a job, etc. There are lots of things that can and do go wrong. It's true whatever you do – education, sport, play, etc.

One response will be to refer the problem to someone else, usually higher up in the organization. The problem will inevitably get resolved but it will take up another's precious time, which distracts them from their role. If that individual has several team members who do that, they spend all their time doing their juniors' work and not their own.

This is neither efficient nor effective yet this would often be a feature of traditional command and control structures.

An alternative response is that the individual, understanding the problem, deals with it quickly and efficiently and only if it proves especially difficult to resolve do they refer to anyone else. It's often said that 99 per cent of problems in the workplace are best resolved by the person closest to the problem and with the best knowledge of the situation.

The four sets of behaviours which supported this were:

Dealing with problems

Figure 3.1 Active problem solving

Active problem solving The extent to which the individual will actively identify, confront, analyze and solve problems.	*Creativity* The extent to which the individual seeks to add new ideas and innovation to your work.
• **High:** Will enjoy solving problems and finding solutions. Will immediately seek to find a resolution when a problem arises. • **Low:** Will dislike trying to solve problems. Will tend to avoid dealing with problems and prefer passing them to others to handle even if they are capable of handling them.	• **High:** Will enjoy playing with ideas, will enjoy trying new things. Will think about their work and the situation in this way. • **Low:** Will dislike playing with ideas. Will find it difficult to think up new ideas.

Doing things right and doing things better

Employers, clients and educators often see this as evidence of a proactive interest in what the individual is doing. People who engage in this way are more likely to be productive and concerned with costs and benefits.

Figure 3.2 Organization and continuous improvement

Organization The extent to which structure and order is important to them and the way they work.	*Continuous Improvement* The extent to which the individual will seek to reflect on what you and others are doing and seek to improve on this.
• **High:** Will enjoy routine and planning actions in advance. Will like structure. Will understand why structures and systems are valuable and why it is important to observe them. • **Low:** Will dislike planning actions, like going with the flow of things. May not respect systems and processes – may not see the point.	• **High:** Will enjoy doing things better next time – even if they already work well. Thinks about what they are doing and why it's done that way and whether it can be done better. Abhors complacency. • **Low:** Will accept the status quo and won't actively think about improving the way things are done. Happy to do what's asked without question.

Drive and motivation

The essence here is the difference between a self-starter and one who has to be prodded into action. Clearly, whatever the circumstance, employers, educators and clients value those who possess a degree of self-motivation and who approach what they do with a sense of wanting to be there.

This includes the notion that individuals take an interest in, and action about, their own personal development.

The four sets of behaviours which supported this were:

The desire to do things right

Figure 3.3 Conscientiousness and standards

Conscientiousness The extent an individual is guided by rules, standards and values. Understands the importance of recognizing what is important and what is urgent. Will strive to keep promises.	Concern for standards The extent to which an individual desires to work to the standards set for their activity. Understanding that working to standards is important for all stakeholders.
• **High:** Will be reliable and complete all tasks to their deadlines. Reliability may be one of their hallmarks. • **Low:** Will not mind missing deadlines or cutting corners. Won't see keeping a promise as important.	• **High:** Will want everything that they do to be perfect and compliant with the highest standards. Less than tolerant about things being 'just enough'. • **Low:** Will be comfortable just doing 'OK', will not mind repeatedly getting things wrong. May avoid giving attention to standards.

Growing capability – achieving potential

Figure 3.4 Growing capability and achieving potential

Ambition The extent to which an individual will desire attainment or seek to be 'the best'. This is not ambition in the sense of wanting to be the CEO. It's more about 'being the best that you can be'.	Continuous Personal Development How likely you are to accept responsibility for your own learning and development in order to maintain and develop capability. Recognizing that standing still may be going backwards.
• **High:** Will be very driven, will aspire and will go the 'extra mile' to achieve. • **Low:** Will aspire for very little and will be satisfied with what they have – even if it is little.	• **High:** Will make the effort to ensure their skills and knowledge are o a high standard and are up to date and see it as their responsibility to do that. • **Low:** Will expect others to develop them and even then may be reluctant to respond positively.

Interpersonal Skills

Almost everything that can be achieved has to be done, to some extent, with others. Employers value those who can appreciate this and who build effective relationships with others – colleagues, clients, tutors, managers, etc.

This is the least surprising of the key employability qualities. Team working has long been recognized as a virtuous quality. Most organizations and networks are essentially teams with a particular focus.

The four sets of behaviours which supported this were:

Working with others

Team working The extent to which an individual will work willingly with others to achieve the groups goals	**Altruism** The extent to which an individual wishes to act in the best interests of others
• **High**: Will enjoy working with others, sharing information and having a common goal. • **Low**: Prefer to work alone focusing on own goals in preference to the teams goals. Unmotivated by team work.	• **High**: Will prioritize supporting others, and will give up their own needs in favour of others. • **Low**: Will act most or all of the time for their own self interest and will ignore the needs of others.

Influencing Others

Emotional intelligence The extent to which you are aware of your emotions & the emotions of others and understand how to respond	**Assertiveness** The extent an individual influences others
• **High**: Aware of when they impact on others, skilled in listening and aware of how they respond to others. • **Low**: Less aware of their own emotions and how others are feeling.	• **High**: Will persuade others to their point of view and stand their ground when needed. • **Low**: Will back down when others challenge them even when they have a strong case.

One observation at this point in the development of the framework is that nowhere was there mention of compliance or 'doing as they are told'. An earlier exercise, some 25 years ago, placed this fairly high on an employer's agenda.

It seems that an emerging aspect of employability is responsiveness and proactivity on the part of an employee, student or provider of services. Many of the attributes described above reflect that interest.

In part, this also indicates the preoccupation of far-sighted employers with ideas such as empowerment, employee engagement and, more recently, in understanding the value and importance of trust. As employers increasingly adopt these models and approaches, they value employees who respond positively to the challenge and the opportunity that an empowered culture provides.

A very good and clear example of this is Cineworld, one of the UK's largest cinema (movie) theatre owners with, in 2012, over £350m in annual revenues and over 46 million admissions to their 80 sites. Their business strategy is clear, simple and focused – 'to create welcoming, contemporary cinemas that movie-goers will want to come back to time and time again... We want the whole Cineworld experience to be smooth, memorable and exciting.'

To see how well this part of their strategy was working, Cineworld undertook research into what their customers thought of them. What they discovered from the research prompted action and significant reflection.

Although customers were very happy with the films and the auditoria, the overall experience of being a Cineworld customer was not scoring highly. What was affecting the customer experience was what was happening before and after the viewing of the film. It was the speed, efficiency of service and empowerment of the staff to respond to customers that was the issue.

Many of the processes and systems in place were based on previous concerns about access to and theft from the tills and stock from the stock rooms. Additionally, many of Cineworld's staff are young and a fairly high turnover of staff meant that cinema managers felt that a high degree of command and control was necessary to ensure things were done properly. This had resulted in a policy and practice of very restricted access to tills and stock rooms – with only one person permitted to use each till. Additionally, authorization for replacement drinks and popcorn which were dropped or spilt could only be given by managers (which they always gave as part of the overall policy to create a good experience).

The result was that although there may have been a lot of serving staff the payment process was highly restricted and customers had to wait to be served. This slowed down service and gave the impression of staff standing around doing nothing whilst queues built up.

This frustrated and annoyed customers. Staff too reflected this lack of trust through lack of engagement – it was 'not their problem'. This all added to the lack of a good experience for customers.

Cineworld did two things. Firstly, they trained their managers and serving staff in trust – ensuring everyone was focused on the need for a great customer experience and on the need for teams to take collective responsibility, including for the tills being right at the end of any shift.

Secondly, vitally, they changed a number of policies and practices to match that investment in trust to show the staff they meant what they said when developing the idea of trust. Tills became multi-user for all team members on a shift. Staff could authorize and supply replacements for spilt or dropped drinks or food without referring to a manager. Keys to the stock room were held by teams serving and sharing a till, so allowing them to re-stock as needed and quickly.

In the cinemas where it was first applied Cineworld started to see a drop in queues, far faster customer resolutions and a drop in the number of tills that were incorrect. Losses of stock (often attributed to staff) also declined. Teams, once trusted, and managers, once focused on both trusting teams to monitor themselves and act in a trustworthy way, transformed the customer experience. Trust was reciprocated and staff in the cinemas also took ownership of the experience and of the decisions made for customers.***

To these three clusters of attributes, we added abilities. The evidence consistently shows that abilities correlate strongly with performance. Employers, educators and clients understand this. Some form of assessment of abilities through the application of psychometric measures is widespread in recruitment and selection for employment in most economies and societies.

Abilities

Abilities are important because the functioning of almost every role (whether in employment, enterprise or further education) depends on dealing effectively with a flow of information which comes to the role in various forms – mainly verbal (written information, systems, processes, etc.) numerical (often in terms of performance data to which job holders should respond), spatial (flow charts, etc.) and diagrammatic.

At one time, data of this type would have only been made available to people designated as managers. As organizations become devolved and employee engagement increases, staff are expected at all levels to be able to read data and information relevant to the effective performance of their role as well as being relevant to the organization's performance and responses.

The possession of a basic level of abilities thus becomes a core requirement for employability.

The four types of abilities which supported this were:

Numerical Ability – Measuring the ability to work quickly and logically with numbers. A wide range of information is provided to individuals in numerical form – often for monitoring and evaluation.

Verbal Ability – Measuring the ability to think, reason and solve problems involving words and letters. Again a great deal of information is provided

---

*Professor Mantz Yorke (2004) *'Employability in Higher Education: what it is – what it is not'*, Higher Education Academy/ESECT
** The USEM account of Employability. (Yorke and Knight, 2004, p.5)
*** *Developing Resilient Organizations* (Strycharczyk and Elvin, Kogan Page, 2015)

to most job holders, students, suppliers of products and services in written form whether this is onscreen or in hard copy. This ranges from agreements, letters, memos, etc through to written information as well as processes, systems and instructions.

Non-Verbal – Measuring the ability to solve problems involving shapes and patterns. An increasing form of communication – particularly with the advent of the internet where information is often shown in symbols, images and diagrams.

Mechanical Reasoning – Measuring knowledge and understanding of physical and mechanical concepts and the ability to solve problems by thinking things through. Essentially this is the ability to envisage how things might work.

The eventual outcome was the formulation of a model – CARRUS – which captures four key areas of employability.

Figure 3.5 Abilities, motivation, skills, problems

Abilities	Motivations and Drivers
Possessing sufficient ability to deal with information coming to the role which needs to be understood and processed for effective performance	Possessing the desire to do a good job and a genuine interest in building capability to achieve one's potential
Interpersonal Skills	**Dealing with Problems**
Demonstrating effective skills in working purposefully with others irrespective of differences and being able to influence others.	Understanding how to deal with problems and possessing the skills to do so. Importantly, wanting to do things right and do things better

This identifies the most important abilities, skills and behaviours – essentially the things an employer, an educator, or a customer would like to see the individual have and do well.

An important by-product of this study and the research that went with it was the development of a psychometric measure, which helped people to assess these qualities. This is known as the CARRUS measure. The measure helps people to assess their employability and to be more self-aware about what they offer. The framework also guides the individual in understanding what others will expect from them.

Models of Employability

For employers, clients and educators the same framework helps to articulate and operationalize what is often described, as we have seen, in vague and imprecise terms. It helps employers to consider more carefully what is important for their business and how they might assess and develop that.

To this we can add the 4Cs from mental toughness which, as we will see, introduces mindset – the way the individual thinks when dealing with situations, which often underpins or determines to some extent their behaviour and their execution of skills and application of abilities.

Figure 3.6 Your Carrus Profile

Your Carrus Profile
This is an overview of your client's profile showing their preference on each of the personality scales and their results on each of the ability scales. Each page will give you a more detailed explanation along with coaching suggestions on how to help your client develop and adapt in each area. Please remember these are not scores out of ten. This indicates their preference on each scale.

Left	Scale (selected)	Right
Inaction	7	Problem Solver
Rigid	7	Creative
Reactive	7	Organized
Self sufficient	6	Team worker
Self-focused	8	Altruistic
Emotionally self-contained	10	Sensitive to others
Submissive	9	Assertive
Spontaneous	10	Conscientious
Casual	10	Concern for standards
Contented	10	Ambitious
Complacent	10	Continuous improvement
Static	10	Continuous personal development
Mechanical reasoning	5	
Non-Verbal reasoning	7	
Numerical ability	6	

Figure 3.7 Assertiveness

Assertiveness

How determined your client is to influence others, including getting their own way.

1   2   3   4   5   6   7   8   **9**   10

Your client describes themself as very assertive and likely to have a strong capacity for standing up for their beliefs and opinions regardless of whether others agree or not. They can disagree with others and are unlikely to back down if their opinions are different to others. They won't give in just to 'keep the peace' and believe that people should stand up for themselves and their opinion.

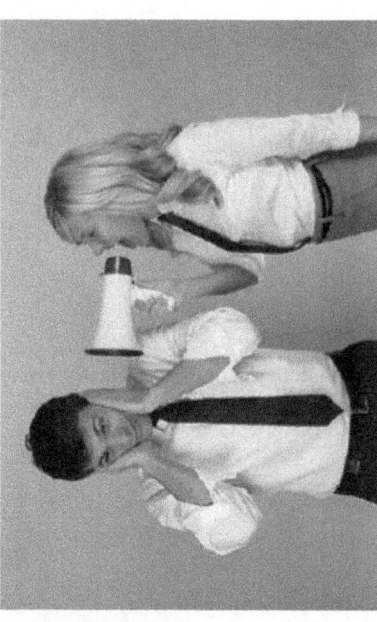

Coaching Suggestions:

- Highly assertive people can sometimes be seen as aggressive. They can seem to be driven to get their own way all of the time. Equally, others who have a lesser sense of self-belief can see assertive types as intimidating, perhaps even as bullies.

Being assertive can be a very valuable quality in many circumstances and in many careers. Examine the interpersonal consequences of the individual getting their own way so much. How can the individual create a greater sense of 'win-win' which is valuable in gaining commitment from others?

Mental Toughness

Where CARRUS attends to the behaviour-orientated attributes which employers identify as important, mental toughness attends to possibly the most important quality in employability – attitude.

Behavioural aspects of personality determine 'how we act'. What is equally important is understanding 'how we think'.

It is clearly very important to understand how we act. Employers and educators alike will want to figure out how the individual will behave when they come to work with them. Indeed most of the psychometric measures used in recruitment are orientated towards this. Behaviour can be comparatively straightforward to assess and confirm. We can see and describe behaviour with reasonable accuracy.

What is more difficult is to assess what is happening inside someone's head. The notion of mindset or mental toughness which comes close to this idea, is more difficult to assess. An individual's mindset can impact significantly on their behaviours, emotions and feelings and ultimately their ability to do the job.

More than 20 years of research and application by AQR International, together with Peter Clough, Professor of Applied Psychology at Manchester Metropolitan University, has led to a practical understanding of what mental toughness really is. This is captured in a unique framework called the 4 Cs which is described below.

The mental toughness concept is consistent with the related ideas and approaches which have entered the world of individual development. These include:

Mindset – Dweck describes individuals as possessing one of two mindsets – a fixed mindset and a flexible mindset. The former captures the idea that ability is all important and that if you can't do something it's because you don't have the ability. A flexible mindset describes someone who is prepared to stretch themselves and work hard to achieve things. Ability is less important. It is about making the best use of the abilities you have and seeking to develop them.

Grit – Duckworth describes Grit in terms of conscientiousness. She has shown that commitment is highly correlated with attainment. If you set your mind to doing something you are more likely to succeed.

Resilience – a long-understood concept from the world of Health Psychology which describes an individual's ability to respond to a difficulty, setback or adversity. Those who can pick themselves up and carry on are described as resilient.

Character – a popular but sometimes vaguely defined concept. It overlaps with the above.

Learned Optimism – Seligman who has championed positive psychology suggests that people fall into two broad camps. Optimists (learned optimism) where they learn to see opportunity rather than threat and take a positive view about the world around them and pessimists (learned helplessness) who see the threats before they ever see the opportunities.

These various models have at least one thing in common. They all suggest that these qualities are developable.

Mental Toughness itself is an umbrella concept that embraces all of these. It is defined as:

> 'A personality trait which determines, in large part, how people respond to opportunity, challenge, stress and pressure, irrespective of their circumstances'. (Strycharczyk & Clough 2015)

Published research and case studies from around the world show that Mental Toughness is a major factor in:

- Performance – explaining up to 25 per cent of the variation in individual performance.
- Positive Behaviour – more engaged, more positive, more 'can do', more likely to volunteer for new or additional tasks.
- Wellbeing – more contentment, deal better with setbacks, sleep better!, better at stress management, less likely to report bullying.
- Aspirations – more ambitious, prepared to manage more risk.

Research carried out under the direction of Peter Clough and colleagues at Hull University and Manchester Metropolitan University has identified the four key components of Mental Toughness. These are called the 4 Cs.

These are summarized below with short explanations for each scale describing what kind of thoughts would be running through the head of the individual:

Table 3.1 Mental Toughness and MTQ48

Mental Toughness Scale	What this means... what does MTQ48 assess
CONTROL	*Life Control* – I really believe I can do it.
	Emotional Control – I can manage my emotions and the emotions of others.
COMMITMENT	*Goal Setting* – I promise to do it – I like working to goals.
	Achieving – I'll do what it takes to keep my promises and achieve my goals.
CHALLENGE	*Risk Taking* – I will push myself – I am driven to succeed.
	Learning from Experience – even setbacks are opportunities for learning.
CONFIDENCE	*In Abilities* – I believe I have the ability to do it – or can acquire the ability.
	Interpersonal Confidence – I can influence others – I can stand my ground if needed.

It's not difficult to equate this with what is commonly described as attitude and mindset.

We are also able to assess mental toughness in terms of these components in individuals and groups through a unique 48-item, high-quality psychometric measure called the MTQ48. Valid and reliable, the measure had been designed to be very accessible to users and clients. The outputs include reports for the individual (with sample development suggestions) and coaching reports for the coach or facilitator which include coaching suggestions as well as sample interview questions to explore an individual's profile with them.

Importantly it is a normative measure which enables users to assess mental toughness before and after an event such as a training & development or coaching programme. This is very useful in behaviour-change programmes. Behaviour change is rarely embedded straightaway – however, if you haven't change mindset it is unlikely that you will see the desired behaviour change coming through. An example of this is shown in the *London Youth Rowing* case study.

Research and case studies are beginning to show a close correlation between the mental toughness of an individual and their employability. In 2013, the Scottish Funding Council sponsored a project at Stevenson College and Adam Smith College in Scotland. They assessed and tracked 50 vocational students on a Media Studies programme and 50 students on a Hospitality programme. The study found:

- That there was a correlation between the mental toughness (as assessed through the MTQ48) of the graduate and the speed at which they found a job and the extent to which they found a job that satisfied them (as opposed to getting any job).
- Interestingly, tracking the students in their first period of employment they found that the more mentally tough the student the more quickly they settled into their new roles and achieved positive assessments from their employers.

This would seem to relate to the wider understanding of employability. Getting a job is one thing, demonstrating employability in the role is equally important.

A fuller description of mental toughness and how it can be developed can be found in *Developing Mental Toughness* (Strycharczyk and Clough (2015), Kogan Page). A summary description is shown below.

Control

Defined: Control is the extent to which a person feels they are in control of their life. Some individuals believe that they can exert considerable influence over their working environment, that they can make a difference and change things. In contrast, others feel that the outcome of events is outside their personal control and they are unable to exert any influence over themselves or others.

Applied: This means for example that, at one end of the scale, individuals feel their input really matters and are motivated to make a full contribution.

At the other end, they may feel that their contribution is of little importance and hence may not play as full a part as they could. An implication may be that one can handle lots of things at the same time and the other cannot.

Ongoing development has enabled the identification of two subscales to this scale:

Control (Emotion)

Individuals scoring highly on this scale are better able to manage their emotions and understand how to manage the emotional responses of others. They are able to keep anxieties in check and are less likely to reveal their emotional state to other people.

Typical behaviours associated with mental toughness (high scores) or mental sensitivity (low scores) on this scale include:

Lower scores	Higher scores
Feel things happen to them;	Feel they shape what happens;
Show emotions when provoked or challenged;	Good at controlling emotions;
Reveal their anxiety;	Difficult to provoke or annoy;
Show discomfort when others 'have a go at them';	Do not appear anxious (but may be as anxious as anyone else);
Deal poorly with provocation;	Impassive when others make comments which could upset or annoy.
Do not respond well to poor marks or the prospect of poor performance.	

Control (Life)

Those scoring highly on this scale are more likely to believe they control their lives. They feel that their plans will not be thwarted and that they can make a difference.

Typical behaviours associated with mental toughness (high scores) or mental sensitivity (low scores) on this scale include:

Lower scores	Higher scores
Find it hard to do more than one thing at a time.	Comfortable when asked to do several things at a time.
Freeze when overloaded.	Good at planning and time management.
Can feel stretched with modest workloads – poor at time management.	Good at prioritizing.
Will tend to blame outside factors for preventing success.	Prepared to work hard to clear blockages.
May panic when given assignments.	Tend to see others as problems – which can be handled.

Commitment

Defined: This subscale measures the extent to which an individual is likely to persist with a goal or work task. Individuals differ in the degree with which they remain focused on their goals.

Some may be easily distracted, bored or divert their attention to competing goals, whereas, others may be more likely to persist.

Applied: An individual who scores at the high end of the scale will be able to handle and achieve things when faced with tough and unyielding deadlines. An individual at the other end will need to be free from those types of demands to handle work.

Ongoing development has enabled the identification of two subscales to this scale:

Goal Orientation

Individuals scoring highly on this scale are orientated towards setting goals and targets for activities. They are likely to be effective at prioritizing, planning and organization.

Typical behaviours associated with mental toughness (high scores) or mental sensitivity (low scores) on this scale include:

Lower scores	Higher scores
Intimidated by goals and measures.	Like goals and measures – these describe what success looks like.
May feel inadequate or 'stupid' when asked to do something.	
Will include terms such as 'if' and 'but' into their response to being asked to do something.	Like the repeated opportunity to measure and prove themselves.
May resent the imposition of goals and targets.	Accept responsibility.
More likely to be late for things.	Set high standards for self and others.
Find reasons to miss the target.	Like being judged or assessed.
May try self-sabotage in order to get out of doing something.	Like the objectivity of goals and measures – avoid being subject to others opinions.

Completion

Those scoring highly on this scale are more likely to deliver what they are committed to. They are likely to 'do what it takes' and gain satisfaction (and perhaps relief) from achievement.

Typical behaviours associated with mental toughness (high scores) or mental sensitivity (low scores) on this scale include:

Lower scores	Higher scores
Unwilling to make an effort or give up something less important;	Will break things down into manageable chunks;
Allow themselves to be easily distracted;	Prepared to do what it takes – will work long and hard if needed;
Adopt a minimalist approach – will do the absolute minimum;	Maintain focus;
Will skip meetings or classes;	Diligent about projects – deliver on time;
More likely to be late for things;	Tenacious;
Attendance can be poor;	Will prioritize effort and activities;
Find reasons to miss the target;	Will do things even if they don't like it.

Challenge

Defined: Individuals differ in their approach to challenge. Some consider challenges and problems to be opportunities, whereas others may be more likely to consider a challenging situation as a threat.

This subscale measures the extent to which an individual is likely to view a challenge as an opportunity. Those scoring highly on this scale may have a tendency to actively seek out such situations for self-development, whereas low scorers may avoid challenging situations for fear of failure or aversion to effort.

Applied: So, for example, at one end of the scale we find those who thrive in continually changing environments. At the other end, we find those who prefer to minimize exposure to change and the problems that come with that – and will strongly prefer to work in stable environments.

Ongoing development has enabled the identification of two subscales to this scale:

Preparedness to stretch oneself

Individuals scoring highly will be open to change and new experience. They are not daunted by the prospect of new situations, meeting new people, etc. They welcome change. They are prepared to manage risk.

Typical behaviours associated with mental toughness (high scores) or mental sensitivity (low scores) on this scale include:

Lower scores	Higher scores
Don't like sudden changes – like routine.	Like challenge.
Don't like shocks.	Provoke change.
Fear failure and avoid risk.	Like problem solving.
Avoid effort.	Work hard.
Dislike being in new situations – new colleagues, new bosses, new premises.	Volunteer self and others for projects.
Worry about the views of others.	Enjoy competition and show it.

Positive about all outcomes

Those scoring highly on this scale will see all outcomes as having a positive element – whether those outcomes are successes or failures. They will see opportunity where others will see threat and will not be deterred by setbacks. They are open to learning – they see learning in most situations.

Typical behaviours associated with mental toughness (high scores) or mental sensitivity (low scores) on this scale include:

Lower scores	Higher scores
Tend to do the minimum.	See the positive in most outcomes.
Respond poorly to competitive people.	Enjoy learning.
See failure and setback as terminal.	Motivated to apply what they know to the next challenge.
Poor or negative outcomes switch them off learning.	Aspirational – would like to have another go and do it better next time.
May get things out of perspective.	Can be competitive.

Confidence

Defined: Individuals high in confidence have the self-belief to successfully complete tasks that may be considered too difficult by individuals with similar abilities but lower confidence.

Applied: For example, individuals at one end of the scale will be able to take setbacks (externally or self-generated) in their stride. They keep their heads when things go wrong and it may even strengthen their resolve to do something. At the other end, individuals will be unsettled by setbacks and will feel undermined by these. Their heads are said to 'drop'.

Again, continuing research has identified two subscales for this component.

Confidence (Abilities)

Individuals scoring highly on this scale are more likely to believe that they are a truly worthwhile person. They are less dependent on external validation and tend to be more optimistic about life in general. They believe in their abilities and in their capacity to develop new abilities.

Typical behaviours associated with mental toughness (high scores) or mental sensitivity (low scores) on this scale include:

Lower scores	Higher scores
Low self-belief. Not confident that they know subject matter even when they do.	Can believe they are right – even when they are wrong.
Produce minimal responses when asked.	Little or no need for external validation.
Will be reluctant to ask questions 'in case it makes me look stupid'.	Happy to ask questions.
Reluctant to do presentations or oral work.	Happy to provide full responses to questions and in exams.
Inner belief missing – need others to build that.	If they don't know, they will find out.
Unsure whether they have grasped a subject or not.	

Confidence (Interpersonal)

Individuals scoring highly on this scale tend to be more assertive – and are as likely to influence others as others influence them. They are less likely to be intimidated in social settings and are more likely to promote themselves in groups. They are also better able to handle difficult or awkward people.

Typical behaviours associated with mental toughness (high scores) or mental sensitivity (low scores) on this scale include:

Lower scores	Higher scores
Easily intimidated. Won't express themselves even when they know they are right.	Will stand their ground.
	Will face down criticism etc.
Lack the confidence to express that they know in writing – will understate a position.	Will easily engage in class and group activity.
	Will use this quality to argue down others more knowledgeable.
Won't ask questions– low engagement.	
Will back down quickly when challenged	Can be assertive.
Will allow others to dominate debates – even when they are more knowledgeable	
Will have difficulty dealing with assertive people.	

MENTAL TOUGHNESS and its relationship with enterprise and employability

The 4Cs framework can be presented as a relationship with key employability competencies. The table below shows how the components relate to those competencies.

Table 3.2 Key employability competencies

Mental Toughness Scale	Subscales	What key enterprise and employability qualities does Mental Toughness assess?
CONTROL	Life Control	**Self Efficacy** – the sense of 'can do'. This is a fundamental requirement for enterprise owners and entrepreneurs. They have a sense that they can control enough of their life and their environment to achieve what they need to achieve.
	Emotional Control	**Emotional Management** – maintaining poise even when circumstances are difficult. Being able to manage client's and colleagues' emotions and feelings to make them feel at ease. People don't buy from or like working with miserable people.
COMMITMENT	Goal Orientation	**Goal Setting** – a sense of measurable purpose. Fundamental to any business role. This also embraces the expectations of others such as bank managers, funders, stakeholders, line managers, tutors, etc.
	Completion	**Tenacity** – doing whatever is needed to achieve goals and targets – including keeping promises to others in order to build a good and trusting relationship. 'I get satisfaction from delivering on time and on target.'
CHALLENGE	Risk Taking	**Open Mindedness** – open (even excited) about entering new markets, territories, clients. Open to taking calculated risks to break new ground. Not being put off by meeting new people, new situations, new opportunities, etc.
	Learning from Experience	**Positive Attitude** – accepting that not everything will go to plan. But taking the view that each occasion is a learning opportunity – you can do it better next time and even failure can be turned into opportunity.
CONFIDENCE	In Abilities	**Self Belief** – nothing is beyond me just because I don't know. I believe in my ability and can grow my ability. This is about not just having abilities but really believing in your abilities.
	Interpersonal Confidence	**Assertiveness** – influencing others more than they influence you. I am also confident about socializing with others in a work setting and will be comfortable networking. I can put people at ease. I can present to others what I do in a persuasive way.

Developing Employability and Enterprise

In summary when employers, educators and clients talk about 'the right attitude', they are seeking to describe a mindset that deals with opportunity, challenge and problems, keeps focused on what is important and does so in a manner which instils confidence. That's mental toughness.

Figure 3.8 Mental Toughness: sample scores

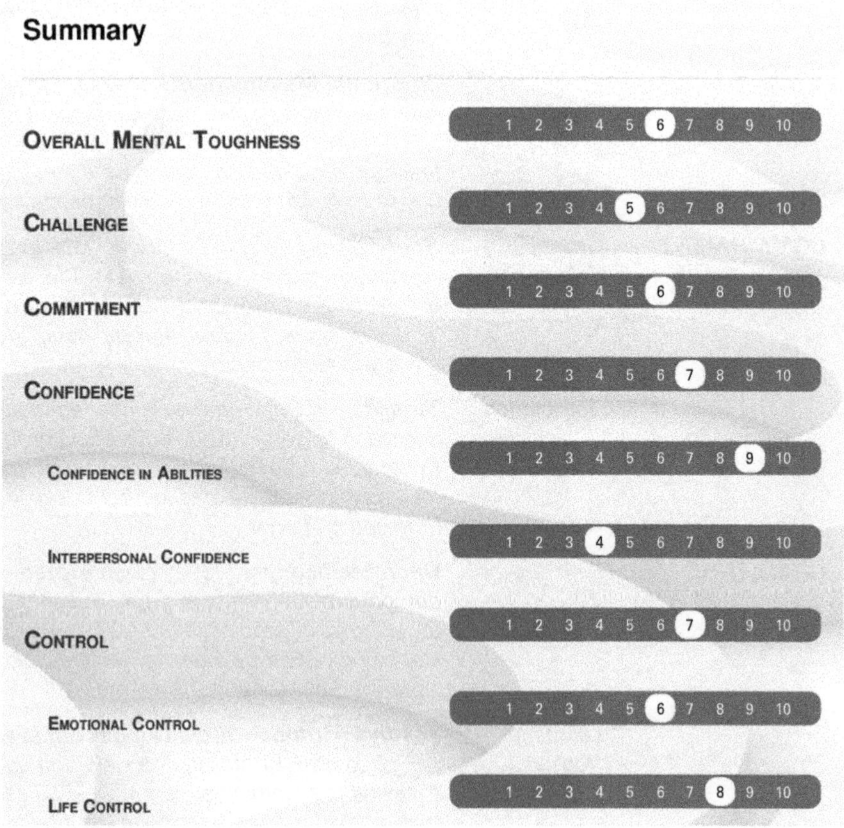

Summary

Scale	Score (1–10)
OVERALL MENTAL TOUGHNESS	6
CHALLENGE	5
COMMITMENT	6
CONFIDENCE	7
CONFIDENCE IN ABILITIES	9
INTERPERSONAL CONFIDENCE	4
CONTROL	7
EMOTIONAL CONTROL	6
LIFE CONTROL	8

Figure 3.9 Coaching and assesser report sample

Challenge

1 2 3 4 **5** 6 7 8 9 10

This individual will be able to cope effectively with most of life's challenges, and may use these as a way of enhancing their personal development. However, at times, they may avoid some of the opportunities which, to them, carry risk. They may at times seek 'change for change's sake', but are reasonably accepting of a degree of routine.

They will be most comfortable in an environment that provides them with a balance of predictability and flexibility, but they will usually be able to react quickly to the unexpected when necessary. In times of high stress or pressure they may tend towards risk avoidance.

Occasionally this individual may take on more challenges than they can handle which might mean that they struggle to complete tasks assigned to them.

If exposed to too much change and challenge this person may become worn down and will lose enthusiasm and interest. If confidence is also low there may be a risk of 'burnout'.

Coaching suggestions will include:

- Helping the individual to review and prioritize their work.
- Getting them to see what they are doing from a wider perspective. Are there others with no greater abilities achieving what they are being asked to handle?
- Introducing simple time management tools and techniques.
- Supporting them in delegating their work to others.
- Encouraging the team to support the individual.
- Getting them to review their goals and targets – are they truly realistic? Are they dependent on others and are the others reliable?
- Check for evidence for 'burn out'. Are activities beginning to take much longer than expected? What can be done to refresh the person?

Figure 3.9(2) Suggested questions

Suggested questions

- What is your ideal working environment?
- Can you give us an example of how you have dealt with an unexpected problem?
- How do you deal with routine/mundane tasks?
- Can you give us an example of how you have successfully coped with a major change in the workplace?
- Describe the last two or three projects/work you handled? How did they finish?
- Describe a routine job task that you are required to carry out regularly. How well is it done?
- What is your reaction when asked to handle large and difficult tasks?
- Describe a piece of work you found particularly stretching. What was so challenging about it? How did you deal with the challenge?
- If asked to do something very different from your nromal or core activity, what is your response?
- Describe three aspects of your work you like most and three you like least. What are the common themes in each group?

A mental toughness case study: Manchester Metropolitan University

Higher Education providers are acutely aware of the need to provide their students with the wider skills needed to gain graduate level jobs. It is becoming an increasingly competitive market and good academic performance is simply not enough to guarantee success.

The Department of Psychology at Manchester Metropolitan University is one of the biggest in the UK, having around 1,250 students and 50 staff. The department makes extensive use of the MTQ48 and the '4 C's model of mental toughness. All first year students complete the questionnaire and it is used as part of the pastoral care tutorial system. Students receive a feedback report and discuss this on a one-to-one basis with their personal tutors.

These discussions lead to the production of a mental toughness action plan that is then followed and refined through the three years they attend. Students complete the questionnaires again in their second and third year to monitor progress.

In general, the students score at the sensitive end of the mental toughness continuum and have particular issues within the confidence domain. This is not restricted to psychology students or Manchester Metropolitan University but rather it appears to be a common pattern across higher education. The challenge is to create a student-centred approach that also delivers the opportunity for students to experience and develop the key coping skills to deal with the challenging and stressful situations that typify the world of work. As stated earlier in this chapter 'Whatever one does (at work), one hits problems, changes and setbacks – often for reasons outside one's control.'

The department supports this with the provision of an extensive employability programme, including mock interviews, career talks and a general mentoring system. The mental toughness concept and measure operate at the core of this preparation for employability.

The embedding of mental toughness has been running for just over two years, starting in 2015 and appears to be successful. It creates a debate and an understanding of mental toughness amongst staff and students, and appears to help graduates find jobs. The figures for 2016 show a 10 per cent improvement in employability compared with 2015.

The CareerEDGE model of graduate employability

What is graduate employability?

If approaching 50 per cent of the young population of the UK were to go on to higher education, it is not surprising that this would provoke thinking about what the particular needs of those who go through this phase of education might be.

As noted above the most widely cited definition of graduate employability is that of Yorke (2006), 'a set of achievements – skills, understandings and personal attributes – that makes graduates more likely to gain employment and be successful in their chosen occupations, which benefits themselves, the workforce, the community and the economy' (p. 8).

This comprehensive pedagogic framework opened up opportunities for a very sophisticated analysis of the aspects of development that teachers and curriculum devisers should focus on in their efforts to enhance and support the nurturing of graduate employability.

Whilst this served the purpose of giving the employability agenda deserved recognition amongst peers in the academic community, it proved to be a weakness when trying to apply it in practical settings.

This problem was highlighted by Dacre Pool and Sewell (2007) who suggested that it did not lend itself to easy explanation to non-academic audiences including undergraduate students, employers and parents, the term 'Meta-Cognition' being a particular case in point.

It was this problem, in addition to their recognition of the importance of emotional intelligence as a key factor in determining an individual's employability that led them to develop the CareerEDGE model of graduate employability (Figure 3.10).

They define graduate employability as: '... having a set of skills, knowledge, understanding and personal attributes that make a person more likely to choose and secure occupations in which they can be satisfied and successful.' (Dacre Pool & Sewell, 2007, p. 280)

The mnemonic CareerEDGE is used as an aid to remember the five components on the lower tier of the model.

Since CareerEDGE is a model of *graduate* employability, **'Degree subject knowledge'**, and **'skills and understanding'** were put at the centre of the five elements. It was hoped that this would reassure academics within universities that this employment-orientated agenda was not intended to undermine the academic rigour of their courses.

Figure 3.10 CareerEDGE graduate employability

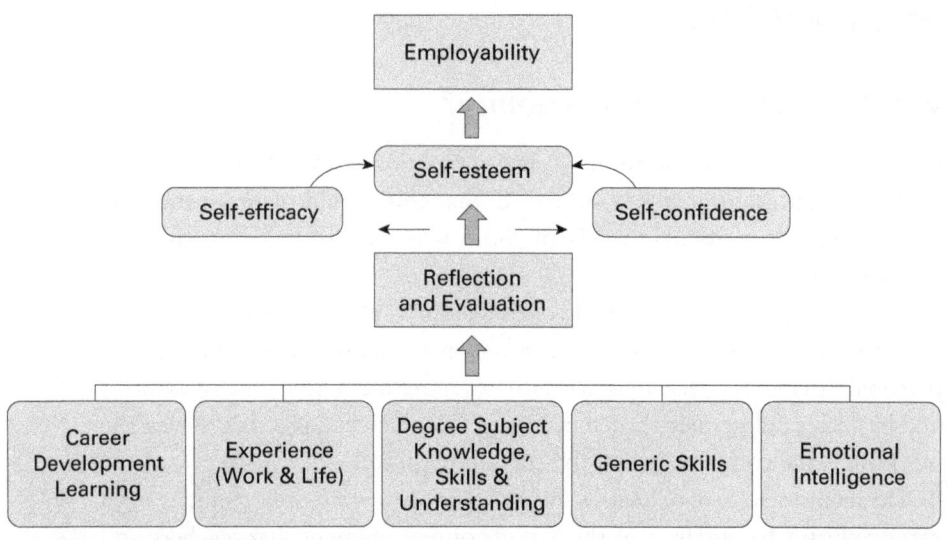

Dacre Pool & Sewell (2007)

Career Development Learning is most effectively summarized by the so-called DOTS model (Law and Watts, 1977), which consists of:

Decision learning – a process of learning effective decision-making skills.

Opportunity awareness – knowing what work opportunities exist and understanding the structure of the world of work.

Transition learning – including job searching and self-presentation skills.

Self-awareness – understanding aspects of one's personality, skills, interests, motivation and values.

The advantage of this simple four-element framework is that it allows for the vast complexity of the career development process to be captured in an easy-to-remember format. Just four topic headings that encompass the vast range of issues, learning and knowledge, that are required to negotiate a path through the world of work.

Work experience is widely acknowledged as a crucial aspect of employability and for students and graduates it has long been accepted that other experiences gained at university are also important, for example through clubs, societies and sporting activities.

In the 2015 High Fliers survey for *The Times* **Top 100 Graduate Employers** it was found that:

'Nearly **half the recruiters** who took part in the research repeated their warnings from previous years – that graduates who have had no previous work experience at all are **unlikely to be successful** during the selection process and have **little or no chance** of receiving a job offer for their organizations' graduate programmes.' High Fliers Research Ltd (2015).

Even for those students who do not seek employment opportunities in such companies it is extremely difficult to provide convincing answers to the frequently used competency application form questions and respond effectively at recruitment interviews without having some, even non-relevant, employment experience.

Graduate recruiters often highlight the **generic skills** that they are seeking in applicants to their jobs and many provide lists of competencies on their websites that they consider as the particular ones that they look for in their candidates. Dacre Pool and Sewell (2007) chose 'The Pedagogy for Employability Group' (2006) list, arrived at from research carried out over the preceding 25 years:

- imagination/creativity;
- adaptability/flexibility;
- willingness to learn;
- independent working/autonomy;
- working in a team;
- ability to manage others;
- ability to work under pressure;
- good oral communication;
- communicating in writing for varied purposes/audiences;
- numeracy;
- attention to detail;
- time management;
- assumption of responsibility and for making decisions;
- planning, coordinating and organizing ability;
- ability to use new technologies (was also added to the list as a key skill).

This list corresponds closely with the outcomes from the research carried out in the development of Carrus (described above) as well as the UK Chartered Management Institute 2011 survey, which sought to examine manager's perceptions about young people and the education system described in Chapter One.

Finally, they argue that **emotional intelligence** is crucial given the high degree of social interaction in the workplace. Whether it is in a manufacturing, sales, legal or commercial setting, a managing, training or other role, emotional intelligence is a critical capacity. The concept of emotional intelligence has developed far greater attention and been popularized by the work of Daniel Goleman (1998), but it is the Mayer and Salovey (1997) 'Four Branch Model' which provides a particularly useful way of making sense of this construct in the context of employability.

They suggest that EI is composed of four abilities: perceiving emotion, using emotion to facilitate thought, understanding emotions and managing emotions. It is this fluid capacity that means that individuals can learn about and develop their emotional intelligence and there is increasing research evidence to support this view, for example Dacre Pool and Qualter (2012).

Whilst studying at university, students should be provided with the chance to access and develop everything on the lower tier of the model. It is essential that in addition to the central subject of their academic study, students are also given opportunities and support to reflect on and evaluate their experiences.

It is this combination of activities which results in the development of higher levels of self-efficacy, self-confidence and self-esteem, which as they see it are the crucial components of employability. Again this is closely aligned with the mental toughness model also described above.

A key innovation in the CareerEDGE model was the far greater emphasis given to emotional intelligence as a vital and previously under-recognized aspect of employability. An important feature of the model is that it is based on sound theoretical research and on the fact that it has been shown to be of particular help to academics, personal tutors and any other practitioners involved in employability.

The main advantages of the CareerEDGE framework are that it:

- Helps to explain the concept of employability simply and clearly to students, enabling them to take responsibility for their own employability development.
- Allows the student to identify personal development areas and make plans to engage with these.
- Can be used as a basis for career planning – identifying aspects that need to be addressed.
- Can be used to help plan applications, write CVs and prepare for interviews.
- Enables explicit links to be made between subject/discipline knowledge and wider employability.

The model has been used to inform the planning of programmes and structured interventions in colleges and universities around the world by providing clarity of information about what needs to be considered and included. It can also be used to demonstrate to employers how the roles of Higher Education Institutions (HEIs) and business can both contribute to graduate employability, resulting in benefits for both parties.

The CareerEDGE model now forms the basis of the delivery of the employability strategies at a number of UK universities as well as in HEIs in the USA and Australia. It has also been used with universities in China and the model informed the approach to employability of the Pan-European, European-Commission-funded, Future Skills in Biotechnology Project.

A tool for measuring graduate employability

There have been a number of attempts to develop questionnaires to assess the employability of students. This is by no means a straightforward task because of the multiple factors that any model of employability inevitably covers.

Dacre Pool, Qualter and Sewell (2014) referred to previous tools that attempted to enable students to assess their employment capabilities, for example, the 'My Vocational Situation' Diagnostic Form (MVSDF: Holland et al, 1980) which was developed in the USA to enable career counsellors to very quickly determine the key career concerns of their clients.

The questionnaire addresses the three areas of 'vocational identity', 'occupational information' and 'barriers' (that might inhibit individual career success). The main problem with trying to use this in a UK-employability context is that it does not explicitly address important aspects such as work experience or generic skills or indeed emotional intelligence.

A tool developed during the 1990s in the UK called 'The Measure of Guidance Impact' (Christophers et al, 1993) was an attempt to determine the effectiveness of school careers-education programmes. Based on the DOTS model it has some potential value in this context, at least in terms of assessing the Career Development Learning aspect of employability. Dacre Pool, Qualter and Sewell (2014) also reviewed other self-perceived employability measures such as Berntson and Marklund, 2007; Rothwell and Arnold, 2007, but concluded that these were not suitable for use with undergraduate students.

The Employability Development Profile (EDP) based on the CareerEDGE model, is a 28-item inventory designed to help students, with the guidance of their tutor or career counsellor, to identify which of the crucial five employability areas they need to enhance. It asks students to rate themselves on the five key areas of employability, as defined by the CareerEDGE model. The goal is to encourage awareness of what these employability areas embrace and to support the user in reflection that is as honest and as objective as is possible.

The final page of the EDP questionnaire includes space for the student to write evidence to support their perceived strengths, an exercise which helps them to prepare for job applications.

A final section encourages them to create an action plan to develop those areas that they perceive as weaknesses. The EDP questionnaire is best used within the context of a course, with support provided to enable the student to identify suitable development resources and activities to provide the necessary enhancement in perceived weak areas. Alternatively, this can be provided by a career guidance adviser. Online adaptations of the questionnaire can provide links to suitable online personal courses and information resources.

CareerEDGE
Employability development profile

1	2	3	4	5	6	7
Strongly disagree	Disagree	Slightly disagree	Neither agree nor disagree	Slightly agree	Agree	Strongly agree

Please respond to the following statements. This is a personal development tool that should help you and your academic/careers adviser to identify possible areas for development over the next year. It is therefore important that you try to answer as honestly and accurately as possible.

The CareerEDGE questionnaire

	Items	Range	My score
Career Development Learning	1–5	5–35	
Experience Work/Life	6–7	2–14	
Degree Subject Knowledge	8–9	2–14	
Generic Skills	10–25	16–112	
Emotional Intelligence	26–28	3–21	
Total Score	1–28	28–196	_____

The data generated guides reflection and action planning.

Now take a look at the way you have scored the questionnaire. For the items you have scored with a 6 or a 7, would you be able to demonstrate your abilities in these areas and give some good examples of these? Choose one of these highly rated areas and write how you would explain this to a potential employer.

Now take a look at the items you have scored with a 1, 2, 3 or 4. What action could you take to help you increase these scores to a 6 or 7? Choose one of these items and write your action plan for this below.

CASE STUDY 1   University of Lancaster

We use the Employability Development Profile with our BSc Economics students quite early in their first year of study as part of the introduction to the careers and employability element of their professional skills module.

All 250 of the students complete the questionnaire and refer to it and the action points arising from it in their personal development reports. It also forms the basis of their action plan, which they have to create as part of their preparation for further careers-related activity in their second and third years.

We are planning to develop an online version of the questionnaire this year to make it easier for the students to use and store in their Moodle (Online learning environment) and refer to as they go through their programme.

It will also allow us to collect results and aggregate them so that we can discern areas of concern amongst groups of students. For example if 200 of the 250 students are showing significant concerns about their lack of work experience or presentation skills when they are asked to complete the survey early in the first year of the course it might help us to target interventions to support them.

CASE STUDY 2 University of Central Lancashire

All of the students on the Level 2, 20 credit elective module 'Planning Your Career' were asked to complete the CareerEDGE employability development profile as a self-assessment tool along with other personality, interest and motivation questionnaires.

With one of the cohorts of students we decided to ask them to complete the questionnaire right at the very start of the first session, then again at the end of the module, ie after a whole semester of attending their Career Development Learning course. As we might have expected and indeed hoped, the scores on the Career Development Learning subscales showed a statistically significant increase, which suggested that the students felt more confident about their career-management skills after completing the module.

What reassured us that the changes were a consequence of the module was that there were no significant changes in the emotional intelligence or problem solving skills of the students, which were not intended learning outcomes of the module. So the students did not simply seem to be ticking boxes to say that everything had improved. What was especially interesting and for the course team reassuring, was that there were significant increases for the work experience sub scale. Indeed further examination of the individual item showing a significant increase revealed that it was the one about explaining the value of experience to an employer which was very much a topic covered in the module.

These two case studies illustrate just two ways that the CareerEDGE model and the employability development profile can be used in everyday practice with students even in very large groups. Dacre Pool, Qualter and Sewell (2014) remind us to use caution when evaluating results using these pre-post evaluation designs.

In one such intervention involving teamwork development they found that the scores of the participants actually went down after a learning experience which was intended to enhance their confidence and capability of working in teams.

They realized that this might not necessarily be a failure of the intervention to achieve its overall aim of learning about working in teams, but it may actually have tapped into the students' realization that they had perhaps overestimated their initial level of confidence. It could be argued that the students had in fact had a useful learning experience, which could be important for their future employability. The point for practitioners is to think carefully about the results of any such evaluation activities using the EDP.

References

Berntson, E and Marklund, S (2007) The relationship between perceived employability and subsequent health, *Work & Stress*, 21 (3), pp 279–292

Christophers, U, Stoney, S, Whetton, C, Lines, A and Kendal, A (1993) *Measure of Guidance Impact* (MGI), User Manual, ASE, Windsor.

Dacre Pool, L and Sewell, P (2007) The key to employability: developing a practical model of graduate employability, *Education + Training*, 49 (4), pp 277–289.

Dacre Pool, L, Qualter, P (2012) Improving emotional intelligence and emotional self-efficacy through a teaching intervention for university students, *Learning and Individual Differences*, 22, pp 306–312

Dacre Pool, L, Qualter, P & Sewell, PJ (2014) Exploring the Factor Structure of the CareerEDGE Employability Development Profile, *Education + Training*, 56 (4), pp 303–313

Goleman, D (1998) *Working with Emotional Intelligence*, Bloomsbury, London.

Hillage, J and Pollard, E (1998) *Employability: developing a framework for policy analysis*, Department for Education and Employment, London

High Fliers Research Ltd (2015) *The Graduate market in 2015*, Annual review of graduate vacancies and starting salaries at Britain's leading employers

Holland, J L, Daiger, DC and Power, PG (1980) *My Vocational Situation (MVS)*, User Manual, Consulting Psychologists Press, Palo Alto, CA.

Knight, P and Yorke, M (2004) *Learning, Curriculum and Employability in Higher Education*, Routledge Falmer, London.

Law, W and Watts, AG (1977) *Schools, Careers and Community*, Church Information Office, London.

Mayer, JD and Salovey, P (1997) What is emotional intelligence?, in Salovey, P and Sluyter, D (Eds), *Emotional Development and Emotional Intelligence: Implications for Educators*, Basic Books, New York, NY, pp 3–31.

Pedagogy for Employability Group (2006) *Pedagogy for Employability: Learning and Employability Series 1*, The Higher Education Academy, York.

Rothwell, A and Arnold, J (2007) Self-perceived employability: development and validation of a scale, *Personnel Review*, 46 (1), pp 23–41

Sewell, PJ and Dacre Pool, L (2010) Moving from conceptual ambiguity to operational clarity: employability, enterprise and entrepreneurship in higher education, *Education + Training*, 52 (1), pp 89–94

Yorke, M and Knight, PT (2002) Employability through the curriculum, *Skills Plus: Tuning the Undergraduate Curriculum*, June 2002 edn

Yorke, M and Knight, PT (2004) *Embedding Employability into the Curriculum*, Higher Education Academy, York.

Yorke, M (2006) Employability in higher education: what it is – what it is not, *Learning and Employability Series One*, ESECT and HEA, York.

Developing employability and enterprise

04

Tackling the challenge of youth unemployment and social mobility

KIERAN GORDON – CAREER CONNECT LIMITED

Two of the biggest challenges facing the UK in terms of the future of its workforce and its economy are those of wasted talent and social immobility. At its core is the way that we prepare young people for a working life. Britain is amongst those nations with the lowest levels of social mobility in the developed world. For every one person born in the 1970s in the poorest fifth of society and going to university, there would be four undergraduates from the top fifth of society. But if you were born in the 1980s, there would be five, indicating a continuing decline in social mobility. Higher education is not evenly balanced either in terms of aspirations – 81 per cent of the richest fifth of the population think their child will go to university, compared to 53 per cent of the poorest. It seems life chances are influenced by a range of factors, not all related to ability.

There is widespread agreement across all sectors of UK political and economic life that the UK needs to build a better qualified and more highly skilled workforce. A recent government target of creating three million new apprenticeships by 2020 is an indication of how serious the problem is. It is greater in specific sectors of the economy, for example the STEM areas of science, technology, engineering and maths. Drilling down further we find an even greater crisis is looming as we face a huge skills shortage in the fast-growing digital and creative industries: an area in which Britain has been a world leader.

The case for better qualifications and higher skills is undeniable, however this is only part of the solution. Qualifications are accepted as proxies for drivers of economic growth; however, employers often go beyond the lack of technical skills when citing their reasons for their difficulties in finding the right people for their workforce. They point to the character of individuals, how well they have been prepared for the world of work and their attitudes towards work. Life skills, or 'soft skills' as they are often referred to, are thought to be lacking in many young people leaving school. These are social and work-related in nature, skills such as communication, problem solving, team working and critical thinking.

More than qualifications

Evidence of the fact that the solution lies in a wider set of factors than mere qualifications is shown in research conducted by Leadership IQ, which tracked 20,000 new recruits in public, private and health-care organizations. The research found that 46 per cent of new recruits failed within the first 18 months. More alarmingly, only 11 per cent failed due to a lack of skills and a staggering 89 per cent failed due to attitudinal reasons. The causes for this were numerous and most often cited as: low levels of emotional intelligence, the ability to understand and manage one's own emotions and accurately assess others' emotions; low motivation, lack of drive to achieve one's full potential and excel in the job, and lack of coach-ability, the ability to accept and act upon feedback.[1]

From personal experience through my work in the field of careers advice for over 30 years I can attest to the fact that all too often people are hired for their qualifications and fired for their attitude. It is time, therefore, that we educated the hirers (employers) and the 'hirees' (recruits) and their educators to invest in developing a wider set of skills, which make people more employable. The reason why qualifications are so often the critical factor in recruitment is that they are easier to measure and can provide objective information on a candidate, even if the actual qualification is not an essential factor in the job match. Conversely, because there hasn't been a universally applied measure for 'attitude', it hasn't been widely assessed as part of the career planning or recruitment process.

My concern has been with how we prepare people to cope with the demands of working life, which have undoubtedly become more demanding.

Technological advances, global competition, fluid and flexible forms of work have all contributed to unprecedented changes in working patterns and forms of employment. The future workplace of 2030 is predicted to be multi-generational, with four generations working side by side for the first time[2] This poses a challenge for each generation in terms of their ability to cooperate, collaborate and communicate. It is conceivably a greater challenge for young people entering the workplace for the first time as they come to terms with hierarchies, real or perceived, and as they learn the basics of the job. Attitudes amongst young people in the 21st century are considered to be different from past generations. Young people entering the world of work will be more flexible and adept at multi-tasking in the way they work and will want flexibility in the workplace; they are more likely to be more questioning and less likely to accept what they are told; they are more likely to learn by doing and prefer interactive media; and will routinely use social media and expect quick responses rather than wait for emails. How they relate to situations and how they cope with challenges will be critical to how successful they become.

Massive changes in labour market and workplace

We need to look at the evidence of how attitudes, behaviours and emotions play a part in the way that people operate at school or at work. The disciplines of psychology and neuroscience are able to provide us with a greater understanding of how we can prepare people to function to their potential; there is a wealth of evidence as to what can make a difference. During my time in the field of careers advice and guidance the underlying theoretical basis of career choice and traditional approaches to careers guidance has changed, due in part to the massive change that is taking place in the labour market and the workplace of the future. Other drivers for change include the advances in the science of personality, with MRI evidence of what causes us to behave in the ways we do, shaping how people are motivated to make decisions and take action. The psychology of personality has been a significant part of the training and tools at the disposal of careers professionals for some time, but the understanding of personality traits has changed with advances in neuroscience. Early on in my career I undertook training to use and interpret psychometric tests; these broadly fell into two types: ability and aptitude tests and personality measurement. The teaching at the time held that one's personality is fixed and immutable, hence it can be measured and used to understand how to influence individual career choice. This somewhat fatalistic belief has since been overturned and evidence produced by neuroscience indicates that our brains and therefore our personalities are malleable and liable to change; the term used to describe this is neuroplasticity. Further to this, the long-held belief that the brain stops developing early in life following adolescence is also proven not to be the case. According to Daniel Siegel[3] the brain continues to physically grow in response to experience and it can be stimulated and nurtured to encourage positive thought and behaviour.

New mental skills can be acquired with:

- intentional effort;
- focused awareness;
- concentration;
- aerobic exercise;
- novelty;
- emotional arousal.

'How we focus our attention shapes the structure of our brain. Neuroscience supports the idea that developing the reflective skills of *Mindsight* [as Siegel describes his model of neural integration] activates the very circuits that create resilience and well-being.'[4] Much of this development takes place in the prefrontal cortex of the brain, the area where complex processing permits us to create concepts in the present, think of experience in the past and plan and make images in the future. The adolescent brain is in flux: it changes especially in the prefrontal cortex regions and does not mature fully, according to Siegel, until the mid-20s.

During adolescence, from early teens, the brain is set up:

1 to be novelty-seeking;
2 for social engagement;
3 with increased emotional intensity;
4 for creative exploration.

Novelty-seeking is conditioned by an increased drive for rewards in the adolescent brain; this is often manifested in thrill-seeking, risk-taking, etc.

It is also evident in a desire for instant or early gratification and can lead to frustrations on the part of the individual who is not able to control this desire, particularly where they are challenged to apply themselves to a task without an immediate reward. When young people engage with peers and have little adult contact these behaviours are more likely to be amplified by increased risk-taking behaviour. By exposing young people to purposeful activities and experiences we can help them manage their impulses and reactions, reflect on their experiences and take control of their lives. The key to resilience and well-being is creating a sense of purpose and adopting a positive mindset. Allied to this is self-efficacy, which comes from a feeling of self-worth and self-belief. To be able to do this one must have a high level of self-knowledge and awareness; this can come from engaging in positive social relationships and exercising control of one's emotions and life situations.

The practical steps towards addressing this involve developing certain skills that nurture the very neural circuits that create resilience and well-being. The skills identified in improving resilience and well-being include:

Table 4.1 Skills to improve resilience and well-being

Goal Setting – the ability to look forward, make a plan and set goals;

Reflection – the ability to take time out to review experiences and actions;

Positive Thinking – the ability to take a realistic rather than a fatalistic view of situations and look for the opportunities in them;

Openness – awareness of self and openness to giving and receiving feedback;

Observation – awareness of the world around you and compassion for others;

Objectivity – the ability to step outside a situation and control emotional responses;

Visualization – the ability to create a picture of an alternative scenario, particularly when faced with difficulty;

Attentional Control – the ability to focus on the task in hand;

Emotional Control – the ability to analyze one's emotional responses to a given situation and to control anxiety;

Perseverance – the ability to stick at it when pursuing a plan or a goal.

At Career Connect, a charity specializing in careers guidance and planning support for individuals, we have looked at ways we could go beyond helping people make decisions to enabling them to make those decisions a success. Career Connect works with thousands of young people and adults every year focusing on helping young people make a successful transition from education to work and helping adults regain entry to employment after breaks in their career brought about by a range of circumstances.

More resilient and self-confident

It became apparent that supporting individuals to make informed and relevant decisions about the career paths best suited to their interests, skills and values was only effective if the individual had the self-belief and personal capacity to put that decision into action and follow it through. Because our work is predominantly with people who are deemed to be in need of additional help and who are often vulnerable to underachieving and making unsuccessful transitions, we decided to extend our approach to address how we could help them to become more resilient and self-confident. In particular we used data and intelligence drawn from our many thousands of interactions with young people to attempt to identify at what point in the transition, failure became evident and to understand what reasons lay behind this failure.

What we learned was whilst there was universally a desire to find and keep work, for many they lacked the underlying behaviours and skills to be able to make this a reality; this was characterized by high numbers of individuals who cycled in and out of education, training and job opportunities without success. The reasons for this were as many and varied as the individuals themselves, but what was common was the realization that the experiences many of these young people were exposed to were limited and provided little instruction as to how to achieve and progress in a school, college or work situation. Many of the young people were below average in terms of school attendance; some had behavioural issues at school and most were less likely to achieve academic qualifications necessary to progress educationally or vocationally. It was apparent that further work was needed to equip them with skills and confidence to succeed. What we needed was a means of identifying the characteristics that were contributing to their inability to make successful transitions. By being able to identify and measure these traits it may be possible to provide support and instruction on how best to harness and develop their talents and make them work in their favour.

Mental toughness

In seeking to identify and measure the factors that could help young people to have realistic aspirations, make plans, set goals and stick at achieving their goals we used the model of Mental Toughness. The application of Mental Toughness grew out of Career Connect's (then Greater Merseyside Connexions) experience of using the MTQ48 measure to assess and develop leadership potential within its own management team at the inception of the Organization in 2001. We had chosen Mental Toughness for its ability to describe an individual's underlying mindset. It is a major factor in individual behaviour, well-being and performance and can be considered an enabler for these important outcomes. There are four elements in Mental Toughness (the 4Cs) – Control, Commitment, Challenge and Confidence, which are described elsewhere in this book.

Mental Toughness, as defined by Professor Peter Clough at Manchester Metropolitan University, is a personality trait, which determines in some part how individuals perform when exposed to stressors, pressure and challenge, irrespective of the prevailing situation. It has a proven link with one's performance, ability to adopt positive behaviours, and well-being. Whilst mental toughness has a genetic component it is also variable and developable and it is this latter fact that encouraged us to adapt the MTQ48 measure for use in our work with young people as a means of increasing their self-awareness and personal effectiveness. Their limitations in responding to stress, pressure and opportunity can have damaging effects on their futures. Risk-taking and poor management of risk often contributes to their inability to recognize and respond to given situations. This can lead to low self-esteem, limited aspirations, poor decision-making, reckless actions and conflict with authority whether in school or in society at large.

The belief that young people can be helped to reach their potential through developing a better understanding of their own behaviours and responses to situations and the consequences of their actions, informed the approach that Career Connect employed in developing innovative solutions to the challenges faced by young people at risk of underachievement. The New Horizons programme was the first programme-wide application of Mental Toughness and the MTQ48 psychometric measure with young people in preparation for transition to the world of work. It was launched in 2012 and operated until 2015, the timescale being determined by the commissioner, the UK Government's Department for Work and Pensions (DWP). The programme focused on young people who were assessed as at risk of underachievement. Based on tracking evidence from our work with school leaver cohorts in the Liverpool City region it was apparent that certain groups of young people were faring far worse than their peers, specifically: young people in care/leaving care; young offenders and young people with Learning Difficulties or Disabilities. Our evidence showed that outcomes for this cohort of young people were worsening at an alarming rate, despite a closing of the gap between them and their peers prior to 2011. The large-scale reduction in public sector funding resources from 2010 meant that programmes of specialist support were markedly reduced and as a consequence there was a polarization in outcomes evident for these young people when compared with their peers. Many lived in families and neighbourhoods where adult unemployment and worklessness was high: some of the most deprived communities in the country according to national statistics. Indeed Career Connect data showed a polarization of outcomes by geographical location as well by individual circumstances.

Return on investment

Our 'New Horizons' response was delivered within the framework of a Social Impact Bond (SIB) where risk capital was secured from a consortium of social investors who contracted with Career Connect on the basis of a detailed proposal which was accepted by the DWP and stress tested by the investors. The investors received payment from UK Government on the basis of individual measurable and evidenced outcomes through a payment-by-results model of funding. These outcomes are detailed in the performance data below and were the product of detailed research by the DWP into the underlying factors that inhibit progression and lead to unemployment and social disengagement. At the time of delivery this programme was the largest SIB in the UK. At the heart of the programme was the application of the Mental Toughness model and the use of the MTQ48 psychometric for assessment, diagnosis and evaluation.

The programme assessed each individual to identify his or her particular needs and from that created a development programme (based on the skill-set described in Table 1 above) over a period of 12 weeks. The programme comprised a range of activities and techniques including: the development of a personal profile based on the MTQ48 questionnaire analysis, bespoke one-to-one and group-based learning activities, experiential learning, including employer-facing activity and personal coaching. By taking the young people through what mental toughness is and providing an insight and understanding in the components of Confidence, Challenge, Commitment and Control, the coaches helped individuals to self-assess their profile in relation to these critical performance factors. These were then moderated by the use of the MTQ48 psychometric test and individual results discussed and analysed to identify a programme of activities designed to work on those areas of development that could have the greatest impact. The range of activities extended from fast-paced activities on learning styles, motivational tools, brain-training exercises, work placements and tasters, to alumni workshops. At the core of the programme young people were exposed to new and challenging situations, using a range of community facilities including those offered by employers. Each young person was helped to create their own learning plan and receive and act upon feedback from peers as well as coaches and educators. The aim of the coaching and mentoring was to support the development of an individual's resilience and capacity towards self-sustained transition as part of a longer-term career plan.

The use of the MTQ48 was instrumental in setting baselines and providing feedback, but it also had the added benefit of motivating and inspiring action. In the words of New Horizons coaches:

> Young people respond to the MT programme well; they liked to talk about themselves and recognizing and relating their behaviour to their feedback... it has the ability to challenge the young people's behaviour and raise their motivation.
>
> Feedback from schools shows a pattern of young people taking a more proactive approach to their learning and taking more responsibility in lessons and in planning for the future'.

Young people and their parents also commented on the positive impact of the programme:

> My son has benefited greatly from the Mental Toughness programme – his confidence has soared, he's really started to believe in himself and with the help of his Adviser [Coach], he's started to think more realistically about how his qualifications match available work opportunities. Thank you.
> Parent, Liverpool

> The Mental Toughness programme helped to improve my confidence – it made me feel stronger. I really enjoyed the brain-training activities and learnt to do things step by step. My friends should do it too.
> Scott, aged 15

The results were evident in the achievement of positive outcomes against which payments were made to the investors who had taken the financial risk to back the programme. Career Connect had made a convincing business case at the outset in which the commissioner and the investors took comfort from the use of a objective measure to establish the baseline and plot the trajectory of each individual towards the achievement of a set of measurable outcomes. Table 4.2 below demonstrates the success of the New Horizons programme in helping participants achieve a range of outcomes that would have been most unlikely without this intervention. The results featured a rate card of outcomes set by the DWP; these were: school attendance and behaviour outcomes; qualifications gained at levels 1, 2 and 3; and entry into sustained employment. The DWP rate card tracked each outcome and its cost and produced a return on investment matrix to identify the cost benefit of the programme in terms of the wider positive returns to government and to society by successful participants benefiting from improved behaviour, increased resilience, improved attainment and entry into employment (See Table 4.2). As the programme focused largely on young people in education the numbers of participants who had left school and were eligible for employment were low in comparison to the total target group. However, the rate of post-16 young people (ie school leavers) completing the programme and securing employment and retaining that employment for three months, six months and longer is high in comparison with their peers. An emerging feature of the programme is that coach support whilst in employment has a measurable impact on retention rates in employment; the dropout rate from employment reduced to zero from an early average of 40 per cent.[5]

Figure 4.1 demonstrates the value of the programme in terms of its social return on investment: the economic value being twice that of the cost of the programme.

Positive impact

The destination analysis Career Connect carried out for the New Horizons cohort of participants indicates that the programme has had a positive impact on the group as a whole. The numbers of New Horizons participants that made and sustained a positive learning or work outcome as measured by education, employment and training participation rates grew as the programme developed. By comparing this cohort of young people with young people with similar characteristics who had not entered the programme

Figure 4.1 New Horizons, social ROI

THE PROGRAMME DELIVERED EXCELLENT VALUE-FOR-MONEY FOR GOVERNMENT

The New Horizons programme ran until April 2015 (though outcomes were tracked for a further six months afterwards). During the contract period, it worked with 4,222 young people to deliver 6,044 positive outcomes. The table below illustrates the value to government delivered by the programme (according to the outcome values in the latest Innovation Fund Round 2 rate card).

	Outcomes delivered	Price per outcome paid by government (£)	Total paid by government (£k)	Value of outcome to government (£)*	Total value delivered to government (£k)
Improved school attendance	1,315	871	1,145	1,400	1,841
Improved school behaviour	1,779	552	982	1,300	2,313
National Vocational Qualification Level 1	1,870	441	825	900	1,683
National Vocational Qualification Level 2	728	1,452	1,057	3,300	2,402
Sustained employment for 13 weeks	198	1,924	381	3,500	693
Sustained employment for 26 weeks	154	740	114	2,000	308
Total Outcomes	**6,044**	-	**4,504**	-	**9,240**

shows a marked difference in the levels of achievement (Table 4.2) over time. The figures below show a comparison of New Horizons participants with young people from the same geographical area and a different area where Career Connect operates who had not had access to the programme and who were assessed as having similar needs.

Table 4.2 Education, Employment and Training rates

Education, Employment and Training (EET) Rates			
	Year 1 cohort 2012	Year 2 cohort 2013	Year 2 cohort 2014
New Horizons participant EET rate	58%	79%	93%
Liverpool City Region control group	48%	51%	54%
Statistical neighbour area control group	68%	71%	70%

Table 4.3 shows the improvement in qualifications for the New Horizons target group, which has impacted positively on the numbers of school leavers remaining in education or training before joining the labour market. For those who have completed a full academic year and taken GCSEs or equivalent qualifications the level 2 achievement rates have grown significantly. The results compare favourably with those from local statistical groups.

Table 4.3 Achievement of Qualifications

New Horizons Achievement of Qualifications			
	Baseline achievements in 2011	August 2013	August 2014
Percentage achieving Level 2 qualification	11%	22%	29%
Liverpool City Region control group	11%	13.2%	15.4%
Statistical neighbour area control group	16%	18.1%	18.4%

At the start of the New Horizons programme there were more than 5,000 young people across the Liverpool City region who were NEET (not in education, employment or training) and on average more than one thousand young people left this group in a month and more than one thousand joined the NEET register. This high degree of dropout and switching (churn) is an enormous waste of resource and was expensive to map, track and support. A key performance indicator for Career Connect in delivering the programme, therefore, has been the degree to which we can stem the cycle of young people aimlessly switching between or dropping out of opportunities. We have done this by fostering greater resilience and persistence in meeting new challenges amongst programme participants; this was measured in the area of 'commitment' via the MTQ48 assessment, which identifies how we can improve levels of 'stick-ability'. The key measure used to evaluate the degree to which the programme tackled the early drop out and switching rate between education, employment and training to NEET was known as the rate of 'churn' as shown in Table 4.4.

Table 4.4 Rate of churn between NEET and EET

	Rate of 'churn' between NEET and EET		
	Baseline achievements in 2011	August 2013	August 2014
New Horizon participants	25%	12%	11%
Liverpool City Region control group	22%	21%	20%
Statistical neighbour area control group	16%	15%	16%

The results achieved by the young people engaging in the programme have been a measure of its success. It has led to a successor programme currently operating in the same region with further investor backing, which is working with young people who have assessed levels of lower-tier mental-health needs. This programme also uses mental toughness and is already achieving positive results.

The New Horizons programme was a step change in our work, which sought to build on the social and emotional capabilities that contribute to long-term success rather than firefight the short-term problems of displacement or disengagement of young people as they leave school and become classed as NEET. It has led to remarkable results in terms of the positive outcomes for some of the most vulnerable and disadvantaged young people in the area. By providing an insight into how individual young people could build their levels of self-esteem, self-efficacy and resilience through the use of the Mental Toughness MTQ48 measure it has been possible to motivate them and shape their behaviours leading to the successful achievement of qualifications and employment.

Notes

1 Mark Murphy (2015) Why New Hires Fail (Emotional Intelligence Vs. Skills), *Leadership IQ*, 22nd June 2015
2 UKCES (2014) The Future of Work and Skills in 2030. *Evidence Report 84*, February 2014. ISBN-978-1-908418-63-0
3 Daniel Siegel (2011) *Mindsight: Transform your brain with the new science of kindness*. E-book Edition, One World Publications
4 Ibid. Location 231/6984.
5 Bridges Ventures LLP (2016) *Better Outcomes, Better Value. The evolution of social impact bonds in the UK*.

Developing mental readiness for the world of work

05

Building confidence and understanding employment journeys

RUTH CARTER, ROS KAIJAKS AND DAVID SUMMERS

The CBI conducts an annual survey with a sample of businesses to identify what employers look for in recruits and how this aligns with the calibre of candidates from whom they receive applications. The 2015 report mirrors 2014, in identifying that the most important things for employers is aptitude and attitude, which rank ahead even of literacy and numeracy. However, in the same report, a third of employers report concerns about young people's attitudes to work. Alongside this, 55 per cent reported concerns about lack of work experience.[1] (CBI, 2015)

These findings point to some very clear conclusions. Many young people are not fully prepared for entering employment and many have no experience from which to draw. In this context, ensuring learners have access to high-quality work experience would seem to be the solution. However, in reality many local employers, in particular SMEs, currently do not offer work experience. The CBI state that 39 per cent of companies 'with 50–199 employees currently have no links with schools', compared with just 18 per cent of companies with more than 5,000 employees'[2] (CBI, 2010, p. 27). It's also known that successful work experience depends on a good match between the learner and the employer – not only in terms of the sector and job role, but also the expectations of both parties.

For a young person, working their way through the multitude of career and job options this employment environment can be intimidating. Jobs, job titles and career options are changing fast and so is information about them. The UKCES 'Careers of the Future' report, indicated that 'we fully expect that new jobs may emerge over coming years as a result of new technology, changing consumer requirements and other trends' (UKCES, 2014)[3]. The use of the internet and websites means that employers have a direct link with future employees. An employer's website is often the first port of call for information about careers and jobs and some companies even dedicate stand-alone sites to their careers and job offers. In many ways, there is now more information available to young people and adults (including their parents) than ever before but searching for this and obtaining the right and relevant information is both a skill and a challenge. So the stakes are high and often this can be very daunting for a 14-year-old. In reality, many are only just starting to think about their future and many won't have a firm idea about what they want to do.

Preparation

So, if work experience is a challenge to organize, how can young people prepare themselves for entering the labour market, choosing a career and above all understanding their own personal employment journey?

There are three key aspects to this. The first relates to learners understanding themselves; the second to learners understanding the requirements of different employment roles and thirdly how learners should present themselves to employers.

Learners need to be able to carry out an assessment of the current level of their own skills or personal attributes. The next stage is to identify how these might transfer into a work setting – ensuring there is understanding about the relevance of the individual's experience. Next, learners also need to be able to identify specific skills or personal attributes for a specific job and be able to produce an action plan to develop their own skills or personal attributes accordingly. Finally, learners need to understand how they should present their personal information in working life both face-to-face and in writing. So planning and preparing for an interview (be it for work experience or a job), learners need to identify the skills or personal attributes that would be needed in that role.

Good self-presentation

A key aspect of preparation is the learners' attitude to how they present themselves, both in written format and face-to-face. Positive first impressions eg being on time and being polite. Personal hygiene and personal appearance show whether a person has the right attitude to wanting the job and showing the employer that they care about wanting to be employed. Learners also need to understand that appropriate communication at interview would include introducing oneself, shaking hands, sitting down when asked, listening to questions, not interrupting, speaking clearly, making eye contact and showing positive body language. It is good practice to support learners by allowing them to experience an interview and reflect on what went well or not well. Finally, learners should identify improvements for future interviews.

Preparing for a specific job role is really important. But before learners reach this point, they must have an understanding about future careers and how their choice of subject and qualification might affect this. For many this is difficult at 14, when they are asked what subjects they are going to choose for their GCSEs or other qualifications route. Again the options here aren't always clear. Many parents know about the 'traditional' GCSE route but many are also vague or not aware of vocational education options at the age of 14. Many of the major Awarding Bodies offer vocational qualifications at 14 as an alternative to GCSE. There are then further choices to make at 16. Does an individual progress onto A-Levels or vocational qualifications (such as Cambridge Technicals) and what is their preferred route after this... university, work, an apprenticeship?

Increasingly, there is a no 'wrong door' option and young people are switching between academic and vocational qualifications, or studying both in parallel. There is an argument that a good mix of both types of qualification makes for a good individual profile and that is attractive to both higher education and employers alike. Good examples now exist of learners going to university with vocational qualifications and likewise, A-level students going on to apprenticeships rather than going to university.

Kick-starting the thought process

All of this can be very daunting for a 13-year-old about to start thinking about their options at 14. However, there are many things that can be introduced both in and out of the classroom that can start that thought process. One such thing is 'Careers Lab', a Business in the Community initiative which aims to bridge the gap between schools and industry by getting more businesses into the classroom to deliver inspiring careers lessons side-by-side with teachers, helping young people to think more widely about their working life. Beyond the Careers Lab initiative, there are also some great examples of companies and employers working with individual schools on specific careers areas. An example of this is the Getting Girls into STEM event which was run by the Islington Business Class Cluster.

Careers Lab

Only 14 per cent of all STEM jobs in the UK are occupied by women and a recent CBI survey of over 500 UK employers reported 42 per cent as having difficulties recruiting STEM-skilled staff (CBI, 2015). One particular challenge identified in Islington was to help young people recognize how the subjects they study at school or college can lead to varied careers.

So the aim of the event was to help young girls relate school STEM subjects to the world of work. By providing real-world examples, business volunteers wanted to encourage and excite them into considering these fields for their academic and professional futures.

Prior to the day, employee volunteers from Islington cluster members and participating businesses were asked to develop a 20-minute practical and interactive activity to give the students from Islington schools an insight into a business or a specific job in their sector. They were asked to focus on activities that symbolize the key skills and talents needed for their job roles.

In the first year, nine businesses and four schools came together to showcase different career opportunities for 50 young girls. Students were able to attend three interactive sessions throughout the morning. The sessions began with an introduction to the industry and a brief outline of the employee volunteers' position and skills which are important in the role. Pupils were then given the opportunity to take part in an activity and ask questions about the products or processes involved as well as what the volunteers' different job roles entailed.

Barclays Bank

Not all employers are looking for the highest flying of graduates. Some companies take a realistic and proactive approach to recruitment, understanding that sometimes school and qualifications don't work for everyone but if they look more closely, they can see talent and potential. For example, Barclays Bank run an apprenticeship programme that offers career options to young people with no qualifications or experience which in turn helps to improve recruitment retention and tackle youth unemployment. It also tackles youth unemployment by providing long-term job opportunities. By engaging with young unemployed communities Barclays promotes the accessibility of careers in banking and financial services and by offering a permanent role and the proposed career pathways, this removes the perception that an apprenticeship is an interim assignment. The Barclays Apprenticeship Programme recruits 16–24-year-olds into entry-level, permanent roles in the Bank: already 1,000 have been accepted since April 2012 and a minimum of 2,000 by the end of 2015.

The initiative identifies young people who are not in employment, education or training and offers a recognized qualification in Financial Services or Business Administration. The programme has evolved to be able to create internal progression pathways through to degree level.

Former Barclays Chief Executive Officer Anthony Jenkins said in 2012, 'We recruit over 4,000 cashiers a year, so we have a real need for talent. And we are finding it difficult to recruit younger people into the organization. We've also found that our apprentices perform very well in terms of what they deliver within the branch or operation environment... the quality of people coming through the programme is very, very good indeed'.

Bradford Pathways

Bradford Pathways is a new initiative that is being embedded in the education, skills and employment infrastructure in Bradford District and is intended to prepare individuals more effectively for changing business and economic needs. It will support young people and adults into a wide range of higher-waged, higher-skilled and higher-demand careers, in sectors that are important in Bradford and the surrounding economies.

It combines academic, employability, leadership and technical skills and allows participants to explore different career pathways designed around high-demand sectors and occupations, gaining the real-world experience needed to compete and achieve success in education and life.

The model works by facilitating collaboration between education, businesses and industry partners to align resources, build shared capacity and combine services to provide a range of interventions aimed at meeting the various needs of employers and job-seekers. Ultimately it helps to fill positions that are available today, whilst closing skills gaps and preparing a flexible and skilled workforce for the changing needs of the 21st century, including jobs that do not yet exist.

The model originated in the USA as Career and Technical Education (CTE) and has been adopted across the country, with extensive evidence of the following outcomes:

- High school students involved in CTE are more engaged, perform better and graduate at higher rates.
- Post-secondary CTE fosters post-secondary completion and prepares students and adults for in-demand careers.
- Investing in CTE yields big returns for state economies; for example, in Washington, for every dollar invested in secondary CTE programmes, the state earns $9 in revenues and benefits.
- CTE addresses the needs of high-growth industries and helps close the skills gaps.

Bradford Pathways aims to work with all relevant stakeholders to develop and embed a CTE model customized to meet the needs of the Bradford District, its residents and its employers.

The development of the model across the whole of the education, skills, enterprise and employment infrastructure is a long-term programme and will be undertaken in a phased approach. Ultimately it will involve the following core elements:

- career clusters;
- career pathways;
- programmes of study;
- individual learning plans;
- personalized learning;
- essential skills and knowledge;

The first phase is focusing on secondary schools to deliver the pathways and on year 6 within primary schools, specifically for the core skills development; full implementation of phase 1 will start in September 2016. Some aspects of the model are currently being piloted in a number of primary and secondary schools throughout the district along with building on the successful work of the Industrial Centres of Excellence.

Next Steps Evening

An example of this was an event held at Titus Salt School (TSS). This event, called 'Next Steps Evening' provided information, advice and guidance in preparation for students making their GCSE option choices. Four external speakers from local businesses representing retail, health, sport and engineering sectors provided information on job opportunities and apprenticeships within the local area, including projections for 5 and 10 years' time. This was the first time such an event had been run and 40 per cent of the cohort attended. Feedback from both students and parents was very positive. Of particular interest to students/parents was the information regarding which group of qualifications might best suit a career path into a specific sector. Presenters made reference not just to the types of qualifications required but also to the grades needed to enter the sector at particular levels. Many parents and students were unaware of the range of opportunities within each sector and the types of jobs that could possibly be available in the future.

In the short term, the school's subsequent Section 5 inspection recognized independent information, advice and guidance (IAG) and links with business partners as one of the school's strengths, noting that this good careers guidance helps pupils to progress. In the medium term Bradford Pathways aims to offer a minimum of 100 hours work-related learning to all young people in Bradford District and schools will take on board the Bradford Pathways Education Journey.

The second case study provides an alternative way of approaching employer/learner interactions.

Sparks fly in Worktree Career WorkOut sessions

Research shows that young people's contact with employers is an important indicator of their future ability to successfully enter the labour market (Mann and Kashefpakdel, 2014)[4]. Young people are known to be especially attentive to the views of professionals they come into contact with in educational settings and overwhelmingly agree that contacts help in career decision-making (Education & Employers Taskforce, 2012)[5]. But secondary schools don't usually have a system for introducing students of all ages to a wide range of employers.

In Milton Keynes, education charity Worktree has developed a scheme called 'Career WorkOut' designed for all students aged 11–18. In a one-hour session, small groups of three to four students meet and interview eight volunteer work guests in a carousel of seven to eight-minute conversations about that guest's personal experience of work. Students can ask whatever questions they like as long as they're focused on work (and the volunteer guest may say 'pass'). Students find it engaging because of the variety of guests and conversations.

Career WorkOut and STEPS

The aim of Career WorkOut is not just to raise students' career awareness and aspirations. It is also to develop their knowledge and practice of the core employability skills 'STEPS': Self management, Team work, Enterprise awareness, Problem solving and Speaking and listening. It is not easy to predict exactly where the sparks will fly in a work-related conversation between a student and an adult, but guest workers invariably talk about one or more of the core employability skills during each short conversation.

It doesn't matter where the volunteer guest has worked in the past. Who can say which guest will spark the imagination and motivation of a student? What matters is that the guest answers student questions honestly and doesn't attempt to teach. Students enjoy being in charge of the questions – even the shy ones who take a while to warm up. This is about students getting independent, personal information about different types of work, not advice.

Career WorkOut is effective. Between September 2015 and March 2016, 2,832 students in three Milton Keynes schools met and interviewed 572 work guests. Results from student feedback immediately before and after the sessions show a 19 per cent increase in students' confidence in career decision-making, a 23 per cent increase in their confidence about talking to unfamiliar adults and an 8 per cent increase in their commitment to learning and achieving.

'I learned many new ideas to help me to achieve my future goals and benefit from the experiences offered to me,' said Matt Snell, a 16-year-old student of The Hazeley Academy.

Sam Rene, another 16-year-old student of The Hazeley Academy, said: 'It was interesting to learn what employers look for in future employees, what skills they look for.'

Confidence and resilience

By asking guests about their experiences in different jobs, students get to understand the importance of being confident and resilient and handling challenge and change. It helps them think differently and plan their futures more confidently.

Tony Nelson, Head Teacher of The Hazeley Academy, said: 'Feedback from our students and staff strongly suggest that Career WorkOut sessions have had a dramatic positive impact on student aspirations, personal vision and drive. In over two decades in education I have not come across a more effective programme for achieving these goals across such a wide range of students for such a minimal investment in terms of time and money.'

Worktree has also observed high levels of satisfaction among employee volunteers, with 62 per cent strongly agreeing they felt valued (99 per cent agreed) and 49 per cent strongly agreeing 'I now feel more positive about my work' (99 per cent agreed), suggesting potential worker-productivity gains for the employer.

'It was easy, interesting and fun,' said volunteer guest Kate Webster of Hewitsons solicitors. 'I came back feeling I'd done something worthwhile.'

Volunteer guest Alan Cusdin of Santander said: 'It reminded me of how fortunate I am to have my job and how much I enjoy it.'

Since Career WorkOut requires work guests to commit just one hour, nearly all stated a willingness to do it again, enabling schools to develop deeper and more productive relationships with local employers.

Career WorkOut has proved effective in Uganda, China and India, where Worktree has been training teachers and trainers since 2012, as well as in the UK. It really isn't difficult. There are two main ingredients:

Recruiting volunteer work guests – ideally at least eight for a group of 30 students. Work guests can be colleagues, people working in businesses nearby, friends or relatives... it doesn't matter what work status they hold, just that they speak authentically about their personal experience of work.

Facilitating the one-hour Career WorkOut session so that students take the lead in asking questions about guests' jobs, and guests feel comfortable giving authentic answers.

In Milton Keynes schools, Worktree recruits the guests and facilitates the sessions, but there are many stories of schools and teachers elsewhere doing it themselves. We believe any teacher anywhere can use the method of Career WorkOut to help his/her students think more actively about their work futures, think differently about different jobs and get better at talking to adults they don't know.

If you're a teacher or trainer, try it yourself! In our 20 years' experience of running education-business link programmes – from organizing 50,000 work placements to running a work-related 'school without walls' for full-time students excluded from mainstream schools – we believe Career WorkOut has the greatest potential to help all young people make the right choices and do well in their futures.

Self-assessment for jobs and careers and for future study is essential and opportunities to do that through work experience or with employer volunteers is even more powerful. A recent cohort study has concluded that on average, for each career talk with someone from outside the school, experienced at age 14 to 15, young people benefited from a 0.8 per cent wage premium when they were 26. (Kashefpakdel and Percy, 2016)[6]

So, in conclusion, there are many different ways for young people to enter the labour market at different levels. As the Business in the Community 'Inspiring the Next Generation' report indicated, four visits from employers during a young person's secondary education means that that individual young person is five times less likely to become a NEET (not in education, employment or training).

With thanks to Business in the Community, Bradford Pathways and Worktree for case studies.

More information can be found on their websites: www.bitc.org.uk, www.bradford-pathways.org.uk and www.worktree.org

Notes

1 CBI/Pearson (2015) *Inspiring Growth Education and Skills Survey* [Online] http://news.cbi.org.uk/reports/education-and-skills-survey-2015/ Last accessed 03/06/2016

2 CBI (2010) Ready to grow: business priorities for education and skills, *Education and skills survey 2010*, CBI, London [Online] http://www.educationandemployers.org/wp-content/uploads/2014/06/ready-to-grow-cbi.pdf Last accessed 03/06/2016

3 UKCES (2014) *Careers of the Future* [Online] https://www.gov.uk/government/uploads/system/uploads/attachment_data/file/452078/15.01.05._UKCES_Career_Brochure_V13_reduced.pdf Last accessed 14/06/16

4 Mann, A and Kashefpakdel, E (2014) The views of young Britons (aged 19–24) on their teenage experiences of school-mediated employer engagement, in

Understanding Employer Engagement in Education – Theories and Evidence, eds A Mann, J Stanley and L Archer, Abingdon, Routledge.

5 Education and Employers Taskforce (2012) It's who you meet: why employer contacts at school make a difference to the employment prospects of young adults [Online] http://www.educationandemployers.org/wp-content/uploads/2014/06/its_who_you_meet_final_26_06_12.pdf, Last accessed 03/06/2016

6 Elnaz T, Kashefpakdel E and Christian Percy (2016) Career education that works: an economic analysis using the British Cohort Study, *Journal of Education and Work, 2016*.[Online] http://www.educationandemployers.org/research/career-education-that-works-an-economic-analysis-using-the-british-cohort-study/ Last accessed 03/06/2016

Giving young people a clear line of sight to work

06

Assessing myself – my motivation, conscientiousness, desire to do a great job as well as my ambitions and aspirations

STEPHEN CARRICK-DAVIES

'What would Richard Branson change if he was the head teacher in this school?' This is a question I asked recently at a Facework employability training session for children who have been excluded from mainstream school and who felt 'pushed-out.'

'Is Branson successful because his companies focus on good customer experience?' I asked.

'No,' said one of the students, 'It's because he tries to have fun and do things differently.' Some of the students laughed. As customers in their alternative provision, having fun whilst studying was clearly something they recognized was important.

Asking a question about how a successful business leader like Branson would run their school is a good starting point when helping young people think about the skills, attitudes, flexibility and resilience needed when starting work. Indeed many of these young people I talk to are fascinated about what skills are needed to establish a business and make money. Darren, one of the 14-year-old students who had been quiet and withdrawn in one of the recent lessons, suddenly piped up, 'I could be earning £60 a day working with my dad right now, if I wasn't in this dump. He says he will teach me to be a plasterer and he needs me because he has tons of work on right now.'

A wonderful learning environment

For a variety of complex reasons, many of these students, taught in Alternative Education, feel they have already failed when it comes to education. But just because their experience of mainstream test-prep schooling hasn't been right for them, it doesn't mean that they won't be successful in a nurturing Alternative Education setting, especially if these centres focus on preparing young people now for the future changing world of work. Indeed it could be argued that for many of them starting work earlier could be the best thing for them. To be accepted in a non-academic, real world environment, to grow up with colleagues at different stages and ages, to receive value through a wage, to be given responsibility; all of these things can contribute to a wonderful learning environment, especially if you need to escape from a chaotic home life. It's just a pity that most schools don't have the staff or space in the curriculum to help to give these students a clear line of sight to work, nor are they able to value the enormous benefit that experiencing work now could give a pushed-out learner.

Within mainstream schooling even the work-experience placement is not mandatory anymore. Indeed, for many schools there is a reliance on parents to find the placements. What does that tell us about 'who you know' as you climb the rungs of the social mobility ladder? Not much equality of opportunity here. Just imagine asking your parents to find a placement for you if your parents themselves are unemployed and are without that wider work-network. Even the number of 16–17 year olds combining work with full-time education has been decreasing steadily since 1998 when around 40 per cent of students did a Saturday job. Today, numbers of young people engaged in part-time work has dropped to 23.7 per cent of girls and only 13.4 per cent of boys (Conlon et al 2015)[1]. If young people aren't earning whilst they are learning, and many schools don't provide employability or effective career counselling anymore, where do they gain the valuable soft skills needed for the hard challenges in the changing world of work?

Conversations make a tremendous difference

Having in-depth conversations about work and connecting young students with employers whilst they are at school can make a tremendous difference. Indeed, recent research produced by the Employment and Education Task force showed that 14–16-year-olds from all backgrounds could be earning an additional £2,000 by their mid-20s, simply through greater exposure to the world of work through career talks at school and engagement with employers[2] (Kashefpakdel and Percy, 2016).

But by the time these young people are in their mid-30s you won't need a futurologist to recognize that the world of work will be at a 'tipping point': computers and automation replacing boring, repetitive and easily learned jobs, driverless cars and delivery drones replacing white van man and globalization eroding the bargaining power for many workers – especially those in low paid jobs. So whilst it is understandable for the government to prioritize STEM subjects and higher academic standards, those who struggle with exams need to rely even more heavily on soft skills, such as imagination, the ability to apply knowledge in novel or varied contexts, resilience and flexibility to handle the unexpected and adapt within changing teams.

Demystifying soft skills

Whilst most people would agree with Peggy Klaus, an expert in workplace development, who says, 'Soft skills get little respect but they will make or break your career', few have answers for how we help pushed-out young people (many with behavioural issues, low levels of self-esteem and special needs) acquire and demonstrate these skills. Many of these young people will have to compete with peers who have better qualifications, self-confidence, certainly a stronger sense of entitlement and, importantly, better networks and links with those in work. So how can we help them to 'leap-frog' their way over further formal education and into successful work environments? Given no one to date has come up with the answer let alone a model, you could do a lot worse than ask the young people themselves to try to codify and interpret what these skills look like to them. And that's exactly what the Facework project aims to do. With funding from Nominet Trust and the Inclusion Trust we worked with 70 students from six PRUs over a two-year period, focusing on demystifying what these soft skills looked like and finding out how young people can gain positive attitudes and mental toughness whilst at school so that they were better prepared for work. The results are a creative, co-designed curriculum of 25 challenges grouped into families of five core STEPS skills:

Self-Management, Teamwork Enterprise Problem-Solving Speaking & Listening.

The students helped us come up with the 25 practical 'ing' activities: things employers wanted you to be able to do and which you could demonstrate practically. Things like being good at admitting mistakes, (not easy when you've been told your whole life has been one) spotting problems, handling emotions, managing time and using initiative. Instead of 'worksheets' we created challenges; instead of far-off inspirational stories we filmed local young people giving advice to their peers and getting students to rate their mates' skills. Instead of banning social media, we collected over 150 examples of apps, films, adverts, songs and quotes all available via social media which can help bring these vital soft skills to life. These are now all freely available on the www.facework.today website, and are cross-mapped to the OCR Life & Living accreditation which means that schools now have an alternative youth-created curriculum which can lead to a qualification.

Creating these resources within the STEPS framework took time and patience, involving deep learning for both the team and students. But as well as the end product (the learning resources) there are some important lessons that emerged from the process and methodology we used. There is no 'silver bullet', only rather simple approaches which teachers use instinctively in all their education and which can be transferred to employability training. These five principles are relevant to educators, employers and government alike, especially if we have a vision for employability as more than just helping the next generation succeed in earning a living, but rather imagine a world where the work they do gives them real value and self-worth, creating greater equality in our society and supporting cultural cohesion.

Figure 6.1 The STEPS framework

Five lessons that we have learned

1 Develop an empathetic understanding of young people and the challenges they face in delivering employability programmes successfully.

Whatever you are born with is normal, and the world in which children are growing up and the one they will start work in, is very different to the world we grew up in. Many of the young people I work with are anxious about their futures, their ability to one day own their own home and their ability to stay in regular employment. Simple techniques for building trust include:

> Validate the soft skills they use every day in social media, as they organize, negotiate, multi-task, upload, publish and create online. Showing how these existing skills can be refined and transferred to a work context helps give a young person confidence.
>
> Whilst trying to help a young person it is easy to suggest a mentor. But don't give a young person a mentor, get them to choose their own. For a start they will have more ownership and it's harder for a mentor to say no to a child.

2 Every young person has worth and potential and whilst qualifications are important, they are not the things which ultimately define us.

Many successful leaders in many different sectors of society left school with few or no qualifications. We need to recognize that, for many students, they will only be ready to learn when they have grown up and had some first-hand experience of proving that they are a success. Employability sessions need to focus on helping young people to find what Ken Robinson terms their 'element'. How you help children discover this 'element' varies from child to child but helping students identify good questions before settling on answers is a positive starting point. Indeed there are no wrong questions and if you can teach young people the power of asking good questions, especially to people who are in work, you introduce them to a network and possibly an insight into work which helps spark this element into life. As Socrates said, 'Education is the kindling of a flame, not the filling of a vessel.'

3 Peer learning is key for helping young people to acquire soft skills.

If these soft skills are viewed as informal and hard to measure, then why not use informal creative ways to demonstrate them and instil them in others? The most effective lessons we delivered when developing Facework was when we took young people from one Alternative school to another school to run the employability session. Throwing them in at the deep end and asking them to run a discussion about work, or sharing from their own experience of work, radically helped to change their mindset. We extended this by using phones to record their advice to their peers. 'Teach once, learn twice' principles came to life and suddenly both the young people doing the teaching, and the adults doing the learning, grew. For many of the students the actual activity of travelling to another school in another part of the country opened up a whole new world of discovery.

4 Bringing the real world of work into the classroom can make a profound impact.

Many of the young people I worked with are kinaesthetic learners and need experience in using their hands and exhibiting their skills. Many schools are seeing the value of the 'exhibition' as part of project-based learning activities and running 'high-stake' activities such as a pop-up café, shop or nail bar, where students interact directly with members of the public, can transform a child's understanding of work. One PRU I worked in recently was beginning to get their students to run a large car boot sale within their playground. The practical skills used in running this – to say nothing of the value of parental engagement – could be phenomenal. But there are other ways to bring work into the classroom. Could well-known coffee outlets donate an old coffee machine to all the Alternative Provision schools and start running Barista training courses for students within school? When I have run Barista training with young people it has been one of the most impactful days of their lives, giving them experience and a foot into a potential 'gateway' job in the hospitality industry.

5 Schools are already places of work

Students are already picking up important messages about work from within their school and there would be opportunities for sharing the work and helping students prepare for work once they leave. Schools often employ local parents, so why can't they also employ a student caretaker to shadow the school caretaker and receive a wage? Why, when repairs need to be done in schools, can't companies run by parents of children in the school be given preference in pitching for this work? Why can't schools use their alumni in better ways to help students with transition into work? Why can't students be given opportunities to run juice bars, produce business cards, take care of school grounds, etc? Introducing paid work and teaching entrepreneurial skills within Alternative Provision is the next step for the Facework project and more could be done to help schools develop a new blend of employability and education.

So returning to Richard Branson, perhaps the Virgin Group should branch out into yet another industry and help us reimagine alternative schools. After all, Richard Branson himself had first-hand experience of struggling in school and left education with no qualifications. If he can rescue our banks, make our trains run on time and start tourism in space perhaps it's time to return to earth and to his roots and help us reimagine a new work-school model.

Facework resources are freely available and can be accessed through the website www.facework.today. For further thoughts on the journey into learning see http://www.huffingtonpost.co.uk/stephen-carrickdavies/conversations-into-employ_b_4205343.html.

Notes

1 Conlon, G, Patrignani, P, Mantivani, I (2015) The death of the Saturday job; the decline of earning and learning amongst young people in the UK, *UKCES 2015* [online] https://www.gov.uk/government/uploads/system/uploads/attachment_data/file/435285/15.06.15._DOTSJ_Report_design_final_EDIT.pdf Last accessed 03/06/2016

2 Kashefpakdel, E and Percy, C (2016) Career education that works: an economic analysis using the British Cohort Study, *Journal of Education and Work* [Online] http://www.educationandemployers.org/research/career-education-that-works-an-economic-analysis-using-the-british-cohort-study/ Last accessed 03/06/2016

Helping individuals develop self-confidence and interpersonal skills

07

RUTH CARTER, ROS KAIJAKS AND DAVID SUMMERS

When recruiting, employers look beyond qualifications and work-based experience. Increasingly employers require a diverse skillset that can almost be as much about an individual's personality as anything else. Employers will often look at how a new employee will slot in to their new environment and with new colleagues. Will an individual be open and share ideas and work in a team or will they actually find sharing ideas and helping others very difficult? How does an individual interact with others and put others' needs first? Employers recruiting within a customer-focused role will often look to see who opens the door for others or who offers to pour a cup of tea for someone else within a group situation. Young people are encouraged to understand the value of teamworking and indeed this is often practised within the classroom on projects and other tasks. It is also fair to say that vocational qualifications studied from age 14 to 19 at school, can provide excellent opportunities to do this.

In big organizations, corporate culture plays an important part in how the business operates and if individuals don't reflect those corporate values, they can often feel uncomfortable in their environment and isolated. Emotional intelligence is now regarded as a key attribute in the world of work and for those who perform to the highest level. Decades of research now point to emotional intelligence as being the key factor that sets star performers apart from the rest of the pack. It is often regarded as intangible but in short, it affects how we manage behaviour, navigate social complexities and make personal decisions that achieve positive results. Emotional intelligence is made up of four core skills that pair up under two primary competencies: personal competence and social competence.

How much of an impact does emotional intelligence have on professional success? The short answer is: a lot! TalentSmart, a US training and development provider (http://www.talentsmart.com/about/emotional-intelligence.php) tested emotional intelligence alongside 33 other important workplace skills and found that emotional intelligence is the strongest predictor of performance, explaining a full 58 per cent of success in all types of jobs.

CASE STUDY   OCR's project approach

OCR has worked with several employers to date on a new innovative approach to qualification delivery. OCR's Project Approach is project-based learning where students work over an extended period of time, for a purpose that is greater than the curriculum, eg they may build something, address a question, solve a real problem or address a real need. The main characteristics of an effective project include: authenticity, a clear purpose, begin with a question/problem, end with a product/solution, have visible outputs, incorporate reflection, revision and feedback and involve employers. The project approach has a number of benefits for the students in that they take ownership, have pride in their work and feel challenged. Because this style of learning is realistic, relevant and meaningful, students can develop ambitions and see how the knowledge, understanding and skills they have developed translate to the world of work. The opportunities to develop the skill sets and mindsets that employers seek, such as problem solving, self-management, working well under pressure, taking initiative, communicating with peers, presentation skills, enthusiasm and resilience are accessible throughout this approach.

With this method the gap between education and employment narrows, with students being able to talk knowledgeably about their project and the approach taken with meaning and relevance that the employer will understand. The school or college also benefits as students are more motivated, their willingness to attend increases as well as the desire to progress and achieve. Employer engagement also brings opportunities to widen community involvement for the school/college, such as employer support for career days, interview techniques and conversations with employers looking at their individual career journeys. The employer benefits too as they can access localized links and nurture and feed their future talent pipeline.

CASE STUDY Volkswagen Group UK and the Outward Bound Trust

It can often be more difficult to measure the positive impact of developing soft skills within the workplace. To give an idea of the importance that companies attach to this, even in younger and newer recruits, Volkswagen Group UK Limited have worked with the Outward Bound Trust (OBT) for ten years to help develop their franchise networks apprentices.

Whilst the company is able to develop the apprentices' technical skills through internal training, the OBT work with them to help develop their key skills, such as teamwork, planning and communication and in particular to develop customer-focused behaviours. In 2013, 250 apprentices took part in a five-day programme during the second year of their three-year VW apprenticeship. An internal evaluation of the programme, conducted by Volkswagen Group's Learning and Development Team, shows that the programme has a positive effect on the apprentices' skills in a number of areas, including communication, confidence, emotional maturity, planning and teamwork. Between one and three months after the programme, line managers were asked to rate any changes they had observed in their apprentices' skills and behaviours at work. Changes in skills were reported from 'partially' through to 'wholly improved'. A total of 94 per cent of line managers reported improved communication to staff and 87 per cent reported improved communication to customers. Furthermore, 94 per cent of line managers reported improved confidence and emotional maturity and 96 per cent of line managers reported improved planning and preparation. One manager commented on how his Apprentice has returned from his Outward Bound week a more confident person. The manager reported that he was 'both delighted and a little amazed that such a change can occur in one week'.

CASE STUDY BAE Systems and the Outward Bound Trust

The Outward Bound Trust (OBT) have also worked with BAE Systems for over 13 years to help their apprentices become dynamic, effective employees. The programme takes place during the first six weeks of their apprenticeship and focuses on building their self-awareness, self-confidence, self-management and skills in working with others, from communication to leadership. It also aims to enhance their understanding of BAE Systems' values and ethical principles.

In 2012, 219 apprentices attended a five-day Outward Bound programme. Six months afterwards, training staff, line managers and apprentices completed an online survey regarding the programme; 150 apprentices and 14 staff (who we refer to as 'observers') completed the survey.

The evaluation showed that the programme is regarded as a highly positive experience that helps prepare apprentices for the many requirements of their apprenticeship. It develops their capacity for independent learning, collaborative working and self-management and gives them a deeper understanding of the organization's values and ethical principles. When asked, 'What was the most useful part of the Outward Bound programme?', 84 per cent of apprentices clearly described the opportunity to develop skills in working with others, from getting to know new people and developing strong personal relationships, to learning to communicate openly, to consider, respect and trust others and to be patient towards others.

The programme also appears to have had a positive effect on the apprentices' behaviour at work, in particular in relation to safety and attendance. Ted Creighton, Head of Learning and Development, BAE Systems, was quoted as saying that 'there seems to be a link between the skills and attitudes developed on the Outward Bound Trust's programme and the behaviours of our apprentices demonstrated in the workplace. The course has enabled these groups of apprentices to have an enhanced sense of responsibility and this has been reflected in an improved safety record and also in our overall rates of absenteeism. Safety awareness has stopped being a 'tick box' procedural chore and become a very real thing'.

CASE STUDY The Luminary Bakery project

As noted above, reducing the parameters of 'employability' to those purely of a qualification outcome, does a disservice to the individual and belies the fact that employers in reality demand far more. Where individuals lack qualification credentials, the other components of employability have an even greater emphasis.

Adults who did not achieve qualifications by the end of mandatory education will have various and potentially complex needs. Many of these will relate to a lack of self-esteem and the impact this has on other 'soft skills' necessary to job-search successfully and, in the medium term, hold down a job.

In this respect, recent changes to funding and job-preparation programmes have acknowledged that solutions need to be far more holistic in scope. In developing underpinning soft skills, the opportunity to do this in a real context, greatly adds to their value.

The Luminary is on one level a fully functioning bakery selling artisan-baked goods to the public. It operates as a social enterprise so all the profits are directly reinvested into the charity. The mission for the social enterprise is to offer training, employment and community to women from vulnerable backgrounds in the East End of London. It runs an employability training programme which takes women on a journey to employment or enterprise. Its aim is to see all women in East London released to reach their potential.

The people it works with cover a range of women with different backgrounds, ethnicities, upbringing and experiences of education/work. Common life experiences include homelessness, sexual exploitation, domestic abuse and/or criminal activity. Many of the trainees didn't complete school and don't have any qualifications or employment history when they come to us.

The programme for each individual comprises several elements and lasts about six months. The Luminary teaches baking skills, food hygiene and OCR-accredited Life & Living Skills through a course called 'MyLife' developed by Reflex – a national youth charity. An enterprise course is also offered to those interested in starting their own business. A key part of this programme is meeting the trainees, finding out where they are at when they arrive and guiding them through all twelve aspects of Reflex's programme, developing their employability through different activities. These elements, combined with tailored support and work experience opportunities, enable the women to grow in confidence and skills for the working world.

From diagnosis to development

It's well known that accurate diagnosis is key to delivering the inputs that are most needed, but also to engage individuals in self-reflection. At the start of our OCR-accredited employability programme we ask the women to assess themselves on their skills: numeracy, communication, baking, IT and teamworking. This helps both us and them to gain an understanding of where their strengths and weaknesses are and we can then tailor their learning to ensure they grow in their chosen areas of improvement. Acknowledging strengths is a powerful confidence-builder as it helps them to remember that they are starting this course with existing skills and building on them. It also helps them to break down their work-readiness in terms of skills and abilities, acknowledging that they might not be ready at that point, but by working on those areas they can become ready.

We also use a character development wheel developed by national youth-offending charity: Reflex. This allows our trainees to assess their character strengths and areas to improve. The characteristics are resilience, self-control, loyalty, kindness, empathy, endurance, integrity and humility. Trainees then choose an area of their character they would like to develop and set themselves targets for how they can challenge themselves to demonstrate those characteristics more in everyday situations. We have seen great success with these targets for our trainees, and this is hugely empowering for them to see that they can change whatever they put their mind to.

Improving by osmosis

We have found that kindness, empathy and endurance are really well-developed in a team environment and, as our setting is a kitchen, there is lots of room for them to develop teamworking, assertiveness, problem solving, creativity and organization whilst baking. Kitchens have to be run tightly, in an organized and clean manner. So in immersing the trainees into this environment alongside other trainees and professional bakers, we see them improving in these areas almost by osmosis. For some it is also the perfect setting for them to work on their targets, actively challenging themselves to be more assertive for example.

Presenting yourself to employers is an area which needs specialist support, for example learning how to write an effective CV or learning how to disclose a criminal record to an employer. These are areas where we partner with other organizations for their expertise, and we have seen trainees become more confident in this area – particularly through practices such as mock interviews and work experience days. We help them to optimize their impact by reflecting with them on how something went, asking for feedback from interviewers for example and talking through what they could improve next time.

In order to prepare our trainees for enterprise, we run a specific OCR & ASDAN-accredited course for those who already have a business idea. Many women are entrepreneurial by nature and aspire to be their own boss, so this course helps them to think through the practicalities of starting up and also sustainability. With our group it has been important to empower them with the tools they need to launch their business – for example going through, as a group, how to create a great pitch and practising with them together in a safe setting. And again giving them the opportunity to develop their character purposefully, with the success of their business in mind. The most common fear amongst trainee entrepreneurs is thinking about the sheer volume of work that goes into starting and running a business, therefore we see it as our job as trainers and equippers to break the work down into manageable chunks. We have also found that encouraging the trainees to voice their vision is often inspiring for themselves and their peers; after all it is the vision that will see them through.

Many thanks to the Luminary Bakery (a social enterprise based in East London providing training and employment opportunities for vulnerable women and Business in the Community for the use of case studies. Business in the Community assists businesses to work together and take action to help tackle some of the key issues facing society today. More information can be found on their website: http://www.bitc.org.uk/.

Further information about Reflex and the Luminary Bakery can be found at http://www.luminarybakery.com/ and http://www.reflex.org/

Examples of the OCR Project Approach can be found at:
Siemens: http://www.ocr.org.uk/news/view/ocr_and_siemens_launch_uk_engineering_skills_partnership/

Jaguar Land Rover:
http://www.ocr.org.uk/Images/209198-land-rover-4x4-in-schools-technology-challenge-project-approach.pdf

HMP Ryehill:
http://www.ocr.org.uk/Images/221475-moving-towards-retirement-a-project-approach.pdf
http://www.ocr.org.uk/Images/221500-moving-towards-retirement-lesson-element-getting-the-most-out-of-your-reading-learner-task.doc
http://www.ocr.org.uk/Images/221499-moving-towards-retirement-lesson-element-getting-the-most-out-of-your-reading-teacher-instructions.pdf

Making the best choices for jobs, careers and study

08

DOUG STRYCHARCZYK

Why is this important?

> 'Choose a job you love, and you will never have to work a day in your life,'
> Confucius

The world of work and study is full of opportunity. This means that there are choices to be made. When the preferred option is chosen it is very important that it is a good option and ideally the best option available.

This is equally true for employers and employees, educators and students.

As Confucius indicates, doing something you enjoy will rarely feel like hard work. It taps into your intrinsic motivation. Whether it is committing to three or four years of study to achieve an important qualification or agreeing to do a job for 40 hours a week, 52 weeks of the year (less holidays) it will either feel like a pleasurable and challenging activity or it will be an unremitting chore.

Some of this down to mindset and the individual's motivation and mental toughness but much will be down to making good decisions about what you are committing to.

It is also the case that at different times and at different stages in one's life one may be involved in work activity that one doesn't enjoy or which feels unrewarding at that time. That is part and parcel of the journey through life. Again it will often be the case that one's mindset determines how to deal with it. There is generally learning in every situation as well as opportunities for satisfaction.

It has been estimated, for instance, that in the UK there are 7,000 different jobs active in the economy at any time. It has also been suggested that most individuals can carry out or be trained to carry out 70 per cent of those jobs. The individual might not want to do many of those jobs or follow those career paths but it illustrates the extent of opportunity out there.

Moreover, this is also subject to flux. In the USA it is already the case that 30 per cent of the jobs available now did not exist 10 years ago. The churn in types of jobs will generally increase as old jobs disappear, often the result of technological development as well as structural changes in a nation's economy. Whole industries can disappear or shrink to a shadow of their former size.

So there may now be an additional challenge for everyone. Individuals need to be prepared to select options and perhaps re-select options at different points in their working lives.

If we look at Higher Education in the UK and Europe roughly 8 per cent of all students starting degree courses drop out of their course within the first 10 weeks having discovered that their choice of study was a poor choice.

Seeking effective guidance is valuable. Professional support can help the individual to consider all the options available to them and steer them through the decision-making process.

The reality is that most receive little effective guidance and even where it is provided it can be limited. Parents, friends and educators can be very influential but can provide their input from a knowledge base which is limited in information, experience and currency.

The challenge for the individual is to take stock of the options available to them – and do this many times in their life and career – and to assess these options as carefully as they can to make the best decision each time. The mnemonic RACPAC represents a process, which captures just such an approach.

RACPAC

Research all the facts and options – the job title alone can be misleading

When investigating jobs there are two levels at which the individual can operate.

Firstly, there is the business of learning as much as possible about what is out there. Most people have a very narrow range of knowledge about the options available – and indeed about trends in employment and opportunity (which includes self-employment).

This can provide us with a high-level picture of what might be out there which suits the our desires and wishes.

Secondly, there is a need to understand closely what a job or career might entail and where it can lead. This will often determine what the individual has to do in order to secure that job which might often require further development, relocation, etc.

In some instances both levels can happen at the same time.

Level one

There is a wealth of written information available through books, libraries and now the internet. Most public libraries also have guides to specific careers (eg How to be... an accountant/ software engineer/ salesperson). These are very useful – for specific occupations only.

Some awareness of individual preferences – either in terms of occupation or in terms of desirable job characteristics is useful and often important.

There are some general databases – often under the title Job Taxonomy – which can be found. Many professional and sectoral bodies will have more specific databases of job titles and job types, which occur in their professions or sectors.

General databases are more likely to enable the individual to research jobs with similar traits – these may be good fits too.

Probably the best source of understanding different jobs and what they entail is the O*Net.

See www.onetonline.org

Developed by the USA Government, the O*NET program is the nation's primary source of occupational information. Central to the project is the O*NET database, containing information on hundreds of standardized and occupation-specific descriptors. The database, which is available to the public at no cost, is continually updated by surveying a broad range of workers from each occupation. Information from this database forms the heart of O*NET OnLine, an interactive application for exploring and searching occupations.

Although American in origin and primarily focused on the US economy it is widely used all over the world and many other regularly consulted taxonomies are based largely or in part on the O*Net. Usefully it is kept up to date and maintains its relevance.

The database also provides the basis for Career Exploration Tools which are part of the O*net offering, and constitute a set of valuable assessment instruments for workers and students wanting to find or change careers.

The following categories are examples of some of the options O*NET OnLine allows the individual to explore:

- **Skills** (35 skills)
    - **Basic Skills** (Mathematics, Writing, Reading Comprehension, etc.)
    - **Cross-Functional Skills** (Equipment Selection, Quality Control Analysis, etc.)
- **Generalized Work Activities** – 41 general types of job behaviours (Organizing, Planning and Prioritizing Work, Interacting with Computers, etc.) occurring on multiple jobs.
- **Interests** – Six occupational types that can be connected with a worker's personal interests to indicate which occupations would be most fulfilling.
- **Work Styles** – 16 work-style characteristics that can connect what is important to a worker with occupations that reflect or develop those values, such as Initiative, Persistence, Cooperation, etc.
- **Work Context** – 57 physical and social factors that influence the nature of work, such as physical and structural work characteristics.
- **Experience and Training** – Five 'Job Zones' that distinguish the levels of education and training connected to occupations. These will be based on the US qualification and education frameworks but it is not difficult to translate this into the requirements in say the UK or another country.

The structure is based on good practice in job search.

Good practice would dictate that you research options under the following headings:

- the work – what would you do?
- work environment – range of places where you might do the work;
- appropriate skills and interests necessary;
- entry requirements and training needed;
- opportunities – what type and numbers of employers offer these jobs – and where;
- pay and conditions;
- prospects for the future;
- related jobs, etc.

Making the Best Choices for Jobs, Careers and Study

Level Two

There is no substitute for talking to people actually doing the job.
RESEARCH – FIND OUT FROM SOMEONE WHO KNOWS!

It is easier if you have friends, acquaintances or relatives who do the work in which you are interested. They should offer information readily.

It is more difficult to contact companies or strangers – but they can often be surprisingly helpful and are very willing to tell you about their work. People asking them for information also often impress companies – it's a good tactic for getting interviews.

When you do take up someone's time, make sure you prepare – both to get the information you want and to ensure you don't waste their time. These are suggestions for a checklist:

1 How long have you been a _____?
2 Why did you decide to become a _____?
3 What kind of training was required?
4 How did you get your first job in this field?
5 What do you like best about being a _____?
6 What do you like least about being a _____? (5 and 6 are the two most important questions you can ask!)
7 How has being a _____ changed since you first started?
8 What changes do you expect to see in this job/career?
9 What other jobs did you, or would you, consider doing?
10 What do you do during a typical day?
11 What does a new entrant earn and what would they expect to earn after, say, 10 years?

Apart from formal training what kind of experience is it worth getting to help me prepare for _____? What could I read to learn more about _____?

There may be other questions the individual would want to ask? They should be encouraged to think of other questions they think are important to them.

RACPAC – Analyse to consider Alternatives – carefully!

Questions should be as open as possible. In other words they should start with the words 'who', 'what', 'why', 'when', 'where' and 'how'.

If they are closed questions they will often only elicit a 'yes' or 'no' response that will be of limited value.

RACPAC – Analyse. You need to be able to sort the data and information you collect about each job and to be able to answer two important questions:

- Will the job meet all or most of my requirements and needs?
- Is it realistic for me to consider this job/career as an option?

Some questions you could ask yourself when considering the list of example jobs

1 How do you feel about them – are there any surprises? Do they seem a good match?

2 Look at the best matched jobs in more detail. Why do you like some and not others?

3 What motivates you towards particular jobs – money, status, people, job satisfaction?

4 What lifestyle do you want in the future?

5 Can you afford to take a step back to enter a new career path?

When you have gathered the information, you need to think about the alternatives available to you and the possible course(s) of action you can take.

A useful technique at this stage is to carry out a simple **Force Field Analysis.**

This is a structured form of brainstorming which generates ideas around two themes, which apply to many situations such as this:

- what are the driving forces/positives about what I have learned about the opportunity and which would encourage me to pursue this as an option?
- what are the restraining forces/negatives that would discourage me from this option?

This technique helps individuals to identify all the factors at play and to put them into perspective. It identifies the 'invisible barrier' to success or otherwise.

Creating a Force Field Analysis

1 Identify the role and all you know about it. Take a sheet of (A4) paper and write the role at the top so that it's always in sight.
2 Draw a line down the centre of the sheet. At the top of the left-hand side write 'Positives' and at the top of the right-hand side write 'Negatives'.
   a Positives are the things you like about the role.
   b Negatives are the things you don't like.
3 List your thoughts, ideas and facts under each heading.
4 Evaluate and analyse each idea/fact to determine how positive forces can be maximized and how negative forces can be minimized, eliminated or circumvented. Take a view on what the balance feels like. Is this still on balance something I would like to do?

An example is shown below:

Figure 8.1 Force Field Analysis

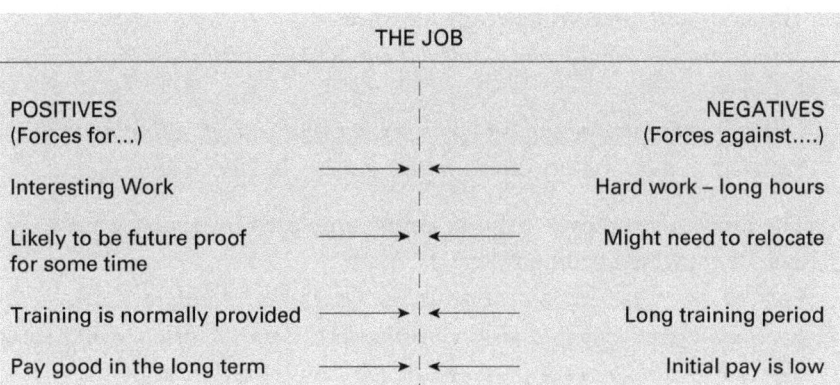

RACPAC – Consider the Consequences – and come to a Conclusion or conclusions

The difficult bit! The individual will now have a lot of information to help them make better decisions. There is no magic formula to offer here. Whatever they decide they will have to move onto the next step and create an Action Plan.

It is useful if they 'test' their decision too.

Does this feel right?

Does it make sense, given everything else that interests me?

Have I missed anything? (Useful to check the decision with a trusted friend, guide or counsellor)

MY ACTION PLAN IS...?

RACPAC – Make a plan of action

A job action plan doesn't have to be complicated. It sets out what the individual needs to do to achieve their job goal and to set milestones. All the work they will have done in the first three stages in this process will now be very useful.

An action plan can consist of the following headings:

Name: John Jo   **Date:** *Today's date.*

My job/career aim is to become:
State your job target eg Administration Manager, Administrator, etc.

Why? – because:
This is one of the jobs that best matches my employability profile – I may already have many of the skills and qualities needed.

The things I need to do to get this career include:
This might include qualifications, experience, personal development, etc.

The skills and interests I already have are:
I am computer literate and can use the following software – Word, Excel, PowerPoint, etc.
I have already worked in an environment that is demanding and I have been left to work on my own – which I enjoyed. I like responsibility.

The kinds of employers who could be interested in what I want to do include (how will you find them?):
Lots of small professional businesses need good administrators as do small manufacturing and service businesses. These will often want people who are flexible and are prepared to accept responsibility.
I will look in the local papers and I will look at small industrial estates and small office complexes. It will be worth registering with one or two agencies.

The possible routes available to me are:

I prefer the following route to achieve my aims:

I need to take the following action:

I will review my progress:
Four weeks from now

Keep your action plan up to date – review it when you said you would, change it when you must.

Like any action plan, it is a live document. It will need frequent review. The individual will learn things as they set out on the journey which will help them to modify or change their plan. Keep your action plan up to date – review it when you said you would, change it when you must.

Reviewing the plan will also provide them with a sense of purpose – -perhaps even urgency. It will also provide a sense of progress.

Remember RACPAC! – approach what you do in a structured way

RACPAC – Action! – Implement the plan.

Ahead of the individual is the process of actually making it happen – a process they may have to, or choose to, go through many times during the course of their working lives. In fact it is virtually certain that this will be a useful process several times over.

To get their preferred job they will have to work hard – applying for jobs, mailing CVs, networking, etc. In terms of the mental toughness model described elsewhere in the book, they will:

- have to create a sense of control – 'I can do it!';
- stay committed to the task – 'I'll do what it takes';
- be prepared for the unknown and for setbacks – 'I'll take them in my stride and I will learn from it all';
- be confident in their abilities and in persuading others to give them a chance – 'I'll show them that I can do it'.

It is often said, 'getting a job is a full-time job in itself'.

RACPAC – Check your decision and the way your plan evolves and be prepared to Change...or confirm that you are doing the right thing.

Possibly one of the most important pieces of advice: it is rare that any of us make a perfect decision every time. And we will sometimes take a path that begins to feel uncomfortable.

It is not a failure to stop, think and to decide that you are heading up a blind alley – and to Change your mind or Confirm that you are on the right path.

As the individual progresses through life their priorities and motivation will change. When they are ready for a change of career direction or within the same career, it's important to review what they have learned about themselves in making decisions and their plans for their future.

The individual can put themselves through the same process again:

- Define who you are, what you have to offer and your current situation.
- Decide what you want.

- Gather information about how you could get to where you want to be and the possible barriers that could get in your way.
- Form your plan to achieve what you want or, at the very least, to get nearer to where you want to be.

Making choices and making decisions about jobs, careers and one's future is not easy. The world of work is awash with opportunities – whether in employment, self-employment or indeed in study. But neither does it have to be unnecessarily difficult. Adopting the RACPAC process, like any process, helps people approach decision making in a structured manner... leading to better decisions.

Presenting personal information for employers

09

HEATHER AKEHURST – OPEN AWARDS

This book provides guidance and tips for people seeking to help prospective employees from all ages and at all stages of their employability journey so it makes sense to deal with this in three stages in this chapter:

- school/university and looking to begin that journey;
- long-term unemployed;
- those wishing to change career paths.

However don't assume the early sections don't apply to your support if you're helping people to look for a career change, there may be some nuggets in there for you.

The start of the journey

Get ready in good time

Firstly, in an ideal world everyone's employability journey should begin at 14 or even earlier. No, we're not advocating a return to changing the school leaving age. Every prospective employer (and more often Universities and Colleges) require people to demonstrate an understanding of employability skills and clearly those who can show they not only understand them but can also demonstrate them have a better chance in what is nearly always a competitive situation. So it makes sense to provide guidance as young people begin to choose their options for GCSEs in England and Wales (and the equivalent elsewhere).

Many schools in England and Wales are now working with the Careers and Enterprise Company, which is a government organization specifically established to link schools with employment and to provide practical support in a number of ways. If working in a school, first find out if the school is connected and if not, why not. If it is, then it is recommended that students are asked to book an appointment with their Enterprise Adviser who will normally come from an employer in your area. Their role is to help students access guidance in the areas they're interested in and they usually have a wide network of employers behind them. When students leave school advise them to take the details of their Employment Adviser with them and ask if they can contact that Adviser again in the future. They are likely to agree to this.

Where are they heading?

Choosing options for study and qualifications requires young people to have some understanding of where they hope to be heading in their employability journey. Clearly if they're hoping to be a Vet they'll take science subjects and if they still believe they have the talent to make it as a professional footballer they'll need do Physical Education at this stage.

However, for those wannabe sportsmen and women, Business Studies, English (sports journalism), Sciences and Psychology will give them additional options, hopefully after a successful career as a sportsperson.

They should be guided to think about how they can gain experience whilst they're still at school so that they can showcase this on their very first CV.

Some schools, but not all, will allow students the chance to undertake work experience during term time and if they do, the student should be encouraged to take up this opportunity. It is preferable to avoid them getting their parents to sort it out with their parents' employer, unless that's what they really want to do.

Encourage them to think outside the box – how can they gain experience (and maybe a prospective employer) in their preferred field? Advise them to email people politely and remember that every piece of punctuation counts. There are a lot of people out there willing to help youngsters who are genuinely interested in their employability. If the school doesn't provide or arrange work experience, remember that students can get up to 14 weeks holiday in the summer. It's worth encouraging them to give up some of that precious leisure time. It's the perfect time to start demonstrating tenacity, drive and initiative.

Lateral thinking is good

Encourage students to think laterally as well and seek to broaden their horizons. Lots of careers, jobs and tasks are interconnected. Something that appears to be peripheral to the young person's main interest may still offer the opportunity to learn something and to practise a skill or acquire knowledge that helps with the main quest.

For instance, if English or Journalism is the interest then encourage the young person to have a look at the plethora of respectable blogs out there and suggest that they write and post articles in an area that takes their interest. They will then have the published article in their CV and portfolio. If it's medicine they're interested in, they may not get a placement within a hospital (although the author of this chapter did before deciding to do physiotherapy). A local care home may be delighted with a young person willing to give a few hours a week or occasional days.

If it's sports get them to look at the holiday clubs available for primary school children and see if they can help there. However the advice is always – aim high – get them to write to Roman Abramovitch, Richard Branson or Boris Johnson. If you don't ask, you don't get.

This is also helping to develop their mental toughness as they are taking a risk and they may not get many replies, but they also have little to lose. A top tip is that everyone emails these days because it is so easy to do. So to send a real old-fashioned but well-written letter in the post is quite a clever thing to do and is much more likely to get noticed. A typed letter will be fine but the writer should pay careful attention to spelling and grammar.

This kind of experience is also tuning them into the job-hunting process. They are beginning to learn about what attracts attention, develops interest and sometimes provokes the desired reaction from an employer.

Clubs and groups add to the employability profile

It's good advice to suggest that young people should join clubs and groups that add to their employability profile. Even Sheldon Cooper went to Science Club. Quite often these will offer the opportunity of taking short courses that all add to their CV. Remind them to keep those certificates safe – they will impress someone.

Again with older students it's useful to encourage them to take the opportunity to help out with younger students.

My 10-year-old daughter moved up to Guides last month but she still helps out at Brownies adding leadership, empathy and loyalty to her CV.

Whether students like it or not employers trust the values that established groups engender and proclaim to provide. Cadet forces are excellent at this but if students get the chance to undertake the Duke of Edinburgh Award or National Citizenship Service then they should be encouraged to do so.

If they don't get offered these chances at their school or college then suggest that the school considers such options.

My silver Duke of Edinburgh's Award still sits proudly on my CV. The scheme offers a wide variety of opportunities that are enjoyable and interesting. It begins to provide young people with the necessary employability skills that they need.

Build a portfolio

An important thing to remember is the portfolio. Students should be reminded to keep all their certificates, no matter how trivial they seem at the time. They should also be advised to keep details of their work experience, always keeping a log of when and where they went, what they did and what they gained from the experience.

The employer may be able to provide a document or letter on headed paper stating what the young person did as well as offering a view about their punctuality, honesty, cooperativeness and friendliness. Such a thing is really useful – this is what employers always say they want. Advise the young person to keep any articles they write or have written about them (if they're good). From 2016 every school leaver in the UK should have a Digital Passport, which captures qualifications and employability experiences. All students should ensure they have one. For more information and advice look at www.careersandenterprise.co.uk.

Final comments on work experience.

It is good advice to suggest that students say thank you in a written letter that employers can retain. The thank-you card and chocolates on the last day are greatly appreciated by staff but taking the time to write and post a handwritten letter the following week leaves its mark. It establishes a good relationship which can be useful in many ways.

The student may want to go back and ask if the employer will act as a referee (always ask, never just assume); they may want more experience in the future, they may even want a job there. It will also create a legacy where the employer will be encouraged to offer opportunities to others who come after them.

The thank-you letter should always be addressed to the 'big boss' and if the student had a supervisor or mentor they should be mentioned by name. It can't help but create a favourable impression.

What do employers really want?

It's probably important to pause at this stage and look at what employers actually want from an employee. This can be puzzling and confusing for those looking for a job; it often baffles those who provide guidance and support! All surveys of employer groups will show that employers ultimately value what are called 'soft skills'.

These include time keeping, loyalty, enthusiasm, politeness, attendance and actually valuing the employer. Work with the student to help them understand that they will be on a learning curve from day one. That might include having to accept that in many new jobs they're going to be making the tea for a while. They should learn to do it with a good grace – but also offer to do it.

Another thing to avoid is being a clock watcher. Employers always know who gives that little bit extra and if they have to leave dead on time mention it to their supervisor so they know it's a rare occurrence.

Having said all this, employers rarely put this in any advert and usually fall back on tried and tested qualifications. It is, therefore, important to make sure people's CVs show that they understand this and can demonstrate that they do. Someone's first CV or application form is obviously going to be thin so they should use the space to set out these points and do it clearly.

Employers may have to wade through hundreds of applications (really) and the more clearly someone sets out how they meet the employer's requirements (stated or not) the easier it is for the employer to find the information that really interests them and the more likely they will be to notice the student.

For instance, I got an interview to be a trainee Quantity Surveyor because I put in a sentence about my tea-making abilities. It was amusing, got their attention but also showed I understood where I'd be in the office.

Nothing to lose

Second top tip – if there's a job someone really, really wants but they don't have the necessary qualifications still think about encouraging them to apply. Advise the student to be upfront about the lack of qualifications and to tell the employer they're willing to study and then go on to stress their other qualifications and attributes. There is nothing to lose and everything to gain.

A friend holds a senior position with Fujitsu, the only non-graduate to do so because he told them about his experiences within the University of Life. Obviously, though, applicants have to be realistic – if someone is applying to be a brain surgeon they are going to need to have a medical degree.

Advice applies to all ages

So far, this chapter has been written from the perspective of the school or college leaver. The advice applies equally, adjusted for circumstances, for almost all ages.

Even if the person left school a few years earlier, they can think about what their school attendance was like. Did they play for a team and do they still do this? They can use this to show loyalty, attendance and commitment. Were they involved with any extra-curricular activities in school?

They should be encouraged to demonstrate to their prospective employer or university/college that they understand the need for these qualities and that they possess them to a worthwhile degree.

Similarly, the advice applies when supporting people who have been unemployed for a while and wish to move back into employment. The first step is to 'normalize' the situation for them. It's a feature of modern life that people will change jobs regularly. Sometimes because it's their choice and decision to do so. Sometimes circumstances mean that jobs are lost for reasons outside the individual's control. Losing a job can happen to anyone and often does.

Accept all help offered

One of the issues which can emerge here is the development of learned helplessness. The individual can develop a view that they are unemployable. 'Why me?', they ask and 'why can't I get a job quickly'.

So it can be important to persuade them to accept all the help they're given at whatever stage it's offered. This means registering with as many organizations, such as Jobcentres in the UK, as is possible. It's evidence of their desire to find a new job.

If the individual is newly unemployed or about to be, it can be a difficult time because the unwanted change is being forced on them. Many do not like being turfed out of their comfort zone. It is important that they accept their situation as quickly as possible. It's happened and it can't be reversed. At the same time the quicker they can engage with positive steps and actions the better it is for their self esteem and their self worth – after all this is what they're now intending to sell to employers and educators. So tell them not to just stay at home; it is better to avoid staying in the house.

Public Libraries are good places to go to. Many offer free internet facilities, which can be useful at this time, newspapers which contain job adverts, volunteering opportunities (more of which later) and lots of information (from books, the internet and the generally helpful librarians).

Taking regular stock of the situation is important too. One good way to approach it is to handle it like a business meeting with themselves. Set a time, get them to arm themselves with paper, pens etc, and carry out the meeting for the prescribed period (say, 30 mins but a maximum of one hour) with no interruptions.

- Is this an opportunity to take stock and consider changing career paths?
- What is it that really gives job satisfaction?
- What is holding them back?
- Do they need new/different qualifications?
- How can people find out more about the jobs that are available?

Even if the priority is to get any job, this is still a worthwhile activity. It creates awareness about the world of opportunity. The RACPAC process described in chapter 10 is a very effective way of achieving this.

Second chance education

There are many who didn't optimize their time in school or college and don't have the qualifications confirming that they possess certain attributes. Here, there are three areas to consider.

Firstly there is no doubt that having Maths and English qualifications are enormously important for almost every job but the emphasis here is on the word 'qualifications'. Most people only know about GCSEs (and their equivalents in other countries) but in the UK there are actually Functional Skills qualifications at four levels below that. People can work towards these, achieve these qualifications and either build towards getting a GCSE or obtain an Entry Level qualification. Ultimately they can legitimately claim to hold a Maths or English qualification.

Secondly, in the UK there is now a whole new range of qualifications out there that demonstrate employability skills to any prospective employer. Sometimes these are described as Life Skill qualifications.

Here at Open Awards we provide Skills For Learning and Employment but there are other brands available. Developed by working with employers to understand exactly what it is they want, these can be delivered from any age from 16 upwards. They're designed in units so that people can pick the units they need and/or take a full qualification in a subject area. A local Further Education College would be a good place to make enquiries about these.

Finally there are Access to Higher Education Diplomas that recognize that the late teens is not always the right time to decide on one's life employability path.

Many social care workers 'fall' into social care because it is flexible and local but have then discovered that they have a real vocation for care and nursing. So a logical and useful next step might be to look at qualifications in this area. There is now in the UK an Access to Higher Education Diploma in Nursing that replaces A levels, which can be completed in a year (often part-time) and which is accepted by Universities. In the UK if someone is over 19 they can usually get a government loan (known as 19+ and 24+ loans) that are wiped out if they do start a degree. More information on loans is available at www.openawards.org.uk.

Valuable experience

Volunteering represents a big opportunity to keep people energized and get some work experience onto their CV, and much of it can be very enjoyable.

The individual should be very realistic about what they can and cannot commit to. If it appears that they will gain employment relatively easily then they should think in terms of a short-term commitment. They may well continue when they have found a job.

For people moving towards retirement volunteering is also a worthwhile option as it keeps them active in all sorts of ways. Again get them to think of it as a business proposition. There is no shortage of opportunity in this sector.

Information can be readily found through library notice boards, local free papers, local volunteer centres or just by spending an hour browsing on the internet.

Not only is volunteering constructive but it builds skills which can be showcased in CVs and interviews. Many organizations in the voluntary or third sector are employers in their own right and quite often they are large employers.

The CV

Advise the job-seeker to prepare their CV in a style that reflects their personality. There's a lot of nonsense written about how to set out a CV. All employers and educators simply want clear relevant information about the person concerned with a list of qualifications and dates of when they were gained. Start with those qualifications. It's still the first thing that employers and educators look for.

If the individual has completed in-house courses awarding less formal qualifications, they should keep a list of them. These might not find their way onto a CV but they are useful to refer to in interviews and discussions.

Next, set out the individual's employment history from the most recent to the earliest, detailing who they worked for, when and briefly what they did. It would be useful to adjust this each time it's sent out to reflect the specific job for which they are applying.

Finally have two reliable referees and make sure that the individual has checked that these people are happy to give them a good reference.

Anticipate what an employer may be concerned about in their CV. Are there any employment gaps? Does the individual change jobs frequently? Did they leave part-way through a study course? If significant these are best dealt with in a separate letter. This puts the applicant in charge of the information and doesn't leave it to the imagination of the employer.

Working with people who are seeking a career change

More people are looking for a different career as we work longer and traditional industries and occupations fall away. The general advice on taking time to think about it still holds true, as does much of the above. Once someone has a plan they can work their way towards it.

It may not appeal but more and more people are going back to college or university to acquire new skills and qualifications. To do this effectively they should look at where the growth sectors are likely to be and check to see if these interest them. So it is important at least occasionally to read the business pages of newspapers or news on the internet. They often provide useful information because it is always newsworthy.

As with the advice given with the RACPAC process, it is always good to speak to people who are already doing the job. The job title might appeal, the job content might not, and vice versa. If they have no personal contacts, the business social media site, LinkedIn, is very effective.

It is critically important to ensure that all the information someone submits as a candidate is accurate. Employers allow a little for exaggeration, we all do it when seeking a new job, but they will make no allowance for blatant or significantly dishonest representations. They have absolutely no view about candidates at the early stages of a recruitment process and it clearly raises concerns if the individual is prepared to lie in the application. What else might they be prepared to lie about later?

The power of social media

Social media is a whole new opportunity – and minefield – of its own. Employers cringe when they receive emails from learners with addresses such as sexygirl@ or barfbrian@. The individual may think this is funny and creative but most people won't. What's funny at 16 and maybe at university just isn't in the world of employability. If the person you're advising has one of these email addresses then tell them to get a new one – even if they just use it for employability-related activities. Do make sure however that it's linked to their smartphone (if they have one) and checked as often as they can. Never, ever, ever let them use text speak in their dealings with a prospective employer. It's just not appropriate and most people over 25 often can't understand it anyway. If I can't read it easily, then, to be blunt, I won't bother.

It is important to check one's social media history. Is there a chance that the applicant could have used inappropriate language or been offensive or told a joke that they shouldn't have? If there's a doubt in their mind then ask them to go through their social media and delete, delete, delete.

Remember, though, that often the offending post is still there somewhere. They should upgrade their privacy settings. Employers, Universities and Colleges increasingly check social media to see what sort of person they're dealing with. They're looking for the kind of post that says 'got trashed last night so took a sickie!' If someone is just starting to use social media then get them to ALWAYS be careful what they post. And remember, employers can get round most privacy settings.

An excellent tool

Having said that, proper use of social media is a great employability tool. Leaving Facebook, Instagram, Snapchat and messaging aside, Twitter and

LinkedIn are extremely effective tools if people use them properly. Create a good profile on LinkedIn and use it as a selling tool, keeping it regularly updated. It's a surprise to learn how often people look up other people on this. Not only can it help gain employment but it can help with all sorts of issues whilst in employment. It gives a chance to collaborate and engage in debate across the world. If someone isn't sure where to start, you'll find all the contributing authors to this book have an account.

Now, I'm going to confess to absolutely loving Twitter: it has opened up new friends, professional opportunities and information for me in a big way. If someone already has an account and they're not sure it stands scrutiny then advise them to open a new one. Then 'follow' as many job sites and organizations of interest as they wish. We haven't the space to go into more detail here but a quick internet search will give you all sorts of tips.

To give you some examples of its power when used wisely:

I recruited speakers for a national event on Skills through Twitter and met many people I'd admired;

I recruited new Trustees for Open Awards through Twitter;

I started a transatlantic Domestic Violence project through Twitter conversations and

I got to meet Sale Sharks but that's a whole other book!

Remember every time someone uses it they are showcasing themselves, for better or worse.

Selection: interviews and assessments centres/tests

10

The employers' and the individuals' perspectives

HEATHER AKEHURST – OPEN AWARDS

So you've done it, someone you're working with has got an interview and they're down to a shortlist of around ten at most. Employers will rarely see more than ten people for a post and six is probably the norm. So firstly give yourself and them a pat on the back because they've done well to get there.

Assessment centres and psychometric measurement

Some employers will use assessment centres as part of their recruitment strategy – they tend to go in and out of fashion. They also tend to be used by large employers, who can afford them.

If someone is considering banking, the legal profession or consultancy then there's a good chance that they will be used. Personally I always find them an artificial environment for the simple advice that I'm about to give you. From the moment the candidate leaves their house to the moment they get home they are on show and there are no times to relax or let their guard slip: they need to be selling themselves the whole time.

Occasionally these assessments will involve an overnight stay or a meal with managers, Trustees or consultants. These are the hardest of all as they're often, but not always, specifically designed to remove people from their comfort zone. So one important piece of advice is never, ever consume alcohol during this process. If someone is driving there's a perfect excuse but, if not, advise them to just decline politely and firmly saying that they never drink in a professional situation. No one can argue with that and it could well earn them some bonus points.

Good advance preparation pays dividends

Get them to prepare as well as they can for the day. Some of the advice I give later on interviews holds the same for here. Often there is no agenda but ensure they know a bit about the organization and in particular any ideals or values that it holds. Advise them to look at the leaders in the organization and what type of people they are, by looking at their social media and websites. There may be little point in trying to appear caring and compassionate if they have a machismo approach to business.

Prepare them to expect the unexpected as in many ways that's what recruitment processes are designed to do. So have them prepared to lead from the front. I've known all sorts of improbable scenarios come up such as being stranded on a desert island, building a raft indoors and designing a new product launch.

Assessment centres are generally, but not always, used by organizations looking to recruit leaders for either now or in the future. This is not the time or place for anyone to be a shrinking violet. Get the individual to show that they can lead by facilitating the discussion – in a group exercise getting hold of the marker pen usually puts you in control. If they're undertaking a team exercise, they should always start it by looking at the assignment and asking the group what they think their strengths are. This allows them to be seen to be leading the exercise event even if they relinquish it publicly to someone else.

I always enjoy assessment centres as a participant because if they're run well they can be a lot of fun. However, you have to almost not care about the job to relax and enjoy them. If someone doesn't get through to the next stage, advise them to ask for feedback because they do learn quite a bit about how people presented themselves. If the event was run by a consultant (and they nearly always are) then get the applicant to ask if they can speak to the consultant direct. They're usually more honest and it could also put them on their books for future jobs.

Ability and personality tests

The final advice is that sometimes Maths and English or ability tests are included as part of the assessment. Ability tests assess numerical, verbal and often spatial reasoning. There's no harm in advising people to call to ask if this will be the case if the joining instructions are ambiguous. If it looks as if there might be ability tests, then get the individual to go online to do a general brush-up. There are lots of really good websites out there aimed at schoolchildren as well as adults that provide free sample ability tests. Simply getting some practice and having a feel for how these tests work will be invaluable to the individual.

Employers of all types often use personality measures too. These are nearly always online questionnaires the answers to which provide information about the individual's personality, predicting their behaviour. Personality tests typically assess:

- introversion and extroversion;
- openness to experience;
- conscientiousness;
- independence;
- emotional stability or anxiety.

There is no right or wrong answer, so applicants should have nothing to fear. They should be advised to respond honestly and usually with the first response that comes into their mind. Employers use the results of these tests to check what they see in interviews and in the CV.

Again, the individual should ask which personality measure is being used. They can look it up on the web and find out what the questionnaire is seeking to assess. And **always** ask for feedback. This can be really valuable whether the individual gets the job or not.

Employers will often use information for personality measures within interviews.

The interview

So what do employers look for in an interview? Well again they'll want it to be simple and made as easy for them as possible. The days of employers playing 'good cop, bad cop' are long gone for enlightened employers: they want to see the real person. That's difficult for candidates but there are a few pointers that should help people. Employers usually set aside one day for interviews for a particular job and that will be a long and mentally tiring day for them. Employers are human and they're having to deal with the stresses of work and home as well as to pay complete attention to candidates.

Some employers will do a test as part of the interview process and this will be part of the day. It could be keyboard skills, an in-tray exercise (more later) or a presentation. Candidates should usually be warned if they need to do one of these but advise them to go prepared just in case. Again if they're not sure, there's no harm in asking.

Do the research

People are often afraid to call organizations in case it reflects back on them in the interview. Well, unless it's a small organization that's piffle. If they need directions to get to the interview, they can call the main switchboard – they won't be the ones interviewing them. If they need clarification on the interview itself they should ask for Human Resources who'll be much more used to an approach than people think. They may want literature on the organization and most of this is available on the internet these days using the organization's website, Companies House and/or The Charity Commission.

People do need to find out about the organization as part of their planning as most companies would expect candidates to know something about them. If they've come across them in business then advise them to refer to that and if they simply haven't a clue who they are or what they do then tell them to do their research but keep their answers generic. There's nothing worse than someone trying to explain to someone else what they do. Answers like 'I know you provide... but clearly I'm not sure on the detail' are fine and even referring to their research shows the effort you've put into the interview. Get people to jot down a few key notes about the organization onto small cards (or paper or Post It notes) so that they can refresh their memory before they go in.

In-tray exercises have their place in the selection process for a range of roles. For example, in administrative posts. Quite simply they will give candidates a pile of paperwork and ask them to put it in order, usually assessing priority. If they've done this type of work before they'll know exactly what to do. If they haven't there's a logic. Any correspondence from regulators or MPs needs to come first, then (and this is personal preference) I'd put complaints, then in order of response required (not received), then order received and finally any junk mail. This type of exercise is increasingly becoming outdated as emails become the business mode of communication.

Good presentations

Presentations are increasingly expected for leadership roles or those involving marketing or training. Employers are testing a candidate's ability to research a topic, their personal knowledge and whether they present information clearly and simply. They will usually make allowance for gaps in knowledge and a good technique is to set out what their knowledge of the subject is right at the beginning. Phrases such as 'I've worked in this sector so I've approached it from my perspective...' or 'I haven't worked in this sector but clearly I've applied my knowledge in other areas and interests...'.

Timing

Firstly, if candidates have a set time for the presentation, then tell them they must keep to it and time themselves. Remember they may have questions asked of them at the end. My advice on tight timing is to ask interviewers to ask all questions at the end and then they're doing it in their time and not the candidate's presentation time. I've certainly had an interview where someone interrupted to say I had two minutes left, but equally I tend to be quite ruthless about ensuring people finish on the allotted time whether they've finished their presentation or not.

Delivery

Secondly, make sure they check how the interviewer wishes them to deliver their presentation if this isn't on the invitation. These days it's usually on a pen drive. Ensure they are completely prepared for a full ICT breakdown. Unfortunately it happens more often than you think and the more prepared they are the less likely they'll get flustered. Advise them always to have a back-up plan – usually in the form of handouts. they should use colour if they can, be concise and be paper-efficient but not using type so small that employers can't read it. They're going to leave these behind anyway so make sure they understand that it needs to look good, to have their name on it and for everything to be spelled correctly. I come across too many people in all walks of life who don't check for spelling mistakes. It shows a degree of sloppiness.

Preparedness includes making absolutely sure that they're going to be able to get there in good time. If they're using public transport then they need to aim to get there 15 minutes early. If they're in a car and there's a car park, I'd aim for half an hour early so they know they've found the right place and they have time to do a last minute run-through, using key bullet points in their mind. Why 15 minutes? Well it gives people a margin of error, time to visit the toilet and sometimes the interviewers can be ready for candidates early. Make sure they always have the reception phone number so if there is an accident, late bus or delayed train they can call. Then, make sure they know who they're seeing and that they take the letter of invitation with them. In my last job we had over 20 departments and often two or three could be interviewing on the same day.

Dress code

What to wear is always a difficult question and depends on the job they're applying for. Whatever they decide on they should make sure it's clean and unlikely to offend anyone.

If they're applying for college or an apprenticeship then I would say smart trousers and a polo shirt is perfectly acceptable. If it's an office job or a leadership role or a University interview then they need to be smart. For the gentleman a suit, although smart trousers and shirt are acceptable; be wary of the flamboyant tie. Never, ever shorts and if they must wear jeans ask them to make sure they're clean and smart.

Ladies have more choices and therefore more dilemmas. A smart suit is fine, as is a dress and cardigan or jacket. Remind them to be aware of skirt lengths as some interviews can be in deep, low armchairs. Equally this is not the time to wear new shoes; tell them to make sure they can walk in them and they're comfortable.

My advice here is to try to add a touch of individuality without going overboard. If employers are seeing 10 people, how they remember individuals is often by what they wore. There's a lot of well-founded research that will tell you that first impressions do count. For the ladies suggest they add some colour or a statement necklace or scarf. It's harder for men but smartness is usually remembered. Remind them to be careful when adding any badges or ties that signify allegiance: I'm sure it doesn't happen but does the candidate really want to be interviewed by a staunch Evertonian on the morning after Liverpool beat them and they're proudly wearing a Liverpool lapel badge.

Think about questions – and answers

So the candidate knows where they're going, they've put together their presentation and they've got their outfit picked. Now you and they need to think about the questions they may be asked.

Employers usually try to start with something simple to put people at their ease. A top tip is to make sure that the candidate's brain and mouth are working in the same order before they start. If they're travelling by car then advise them to ask themselves questions and answer them out loud. If they're on public transport they need to either resign themselves to people staring strangely at them or make a determined effort to chat to the receptionist. So questions employers consider easy can often be a death knell and candidates do need to give them some thought.

Most interviews will begin with one of two questions: either 'tell us a bit about yourself' or 'what attracted you to this job'. Get them to rehearse their answer and it should be about two to three minutes long. Remember an employer doesn't want to know about their holidays or their pet, they're after something work-related. If the person you're working with is seeking to switch careers or move into a new career this is a good chance to say why, upfront, particularly if an event has begun this journey, but keep it brief.

Chances are they'll ask candidates about their skills and experience at some stage. Ensure they rehearse the good things they want to bring to their attention and have some examples ready. If 'team player' was part of the advertisement or person specification then ensure they have an example ready. If they're a school leaver they still need an example and playing football/rugby/cricket is not it! However dealing with an issue within the team is.

'What can you bring to the job' is another likely question and again ensure people are ready for it. Stress their good points and don't forget the earlier advice about employers valuing such life skills as timekeeping, good attendance or enthusiasm. Make sure they don't use the phrase 'I believe'. This occurs most often when an employer asks someone about their skills and they reply 'I believe I have...'. This is really wishy-washy but too many people do it. Get them to have conviction, say 'Yes I can/have/will' and say it firmly.

Remind people to look at the advertisement for the job and anything sent to them, usually a job description and/or person specification. These will tell candidates what an employer is looking for and help them to try to guess what questions may be asked. Again get them to practise their answers out loud as this gives them a feel for their answer and can prevent the 'umming' and 'erring' that can slip in.

Work with them to think about what examples they could offer from their previous work or voluntary sector or school/university life to illustrate how they would deal with an issue.

Be ready for unusual questions

Very occasionally employers will throw in a nonsensical question that is clearly designed to either throw people or test their quick thinking. It's never happened to me but I do know people who were asked about what skills you would use on a desert island, who you would invite to a dinner party and what TV reality show they would most like to appear on and why. There are no right or wrong answers to these and my advice would be to tell people to enjoy them for the nonsense they are. Get them to embrace them and let their imagination do its work and never, ever worry about them after the interview. If there's one question not to reflect back on, it's that one.

Common questions include 'What three things are your biggest attributes?', so ensure they have some examples ready. Equally common is something about your biggest fault. Get them to think about this in advance and turn a negative into a positive. 'I can't leave until a job's done' or 'I know I can on occasion pay too much attention to detail' are good examples but make sure they don't go overboard. Attention to detail is good, an absolute perfectionist can be a pain unless you're interviewing to be a copyreader, brain surgeon or something that requires perfection.

Practice makes perfect

Body language is important in all areas of life and employability is no different so do spend some time getting them to think about it. Get them to practise sitting in a high backed and low chair. They want to lean slightly forward and appear alert and interested at all times. This can be harder in a low chair or armchair so do think about it. Equally perching on the edge can make it easier to exit gracefully.

Employers who pride themselves on informal interviews tend to use this sort of set-up and I have to say I find it makes it very difficult for all concerned. All advice will tell you to try to look at all the panel members whilst replying to a question but this is a skill that can be hard to acquire. Eye contact is vital to create a good impression so do try to get them to practise looking around but if nerves get the better of them then ensure they can maintain eye contact with the person who asked the question.

Firm handshake and the best smile

The best advice I can give is to ensure you have a firm handshake and smile frequently. The number of people who say to me that the interviewers didn't smile once is huge and my response is – did you smile at them? Smiling indicates that you're relaxed and very few people won't smile back if you smile first, which helps. Smiling is usually contagious. Win–win.

Shaking hands is a difficult one. I would recommend that people do at the start of any interview and particularly when they meet the person who comes to escort them to the interview. Ensure they are clear that they are going to do this and stick their hand straight out. This signals their intention and the interviewers can respond accordingly. There's nothing worse than a clumsy 'is he/she or isn't she?' scenario.

Drinking water, if offered, is another tricky one and my advice is unless people are giving a presentation just don't! I've had people spill it on themselves, knock it over and on one memorable occasion a lady that continued pouring as she spoke until it overflowed onto the table and floor. However if they're delivering a presentation they may want to take a sip after the delivery and before the rest of the interview.

What about asking questions?

People struggling with deciding whether to ask questions or not is common and my advice is to decide before the individual goes into the interview. Never ask about terms and conditions of employment during an interview. The time to do that is with Human Resources before the interview or to save negotiations until they get a formal job offer.

For many years the advice was to always to ask a question because it demonstrated your interest. Utter rubbish. I've never been remotely tempted to employ someone on the basis of a question that they asked. Often it comes across as trite and wearisome. People can always say that they did have some questions but they've been covered in the interview. Equally if there's something that hasn't emerged that is important to them, then do ask. Examples of this usually include the opportunity to undertake training, induction, requirement to travel or location.

After the interview: what's next?

Once the interview is over there are still things to do. A quick reflection on the questions asked is useful whilst they're fresh in people's minds, particularly if there was something completely unexpected that came up. Do get them to bear in mind that they will be their harshest critic at this stage so ensure they don't dwell on the experience too much but try to see it as learning.

Feedback?

If they're not successful should they ask for feedback? Most employers are risk adverse and can often see a request for feedback as an opportunity for a claim against them, falling back on 'there was someone who answered better on the day' and sometimes that is true. Encourage them to ask by all means but make sure they're not too disappointed if the feedback is vague or unhelpful.

If this was the job they really, really wanted or in the sector that they really want to work in there are a number of things that they can do. Much will depend on their current employment status. Do encourage them to write and thank the interviewing organization for their time and ask for their details to be kept on file. Employers need permission to do this. If they used an application form to apply, send their full CV with the letter. If they are unemployed get them to ask if they can do some work experience with them. It shows willingness and if nothing else gets some appropriate work experience on their CV. Moreover, I know many, many people who gained employment by starting this way.

Above all ensure that people don't get disheartened. There will be other jobs and something better may be just round the corner. Focus their energy positively into getting the next interview.

Work placements and internships

How to optimize their impact

HEATHER AKEHURST AND ANTHONY MANN

In the previous two chapters I've stressed the importance of work experience in boosting people's employability factor and work placements and internships are two excellent ways to do this. However, I have given plenty of advice if you don't feel that your candidates fit either of these categories for gaining that kind of experience.

Work placements can be arranged in four different environments: school, apprenticeships, university or, for job seekers, linked to the Department of Work and Pensions. I don't propose to cover school opportunities in any more detail as I have already described those earlier in the book. All I'd say is do encourage people to take every opportunity that they can!

The apprenticeship route

Apprenticeships come in all shapes and sizes these days and are an excellent career path to consider. My nephew turned Oxford University down to take an Advanced Apprenticeship with BAE Systems and has never regretted it. Good salary, placements abroad and no student debt. You could argue that as all apprenticeships are linked to employers they're all work placements. However, look closely at the offer. Advanced apprenticeships are clearly with a reputable employer and offer not only an excellent structure but also a career path with that employer. They are making significant investments in their apprentices and hope to reap that investment through gaining employees with the skills they need for their succession planning.

I would issue a word of caution about apprenticeships at Further Education Colleges and urge people to talk to them very thoroughly to understand what is required. I hear from too many young people who successfully complete their first year entirely in college and then struggle to find an employer to provide the work experience element in year two. Equally some colleges have enterprising business models that have restaurants, beauty salons or car workshops on site and whilst these provide the work experience elements they are very unlikely to provide sustainable employment after completion of the apprenticeship. What they do, of course, provide is work experience, of variable quality in a simulated work environment. If candidates are considering this route and have a choice make sure they check the latest OFSTED report and specifically look at the apprenticeship section of the report. That said, there are many excellent apprenticeships and advanced apprenticeships out there that can provide people with valued, vocational qualifications and very good work experience. After completion, refer people back to my section on Access to Higher Education Diplomas.

University work placements

It is increasingly common for universities to offer work placements in second and third years now. These can be an integral part of the degree course or in place of a final dissertation. Employers are very late on getting switched on to these as I have used them for several years now with two organizations and always find them to be an excellent partnership between university, employer and student. The student gains work experience in their subject and the employer gains a fresh and usually innovative pair of eyes to bring to a piece of work. At Open Awards we work with three different types of work placement activity. With Liverpool John Moores University's World of Work programme we will work with a group of students on a discrete piece of work that will contribute to their final grade. For example, we commissioned them through the Manufacturing Futures Board to design marketing materials specifically to attract younger people (aged 14 upwards) into manufacturing and engineering. With Chester University we take students for a month in May in their second year to work on research-based study that we need to be done and finally through the University of Liverpool's Interchange programme we take a student during their third year for one day a week to undertake some research and operationally based study, the findings of which the student will use for their dissertation. As an employer this gives us the chance to undertake research we couldn't fund otherwise and the student gains experience of working in a busy, national Head Office as well as getting a reference at the end of it.

I know from talking to our students just how little they had appreciated what the world of work was going to be like and this gives them a real taste of it and allows them to understand the employability skills that employers are looking for. They get their first taste of office dynamics, working with all ages and committing to a project that makes a very real commercial difference. Some of our students have returned to undertake casual employment during their holidays and this allows them to build up their CV.

Internships

Graduate internships are increasingly popular these days, both paid and unpaid as employers have been able to capitalize on excessive demand and savvy students realize that, as well as a degree, they need work experience to gain good employment. Traditionally some sectors have always offered internships, for example, the legal profession, politicians and large consultancy firms. They have been seen a way into the market and there is undoubtedly a lot of truth in this. I would always promote an internship to gain practical work experience and would recommend that students begin to consider this in their second year. Again there are ways to build it into people's CVs before they leave university so that they have it to offer straight away. As shown above some courses provide the opportunity to do this as part of the curriculum; for others you will need to advise people to consider using some of their very, very long holidays to do it in.

Consider carefully what people's thoughts are about their career after completing university. If they still have no idea – and many students don't – then get them to look at options that will broadly enhance their CV in whatever direction they choose to take. Politics is useful if people can get a placement as not only does that give them a broad range of skills and experience but it generally intrigues employers. A placement in the Head Office of a charity (the better known the better) shows an altruistic side and will often give them the chance to take on quite significant duties quite quickly. If they have a clear plan then they need to pitch to those organizations. Polite enquiries by email is fine at this stage but they should also have a short covering paragraph and CV already prepared.

Within the covering paragraph I would get them to state what they are looking to gain out of a placement. This gives an employer a clear sense of how they could integrate someone and a decent employer will want to make sure they're getting something positive out of it. Ensure they do their research; the Personnel/Human Resources team will be used to dealing with this so ideally they want to pique the interest of the Chief Executive, MP or senior Director within the organization. The main fear employers have is that they will need to commit their precious resources to 'looking after people' and unfortunately many of them can have short-term views in this respect. Make sure people address this concern head-on and make it clear in their approach that they are capable of picking things up quickly and are a real team player.

Potential route to a job offer

Not only do these internships give practical work experience, I know of many examples where they turn into firm job offers. This often happens with legal and large consultancy firms who've had a good chance to have a look at people's capabilities in advance of the graduate deluge. I also know of one young man who badgered his local MP for work experience whilst at school, went on to do work experience during his holidays from school and university, worked as an unpaid intern for six weeks after leaving university and is now employed full time within the MP's office. It was his tenacity that paid off.

There used to be a plethora of organizations that specialized in graduate placements at relatively low wages but with the clear aim of the student gaining work experience. In these times of austerity they have largely disappeared but it's still worth seeing if there's one near your candidate that they can register with. Certainly at my last organization we took on several of these and they all gained employment with us as soon as vacancies became available.

Work placement schemes have become much maligned over the last few years and whilst it's true there are some unscrupulous employers out there who are simply exploiting the scheme for cheap labour, there are many more who are offering genuine opportunities. Get people to do their homework. If there are Department of Work and Pensions placements offered then they should be vetted on a regular basis so if they do have concerns they can raise them with their Job Broker. Get them to look at the organization: a simple search usually reveals lots of comments from existing and previous staff. Be aware, however, that ex-staff may have a grudge so ensure they look for similarities and volume. If they can, visit the shop or office and get a feel for the place. Do the staff look happy? If it's a shop, they can visit it without an appointment and it's surprising what gossip/information people pick up browsing the aisles. If they have a Job Broker get them to ask if they can fix up their own work placement; it takes more work on their behalf but does give them more control.

A good commitment

If you've made it this far then you won't be surprised to hear that I thoroughly recommend that people take advantage of work placements. They give people current work experience, develop their employability skills and can sometimes open new horizons. Whilst you clearly don't want people to be taken advantage of, there is still something positive to be said for them committing to a period of time and sticking it out. If they're unsure, confirm that they are absolutely clear about the length of time they are supposed to commit to and check what their options are if it doesn't work out. Even if it's terrible, make sure they (or you) never publicly trash the employer as it will also reflect on them.

With all of these examples people need to treat them seriously as employment. They need to check the employer's expectations before they start in terms of attendance, dress code and their role. For the first few weeks at least, they need to treat every day as a work trial and take opportunities to showcase their work ethic and abilities. Remind them to be wary of being drawn into other people's issues (particularly if they're a smoker – smokers tend to know all the gossip by virtue of grouping in solidarity together in the freezing cold) as often there will be things that they're not party to. Also remember, whilst it's important that they get on with their colleagues, it's their manager and employer that they need to impress at this stage. Tell them that they should never pass on gossip or express an adverse opinion about colleagues as you just never know how the office, factory or shop dynamics work.

Seek feedback and references

Shortly before the placement/internship/apprenticeship comes to an end recommend that they make an appointment to see the most appropriate senior person that they can. Hopefully they've sussed this out in their time with the organization and if not, then they should approach their immediate supervisor. This is a chance for the candidate to hear from their supervisor's point of view how it's gone and what else they could do to improve their CV. Remind them to find out if any employment opportunities are likely to come up in the future and ask how they can register for these. Advise them to ask if their employer would be willing to keep their (now updated) CV on file and contact them if there are any opportunities. Importantly, remind them to ask if their supervisor would be willing to give them a reference when they apply for jobs in the future and if they'd be willing to write an open reference for them to take away with them. If the employer asks for their feedback on their time there, then ensure they know always to be constructive, praise where they can and if something didn't work out, to be prepared to offer a suggestion or an improvement rather than being negative. They should always end the meeting by thanking their employer for the opportunity.

If you've read the previous chapters then you'll know I'm a fan of positive use of social media. So encourage them to connect with people in the organization using LinkedIn and to make sure they update their profile. If they're using Twitter, remind them to follow the organization and people in it, making a note to retweet where appropriate and use it as a public thank-you. They should never, ever, use it as a tool to castigate their employer; this just creates fear amongst other employers.

Advise them to keep in touch and not just with new friends that they may have made. If they're invited back to anything, encourage them to try to attend. If something big is coming up after they leave and it's appropriate, get them to ask if they can attend. As I said before using social media is an easy way to maintain gentle contact and remind people who they are. If an opportunity for employment does come up then ensure they shamelessly exploit their contacts within the organization to see if anything's changed and what the current management issues are.

Finally ensure that they update their CV. They have new experiences to add and hopefully a potential referee. Check that they make it clear what type of work experience they had so that future employers don't get confused and see it as just a short period of employment. Not only that, but remind them to keep a list of all the jobs they undertook, no matter how trivial. They shouldn't put them all in their general CV but it's useful to refer back to for covering letters, more specific, targeted CVs and for examples to use in interview situations.

Delivering effective work experience

12

Work placements and internships – how to optimize their impact

For young people, work experience is an important and complex thing. It can lead directly to employment or help them to get into a university of their choice. It is highly influential in making decisions about immediate educational progression and long-term career ambitions. For many teenagers, it represents their only real experience of 'employment' before they leave school. When asked, teachers routinely testify that placements often have a deep and immediate impact on pupils, changing attitudes towards education and career aspirations. Work experience is important, but it is also complex. It only happens because of the goodwill of employer hosts who will provide widely differing experiences for young people depending, of course, on how that pupil responds to the opportunity presented. It is complex too, because work experience can be seen to contribute to multiple objectives and the context in which it is delivered is changing rapidly. When work experience was first introduced as a funded UK government programme in the 1960s, most pupils left education in their mid-teens. Work experience gave them a taste of the sort of employment they could expect in an economy which wanted the skills school-leavers possessed. Move forward 50 years and most pupils now stay on till 18, half go on to university and high proportions of jobs demand graduate qualifications. In moving from a manufacturing economy to a knowledge-based economy, what it means to be effective in delivering work experience has changed too.

When to do it

When asked, young British adults who went through work experience over the age of 16 felt it to be more helpful to them than peers who only did it when younger. Young adults who did it at both ages report the greatest benefits. This makes sense when considering how rare it has become for teenagers to leave education at 16. With the great majority of teenagers now staying on, work experience placements which occur closer to their ultimate full entry to the working world can be seen to have greater impact on ultimate outcomes. But this is not the whole story. Pre-16 work experience is highly valued by many practitioners as a valuable aid to decision making at 16 (not just whether to stay on, but what and where to study – choices that can be crucial for later careers) and to support a process of maturation.

Table 12.1 When work experience was done
Views of 1,000 young British adults (aged 19–24) on how helpful work experience placements were in career decision making.

Age undertaken	Getting a job after education		Deciding on a career		Getting into higher education	
	Helpful at all	Very helpful	Helpful at all	Very helpful	Helpful at all	Very helpful
Pre-16 only	22%	6%	50%	14%	17%	21%
Post-16 only	39%	16%	78%	37%	54%	3%
At both ages	43%	23%	82%	41%	51%	22%

SOURCE: Mann and Kashefpakdel (2014)

A second key question surrounding the timing of work experience is when during the school year it should take place. It is common practice for placements to happen in summer terms. There is a strong case for running placements much earlier in the school year. For a young person, a placement is a rare opportunity to see for themselves how the labour market works, whether a specific careers area is right for them, but also to relate new information to their schooling. It encourages them to secure professional careers advice to make best sense of what they have learned, but also for changes in attitudes towards schooling to have an effect. A survey of 15,000 teenagers in 2008 found 95 per cent agreeing on return from their placements that they had changed the way that they saw education and qualifications and planned to work harder in school as a result (Mann 2012). The earlier work experience takes place in the school year, the greater the likelihood that changes in motivation will be played out in improved attainment.

What to do

A period of work experience is a big investment of time, energy and resource for both young people and their schools. With part-time employment becoming a thing of the past for many school pupils, it may represent the single most significant experience of the world of work that a young person has before they leave education. To get the best value out of it, it should not be their first exposure to the world of work. Rather, in preceding years, they should have the opportunity to explore the labour market through careers talks, fairs and especially careers carousels and workplace visits. When it comes to thinking about their placement of choice, they need to be able to make informed decisions and be encouraged and counselled to consider stretching placements aligned with their informed ambitions. In discussing the placement in advance, thought should be given to why and how it can be useful to the young person: is it to help get a job straight from school? To get into a university of choice? To explore or confirm a possible career? Is it to gain experience or insight? Is the purpose more for the young person to explore an occupational area or to demonstrate that they can do a job which slightly older workers do on a full-time basis? As a consequence, would it more advantageous to job shadow a number of different professionals or to undertake a traditional placement? For practitioners, the implication is clear: closer management of work experience and greater pupil self-reflection can help increase the chances of benefits being incurred. By way of example, can planning help to give a young person the opportunity to complete a task which could feature on a CV or gain a reference of relevance to future employment? If a young person is planning to go into work immediately from education, are they taking part in work experience with employers who actually take on school/college leavers?

Who does it?

Over the last decade, a declining proportion of teenagers have taken part in work experience. Pupils planning to take 'A' levels, in particular, are much less likely now to do a pre-16 placement. One of the less well known functions of work experience, however, is how helpful it is to pupils trying to get into competitive undergraduate courses. A review of the admissions requirements of the then 20 Russell Group universities in 2011 showed that it was frequently mentioned as something which was either essential or desirable across a range of different courses.

Table 12.2 Relevant experience
Proportion of Russell Group universities asking for relevant experience of the world of work within admissions requirements if offering the following undergraduate courses of study (Mann 2011)

Subject	Essential	Desirable
Veterinary Medicine/Science	83%	17%
Dentistry	55%	36%
Medicine	22%	66%
Engineering	6%	22%
Law	0%	37%
Business/Economics/Management	0%	21%

When there is so much competition to get into Russell Group universities, it would be reasonable to read 'desirable' as 'essential'. The review shone a light on some of the thinking behind such admissions criteria:

> Medical Schools expect applicants to have a range of work experience for two reasons. Firstly, this demonstrates that you have a realistic insight to the profession – you are after all committing to a lifetime career when you apply to study Medicine. It is important that you have an understanding of the complex nature of a doctor's role, as well as being aware of the highs and lows of the profession. Work experience is also important in enabling you to develop (and to demonstrate that you have) the relevant skills and qualities that are essential to becoming a good doctor.
> (University of Sheffield)

Other studies show that independent schools overwhelmingly get why it is so helpful for pupils to gain relevant work experience. The University of Manchester's Dr Steven Jones (2014) looked at the personal statements in the UCAS applications of hundreds of young people applying to get into one Department in one Russell Group university. Jones found that pupils attending independent schools were considerably more likely to have had relevant workplace experiences of work to draw upon in their applications.

Work experience to help to get into university should take place in key stage 4 and/or the lower sixth and be designed to help a young person confirm that their career aspirations do lie in arenas linked to the undergraduate course of study they have in mind. Schools need to help young people access experiences of relevance to their university ambitions and consider one-to-three day job shadowing as an effective alternative to traditional work experience.

How to do it

One of the most consistent insights to emerge from research over recent years is simple: when young people are asked to source their own work experience, what they find will typically reflect their social background. As Tricia Le Gallais (Birmingham City University) has powerfully demonstrated, when pupils are asked to find their own placements, social reproduction commonly ensues. Middle class kids get access to the middle class work experience, especially in the professions and very often through their family networks. Pupils from less affluent backgrounds lack both the networks and sometimes the confidence to find ambitious placements in keeping with what are often high aspirations.

It is the job of the school to intervene and help break the cycle. In her ground-breaking 2008 study, Le Gallais (2008) found that where pupils are counselled before placement, encouraged to seek out placements which are stretching and matched with placements which are sourced by the school, then it is much more likely to see young people from deprived backgrounds not only gain access to white collar workplaces but to undertake experiences of real value.

Many practitioners will argue that it would be detrimental to young people to prevent them from sourcing their own placements. The argument follows that pupils have something to gain from being required to approach employers by phone, email or in person and it is undoubtedly true that increases in maturity can be experienced from having to step up. It is a quandary but one which can be solved, by running work experience as an enterprise project: pupils working entrepreneurially and competitively to source the placements which their peers especially value.

Conclusion

This chapter draws on recent research to look at how work experience can be most effectively delivered in this changing environment. It has focused particularly on school, rather than college-based, academic secondary provision as this is an area where government policy is loosest. The chapter challenges schools to recognize the importance and complexity of work experience and to take a greater role in managing work experience placements, in personalizing approaches and considering the placement in the context of wider engagements with employers. Recent evidence shows that young adults feel that work experience is more effective if done after the age of 16 or ideally at both pre- and post-16. Placements held early in the school year are more likely to harness positive changes in attitude. In reflecting on the purposes of placements, which will vary by individual pupils, schools should give thought to the range of different opportunities to engage with employers, both prior to placements and in considering job shadowing as an alternative to work experience. Job shadowing can be especially valuable to pupils aiming to progress to higher education who need to be able demonstrate understanding of careers linked to specific courses of study. For all pupils, consideration must be given to how placements are sourced. A work experience placement can make the difference between the career ambitions of a young person succeeding or failing – it is up to schools to ensure that, as much as possible, all young people have a fair chance.

References and further reading

To access research on the impact and delivery of work experience, visit: http://www.educationandemployers.org/research-type/research-library/

Archer and Moote (2016) *ASPIRES2 Spotlight Study: Year 11 Students' Views of Careers Education and Work Experience*, King's College, London

Huddleston, P, Mann, A and Dawkins, J (2012) *Employer Engagement in English Independent Schools*, Education and Employers, London

Jones, S (2014) 'The role of work experience in the UK higher education admissions process' in Mann, A, Stanley, J and Archer, L eds, *Understanding Employer Engagement in Education: Theories and Evidence*, Routledge, London

Le Gallais, T and Hatcher, R (2014) 'How school work experience policies can widen student horizons or reproduce social inequality' in Mann, A, Stanley, J and Archer, L eds, *Understanding Employer Engagement in Education: Theories and Evidence*, Routledge, London

Mann, A (2012) *Work experience: impact and delivery – insights from the evidence*, Education and Employers, London

Mann, A and Kashefpakdel, E (2014) 'The views of young Britons (aged19–24) on their teenage experiences of school-mediated employer engagement' in Mann, A, Stanley, J and Archer, L eds, *Understanding Employer Engagement in Education: Theories and Evidence*, Routledge, London

Mann, Awith Spring, C, Evans, D and Dawkins, J (2011) *The importance of experience of the world of work in admissions to Russell Group universities: a desktop review of admissions criteria for six courses*, Education and Employers, London

Enterprise – more than being Richard Branson

13

RUTH CARTER AND ROS KAIJAKS

Educating about 'Enterprise' is a government priority. A BIS report from 2013 noted that 'while the proportion of the working-age population involved in starting or running a business in the UK compares favourably with many of our international competitors, levels of enterprise ambition compare less favourably.' (BIS, 2013)[1] Amongst the barriers identified were a lack of awareness of opportunities or support and a lack of understanding about the benefits of running their own enterprise or how to go about it.

Studies suggest that individuals find active learning to be more effective in developing both an entrepreneurial mindset and skill set (self-belief, risk taking, creativity, identifying viable opportunities) and in encouraging individuals to go on to set up their own enterprises (see, for example, Levie, J, Hart, M and Anyadike-Danes, M, (2010)[2]).

Vocational qualifications are an excellent way to provide learners with practical and engaging activities. In response to developing the skill sets and mindsets of young people, OCR has embedded entrepreneurial skills within a number of qualifications to help students know what it takes to be entrepreneurial and how to pitch their ideas.

The approach is for learners to be imaginative when coming up with viable opportunities and to understand how to overcome barriers and risks. Viable approaches could include solutions to a problem, to meet a need or fill a gap in the market, then investigating the feasibility of this opportunity before pitching their chosen idea to others. In pitching, students can demonstrate the use of a range of verbal and non-verbal communication skills and answer questions about their pitch.

From this students learn the essential transferable skills that can be applied in future learning and everyday life. They are provided with the self-belief, determination and the initiative to find out about what it is to be entrepreneurial. This set of skills can be applied to all aspects of everyday life.

This approach has for example been a good match for schools and colleges taking challenges such as The National Enterprise Challenge, Micro-Tyco and NACUE whilst wishing to gain other external recognition through qualifications.

The following case studies examine how NACUE has supported institutions in delivering impactful and practical enterprise education, some of the approaches taken and responses from both the individual students and the educators involved.

NACUE (National Association of College and University Entrepreneurs)

NACUE is a membership organization for engaging students in enterprise, originally set up by students for students. It gives college and university students the opportunity to boost their skills, confidence and aspirations through supporting student-led enterprise societies, running inspiring events and advocating practical learning. Over the last six years it has engaged over 180,000 students in enterprising and entrepreneurial activities, supported a network of over 260 enterprise societies, and seen over 15,000 people attend its events. The community alone has to date generated over 1,600 businesses in innovative spaces, creating hundreds of jobs.

The NACUE programme starts with the fundamentals about what 'Enterprise' means and students' evaluations of their own enterprising mind and skills sets, then takes students on to generating and developing business enterprise ideas and implementing these. Students, therefore, have the opportunity to gain confidence, improve their own employability skills and business knowledge and raise their perception that an enterprise might be a viable career option.

One of the early sessions is called 'Inspire'. This seeks to debunk some of the myths around enterprise and entrepreneurs which would otherwise hold learners back. Learners are asked to think about what working life might mean for them and what they understand by 'Enterprise' and 'Social Enterprise'. These words come with a lot of baggage – one of the key messages is that 'Enterprise' means *using creativity and making an impact* – not necessarily becoming Richard Branson. Another myth busted is that enterprise is not the preserve of business studies students. Where cross-college enterprise programmes have been the most successful is when they are truly inclusive for students of all disciplines.

The programme also develops an entrepreneurial mindset. Learners need to be able to ask questions, take risks and be resilient enough to carry on when things don't go to plan or fail altogether. Initially, students are asked to think about challenges such as a key speaker for a big event cancelling due to illness. Students are then encouraged to explore how they would deal with this. As this is in a safe space, they can take more risks to solve this problem creatively than perhaps they would normally. This example is both a useful exercise in scenario planning and it also encourages a number of other key skills and behaviours which are part of the entrepreneurial 'toolkit'. Follow-up activities allow participants to reflect on their experience and identify what they have learned from the day. The outcomes from this session are not about having become an entrepreneurial millionaire but about developing a group of core skills which includes teamwork, presentation, leadership, networking, communication, problem solving, creativity, positive thinking, organization, planning and risk management.

The programme then moves into exploring ideas for the students' enterprises. This is easier for some than others and it can be daunting to sit facing a blank sheet of paper. To tackle this there is a session on ideas generation. Students are asked to think about what activities or events they think would be good for promoting enterprise or would give students the opportunities to be enterprising. For some students this stimulus is sufficient but for others there is further support from asking students to think about their own different types of skills and knowledge and how existing interests and contacts might be used. Students are also asked to consider their local or even national environment – what they like and dislike, what they would change and how this might be part of a business opportunity. Research on millennials shows that many have a strong sense of social responsibility and this aspect can be particularly motivating (see for example, Deloitte, 2016[3]).

Further practical support is provided whilst students create their mission statements, their vision for their business and some tangible aims. These need to be negotiated by the group, which helps develop teamworking skills and they clearly need to relate to their vision. One of the aims might, however, be no more complicated than 'to have fun'. Students who enjoy what they are doing are far more willing to carry on doing it when things get difficult. As with most enterprise programmes, students must allocate roles amongst themselves through using their own self-evaluations to match skill sets to tasks.

Finally, at the end of the programme, students are asked to reflect on their journey and progress, both from their individual perspective and from that of their enterprise society. Students are then asked to think about their own goals and that of their enterprise society for the following year and life beyond.

The following college case studies illustrate how this programme has been delivered in different institutions and were prepared by NACUE and Dr Maria Hudson.

CASE STUDY 1   Northbrook College

Northbrook College has 1,000 HE students and 6,000 FE students and is based in West Sussex. A group of students from a range of subject backgrounds launched their own commercial radio station in order to gain new media skills, learn about setting up and running a commercial venture and to engage the student body with the local community. The students approached NACUE to help with funding their project and five students were invited to Google Campus in East London to take part in NACUE's Innovation Day. This event gave enterprise societies the opportunity to pitch their project ideas to a panel of judges and win a share of the Innovation Fund. Two students from Northbrook pitched to a panel of expert judges, whilst streaming live on their student radio station (NSR.FM). The students were given £5,000 towards their project and won the prize for Best Pitch in the Further Education category.

Mike Pailthorpe, Course/Pathway Leader at Northbrook College found the Innovation Fund helped to progress enterprise across the whole college. He said: 'As for how the Innovation grant is expected to enhance entrepreneurial activity, it is huge. Quite apart from the boost it has given the individual students who were involved in the bid and the day, there has been a swell of excitement at the college's success and this has brought about much more participation [in enterprise activities] already. Most importantly from my perspective, the grant has placed student entrepreneurial activity at the centre of the College management's attention, and initial worries as to whether the radio station was an acceptable academic activity have now been eased and our students' entrepreneurship is firmly embedded into college life.' Angela Crane, Specialist Skills Coordinator in Business & Enterprise at Northbrook, saw the project as a gateway to further entrepreneurship. She said: 'From here onwards I think it's "watch this space"'.

'The students are working hard to get the radio station live on FM and this will be an excellent leap forward, for both the local community and for students across the college to promote all the individual enterprise activities they are involved in. For example, the college has a Market Stall based in our canteen that students use to sell cakes/jewellery – anything really – as part of their enterprise activities and curriculum. I think this year will be a very enterprise-led year for students and I have no doubt there will be a lot of success stories!'

CASE STUDY 2 Westminster Kingsway College, Vin2 Enterprise Society

Westminster Kingsway College is a further education college in central London with approximately 15,000 students aged 16–18. Students from both campuses: Vin2; the Victoria Centre Enterprise Society and the King's Cross Enterprise Society, came together to bid for £5,000 from the NACUE Innovation Fund. Their bid was a success and the money has been used to sustain the activities of the enterprise societies and to encourage more students to engage with their projects.

One of these projects is the Vin2 Enterprises' annual Enterprise Festival. In 2014, over 200 students from across London came together to learn about the process of starting a business. Delegates listened to entrepreneurial speakers from various industries, including Maria Allen from Maria Allen Jewellery, Masie-Rose Byrne from Unilever and Levi Roots. Student business owners were given the opportunity to promote their products in the 'Entrepreneur Market Place', giving them practical experience in pitching and selling their wares. Other students were invited to pitch their business plans to a panel of judges. The winner was 23-year-old Peter Jones Enterprise Academy student, Joshua Ousley. His business plan for a new health food business impressed the judges and won him the top prize of £500 to invest in his business.

Andy Wilson, Westminster Kingsway College Principal, said: 'We are delighted that our students have been awarded this innovation fund award to further the college's enterprise activities for students. Westminster Kingsway College puts enterprise at the heart of its activities and is the central London home of the Peter Jones Enterprise Academy. We run a number of business and enterprise courses for young people and adults and the enterprise theme runs through all of the courses at the College. There are also a number of entrepreneurial activities through the College's Vin2 Enterprise Society, the King's Cross Centre Enterprise Society and the College's partnership with Camden Into Enterprise.'

CASE STUDY 3   Uxbridge College

Uxbridge College is an Outstanding FE College in west London. It encourages all their students to engage with enterprise activities and thinks it is fundamental to their future employability to take part in and lead in these opportunities. A group of self-led students came together to launch their own company in order to gain practical work experience whilst studying. The group of BTEC-level Production Arts and Design students successfully applied for £5,000 from the NACUE Innovation Fund, which they put towards their company Frock & Roll. Frock & Roll provides vintage clothing, dating back to the early twentieth century, for sale or rent. They also offer hair styling, make-up and event production. The venture will help the students to apply for jobs within the creative industries, whilst providing hands-on business and enterprise skills.

Charlotte Reynolds, 19, is a Production Arts Student and one of Frock & Roll's founders. Speaking about her experience she said: 'Being part of Frock & Roll is a unique experience. Getting into this industry is really hard, so freelancing and building a company when we are young will give us a fantastic grounding. By the time we have come out of college and graduated we'll have the experience to compete for the bigger jobs. It is a great opportunity for us to gain experience and learn about how this kind of business works, so we're so glad to have the Innovation Fund to make this a reality.' Sharon McCann, Volunteers and Citizenship Coordinator at Uxbridge College, has supported the students through the process.

CASE STUDY 4   Chichester College

Embedding student-led enterprise into the institutional culture in Further Education

Chichester College has taken a holistic approach to enterprise development as Helen Loftus, Assistant Principal, who takes a strategic lead on enterprise, explains: 'We felt it was important to embed enterprise and a strong work-readiness culture within curriculum teams and across all study programmes, which is in essence a vertical approach to aligning and mapping enterprise competencies to qualification specifications. However, we soon realized that students would also benefit from a horizontal structure, an enterprise society that would touch so many more students' lives by providing a broader range of enterprise opportunities.' There is a strong staff steer for student-led enterprise at Chichester College, in an approach which, drawing on the support of NACUE and curriculum leaders, engages with the challenges of supporting student leadership in the further education sector.

Students were less receptive to running the enterprise society than actually taking part in the activities championed through the Society. Much of this is attributed to their focus on their studies and part-time work commitments. However, student focus groups gave the staff team and Entrepreneur in Residence a strong understanding of student expectations of an Enterprise Society, which helped to form a strong enterprise framework that supports the College's entrepreneurial culture and allows enterprise participation to grow.

Students suggested the Enterprise Society 'Xpressyourself' should champion four key activities: the development and growth of student-led curriculum companies; the offer of business start-up programmes and funding opportunities; engagement with local employers to support pop-up enterprise and opportunities for social enterprise. A current student of the College (aged 21), is the Entrepreneur in Residence and President of the Enterprise Society, who also provides a point of day-to-day support for the students, who are typically aged from 16 to 18. The College's Enterprise Society champions the growth of student-led curriculum companies by providing start-up investment, mentorship and links to local and national businesses. Each company is expected to generate a return on their investment but it's the development of employability skills that is paramount and pivotal to each company's success. The Enterprise Society gives learners the opportunity to develop their enterprise skills in a cross-College context with invaluable stretch and challenge benefits. After three years of development, there are currently 13 companies. Seeing the success of the first few companies has encouraged more staff and students to get involved.

One of the first curriculum companies was Cee Cee productions, a digital media company. This thriving business responds to both internal and external briefs, providing income to the society and excellent work experience opportunities for the students. To date they have produced a College news channel, a Goodwood Golf promotional video, four curriculum promotional videos and a community video commissioned by local residents.

With an initial investment of £500 from Xpressyourself, sports students have set up a 'Kit Shop'. Two students open the shop daily during the lunch period, selling kit to their fellow students and by September 2015, they were able to start repaying that investment. Another sports student set up her own personal fitness company, using college facilities and has been able to build up a student client base, as well as confidence and business acumen.

Some of these business activities actively engage with external employers for support, for example some business students set up as a college chocolatier. They are working with a local chocolate company which allows them to use their premises to design and make a range of chocolate products. They sell chocolates to their fellow students, with a focus on key events such as Easter and St Valentine's Day.

The society also engages in social enterprise. Students have been involved in the development of a local play park which was designed, funded and built through collaboration between college departments and local businesses.

All 13 curriculum companies are sustainable and sustainability is a key priority for the Society, both in financial and structural terms. Fifty per cent of company profits are kept by the College, forming a central pot to invest in new companies, enabling students to make funding pitches to staff for new projects, with the remainder left to the individual companies to reinvest as they wish. A special recruitment process has been set up in the Human Resources department, engaging students as Enterprise Officers on college contracts. Staff mentorship is also a key feature of the structure which allows the companies to function, despite annual student turnover, although importantly there is now a culture of existing students training new students to hand over the business. 'Students do leave,' explains Helen Loftus. 'That's absolutely fine but there's a structure in place, which means that the company remains in place and ready for the next year's cohort.'

An outcome of the greater vocational activity at Chichester College is the growing learner interest in business start-ups. Two years ago, 22 students attended the college's first business start-up-day programme. This year 112 students attended.

This is of significant interest really, in terms of the number of students who now think, 'Oh, actually, do I need to work for somebody else? Have I got the skills that would enable me to set up on my own?'

Embedding an enterprise culture and orientation

Other curriculum developments have also been key for including an enterprise orientation and culture into teaching at the college. For example, the Enterprise Passport is an initiative which aims to encourage students to reflect on and record what they have done to practise enterprise eg on their course or activities linked to the enterprise society. There has also been a drive, from level three and four courses upwards, to ensure that key employers are involved in every curriculum area, as Helen explains. 'Those employers are working with lecturers to look at the content of the specification that they are delivering, making sure we are involving up-to-date, industry-relevant skills. This is more than students working on an assignment, they are working towards a qualification in collaboration with employers, which makes it more realistic, more worthwhile. We work very hard to bring industry and curriculum teams together and introduce enterprise that way'. Initial funding and support from NACUE on the Strategic Growth Project for the enterprise society development has been pivotal in making this progress. 'If we hadn't had the NACUE money... we would have designed and implemented the Enterprise Passport to support the introduction of study programmes. We would have engaged with employers to support the design of assignments, but I suspect we would not be as far forward as we are. We certainly wouldn't have been able to invest in curriculum companies or start-up initiatives.'

CASE STUDY 5 Experiences in developing a student-led enterprise society and supported student-led enterprise at Newcastle under Lyme College

At Newcastle under Lyme College there is a considerable emphasis on employability, described by the College's Assistant Principal, Val Tomlinson, as 'the preparation of students for work.' A testimony to this is the 1,800 students who are undertaking apprenticeships for a student body that includes 4,000 16–18-year-olds. The College began to engage with NACUE three years ago, receiving start-up funds for student-led enterprise from the Innovation Fund. Luka, a NACUE Regional Enterprise Coordinator, helped the students plan and develop a funding bid. Some of the funds were used to establish the enterprise society, called NOVA, supporting team-building activities, including paying for a venue and refreshments. Acting as a sounding board for the College, Luka ran a student workshop that provided advice on ways that a society could be run and also supplied start-up materials and online links to further resources.

'Luka was very enthusiastic, very bouncy, very bubbly,' said Val. 'Students took to her straight away. And she did some work with staff as well, about... models and the ways that they could work'. NACUE brings a distinctive approach to student learning: 'For our students, I think the enterprise society gives them the chance to meet, interact and work with other students, who are not on the same course as them. Though they have probably never met each other before, they develop teamworking, communication and listening skills; just through working together... NACUE's way of doing things is quite different from how we normally deliver and it did get them thinking in a new way and gave them a chance to do something alternative, instead of sitting in a classroom, in the normal college environment'.

Both continuity of enterprise-society-leadership and staff support have been an issue. 'One of the challenges is that, the students are, generally, on two-year courses, some are just on one-year courses' Val explained. 'You haven't got them for three years, like university students... How do you get that continuity? We struggled both in terms of student cohort but also the staff, because obviously staff move, they have new responsibilities. NACUE support for staff has been helpful. To be honest, staff need support as well because they need to understand that working with students through an enterprise society is very different from teaching them. So they need to understand their role, how they can support the students to run their own society. We have on-going support and I would say that it's been helpful.'

There are currently 20 students who are active in the enterprise society and a wider community of students with whom the society communicates. Newcastle under Lyme is an area with pockets of deprivation. Some students are from low income families and trying to juggle part-time jobs with their studies. In this context, extracurricular activity with the enterprise society can be a lower priority for students. Other participants are able to prioritize the enterprise society and are very passionate about it. In seeking to address leadership-continuity issues, college enterprise champions are trying to identify first-year students who can go on to develop the enterprise society in their second year.

The NACUE Innovation Fund was also used to set up pockets of funding that students could apply for. For example, one student had designed a mug and the enterprise society lent her the money to get this manufactured. There is a lot of enterprise activity in the curriculum, though Val Tomlinson feels that the College does not label it as such but should do. Students undertake the £10 challenge, for example, producing and selling things and donating the money to charity. Since 2013 the College has had a pop-up shop in Newcastle under Lyme town centre, having negotiated with the borough council to take on an empty retail unit. The shop sells a mixture of photography, print, jewellery, original artworks, some ceramics and textile work that fashion students have created. Joinery students produce items such as wooden tea light holders and breadboards and engineering students produce metal sculptures. Two members of staff in the College's art club act as enterprise champions and their job is to liaise between the student body and the shop manager. The A-Level product-design students are set a project. They are linked with a local sheet metal company and go on a site visit in their first term at college. Following a tour around production processes, the students come back to college and they have to design an item that can be produced by this company and sold at the shop. They do all of the design work on their computer, send the images to the company and get staff help to select the items that are likely to sell well.

While valuing the benefits of student engagement in an enterprise society, Val Tomlinson feels that it is one of several approaches to support student-led enterprise. 'You can do activities with students that aren't badged "enterprise society" but you still deliver a really good experience for them and something that they can then take with them. It's not all about having a very formal society and meetings and structure. Sometimes, it's about pulling students together, giving them the freedom to do something new, with support.'

CASE STUDY 6 Student Engine

Nurturing employability and labour market progression

Chris Foster, the founder of Student Engine, was a student at a Peter Jones Academy where he joined the enterprise society. 'Going into the enterprise society opened a lot of doors and gave me a lot of skills,' he said. Over the last couple of years Chris has participated in NACUE Leaders' Summit events and been a member of the Student Advisory Board. Participating in these forums, he has found it inspirational to network with other young people engaging in enterprise activity, a life-changing experience. 'That for me has been the most transforming experience, seeing that young people do want to make something. You know, it's being in a room full of young, creative and talented young people... [NACUE] have all these meetings to connect young people together, building their skills and guest speakers come in as well. It's highly beneficial, just linking with like-minded people. It obviously increases your own motivation.' Over the last year, alongside his further studies at Chichester College, Chris has been working as an Entrepreneur in Residence, providing support to students involved in 'Xpressyourself', Chichester College's Enterprise Society.

He has also been developing his own business start-up. Student Engine is an online platform which connects students in education with businesses. With an initial main focus on the Sussex area, the platform was launched in June 2015. At this time 350 students and 200 businesses had registered. It aims to help students build their employability skills and gain a portfolio of labour market experience as well as client recommendations. It does this in two ways. First, it enables students to build experience through freelance work by advertising their skills on the platform, for example in accounting, logo creation and website development. Businesses can upload current projects to the platform, providing a project description and a guide to the budget available. Students can then bid for the work, signalling the services that they would offer and the rate that they would charge. Businesses can select students to undertake the project by searching through the platform database. 'We mainly focus on the freelance section purely because, while they are in education, students need to build skills, they need to build their portfolio'. The students charge one third of the price of a full-time freelance. 'Obviously [the businesses] get a good deal, but they also know that they are helping to build someone's future. It gives them a chance to test young people and see what they want. And then if they feel that they connect with them quite well, they may offer them firm employment.'

The second strand of Student Engine's work involves providing a platform for employers to advertise full-time jobs, internships and apprenticeships. When students approach graduation, they again use Student Engine to support their further progression into the labour market and apply for positions, drawing on the profile of skills' recommendations and endorsements that they have built up. Complementing this activity, Chris has also been involved in Xpressyourself's development of a Young Person's Chamber, in essence a youth section of the local Chamber of Commerce. Guest speakers give talks at monthly meetings, for example, on finance and business planning, interacting with the students.

'The Chamber of Commerce has been a massive support in helping us arrange everything,' says Chris. The response that we got from the members was actually phenomenal. They all wanted to get involved, all wanted to help and all wanted to sort of give back. I thought that was amazing.' These links with the Chamber of Commerce have also helped to build business interest in Student Engine's Platform.

With thanks to NACUE for providing the case study information. For further information see http://www.nacue.com/

Notes

1 Department for Business, Innovation and Skills (June 2013) 'Enterprise Education: Impact in Higher Education and Further Education: Final Report' [online] https://www.gov.uk/government/uploads/system/uploads/attachment_data/file/208715/bis-13-904-enterprise-education-impact-in-higher-education-and-further-education.pdf Last accessed 03/06/16

2 Levie, J, Hart, M and Anyadike-Danes, M (2010) 'The effect of business or enterprise training on opportunity recognition and entrepreneurial skills of graduates and nongraduates in the UK', *Frontiers of Entrepreneurship Research2009* pp 749–759

3 http://www2.deloitte.com/global/en/pages/about-deloitte/articles/millennialsurvey.html

Coaching for employability and enterprise

14

DOUG STRYCHARCZYK

Coaching is a particularly apt activity for developing employability and enterprise. Both require a combination of skills and knowledge, which can be taught, and mindset which is predominantly learned.

The last has to come from within the individual. This means that the individual needs to be self-aware about what qualities they possess in this area and what are the implications of such qualities; and then they need to be minded to do something which brings its own benefit. Telling doesn't work.

Looking at the examples of very successful projects described elsewhere in the book (New Horizons p XX and London Youth Rowing's Breaking Barriers programme), we find that coaching activity is built into these projects and is focused on mindset or the development of mental toughness which is necessary for achieving the project outcomes.

One issue is that coaching can be by its nature 'labour intensive' and costly. If seen as a cost and not as an investment then it won't be used. Building evidence for its effectiveness and its efficiency for ROI is important. Projects like the New Horizons project are beginning to do that. Another issue is that it must be done properly. A skilled coach understands the process and how to work with someone so that 'coachee' feels they have found their own solution which works for them.

So... what does a good coaching process look like?

Coaching is a continuous process which is used to bring out the best performance in others. Coaches guide and support people who possess the knowledge, skills and abilities they need to perform effectively but may need help to:

Recognize where they need to improve and develop their performance;

Overcome barriers to effective performance improvement;

Achieve long-term and sustainable change;

Develop strategies that help sustain their potential.

Identifying the desired outcome(s) of a coaching intervention is often a vital component for measuring success.

One of Stephen Covey's Seven Habits states 'Start with the end in mind'. How often do you set out on a journey without knowing where you are heading off to? Rarely, we would guess. So this is sound advice and it is equally important that you enjoy the journey that takes you to your chosen destination.

Coaching is the very opposite of telling someone what to do. It is frequently described as non-directive. Although some would argue that simply by asking questions, even open questions, the questioner is bringing some direction to the conversation. The best coaches use questions to:

- Raise self-awareness in the individual
- Develop understanding – particularly of the implications of what has been (self) discovered
- Provoke thinking – about the consequences of those implications and how that impacts on the coachee. Important here is establishing the coach's commitment to doing something
- Help to form actions which are realistic and achievable.

Coaching is based on the use of good structure which is supported by open and structured questions. The material in AQR's workbook seeks to do that and provide the structure for the coachee to record and use the answers to those questions. This is illustrated below.

Primarily developed to support the work of the coach, this workbook can, with careful use, be used as a standalone device by the coachee.

There are many useful coaching models around. For the purpose of illustration we are using the GROW model but this works equally well with other structured approaches.

This material is drawn from AQR International's Coaching Workbook. This is a resource developed to support coaches and coachees on their journey.

The material is designed to support a flexible coaching approach for both parties to the coaching discussion. It is often used as a workbook for reflective notes when working with the support of a coach.

It is particularly suited to the style of coaching that might use 'step by step' models and focus on goals and outcomes.

The GROW coaching model

First, just a few words of introduction to the GROW model (Whitmore 2002) which is perhaps one of the more familiar models used to structure a coaching conversation that is focused around clear outcomes or goals. It is particularly useful here.

It proposes that a coaching conversation can proceed purposefully through four distinct stages.

- **Goal** – At the start of the process we define the goal or outcome – this helps us to stay focused. It also begins the formation of motivation – it can clarify direction and provide purpose for the individual;
- **Reality** – This is about what is happening now that you would like to change and establishing what this would be like in the future;
- **Options** – Identifying and exploring the options available, the barriers and how they might be overcome and the challenges you might face;
- **Way Forward** – A commitment to specific actions and an action plan for building motivation.

Whilst described as a linear process it is actually iterative and coaches may find they need to move backwards and forwards between the stages to clarify and refine the best course of action.

This can be diagrammatically shown as:

Figure 14.1 GROW coaching model

WRAP UP		GOAL
Commit to action		Agree discussion topic
Identify possible obstacles		Agree specific objectives for session
Make steps specific and define thinking	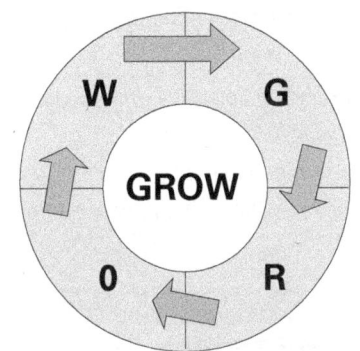	
Define Support		Set long-term aim if possible
OPTIONS		**REALITY**
Cover full range of options		Invite self-assessment
Invite suggestions from coachee		Offer examples of feedback
Offer suggestions		Avoid or check assumptions (yours and others)
Ensure choices are made		Discard relevant history

Preparing the coachee for the coaching experience

A fairly fundamental step – the coachee must be ready for the journey. The Mental Toughness framework and the associated MTQ48 measure can provide insight here as to the coachee's mindset, their potential state of readiness. Read it carefully before considering this:

> *To what extent am I in the right frame of mind to get the most from this coaching process? Do I accept that I have areas to develop? Can I see the benefit in so doing?*
>
> *What can I do to improve this mindset? How important is development to me?*

G – Goals

Take a moment to think about what you want to achieve in your life and where and how you would like to work.

Consider any challenges you are facing or potential changes that you might need to respond to and when you are ready answer the following questions in the space below.

> *What specifically do you want to achieve from working through this guide? (short-term/long-term)*
>
> *How will you measure it? Can you think of SMART goals? If not, why not?*
>
> *How will you know when you have achieved it? How do you think you will feel when you arrive?*
>
> *When do you want to achieve it by?*
>
> *How will you best use your time on this workbook?*

Goals – and Mental Toughness

Several of the components of Mental Toughness are relevant for this stage in the process.

Control

To launch the GROW process, you do need to have a sense that you know where you are going and that you believe that you can achieve. Others do it; so can you.

- To what extent do you believe that you are in control of your life and your environment? Or do you believe that it's the environment and others who shape you?
- It's hard to sets goals and targets. Will you give up in a fit of pique or do you have staying power?
- Will you be able to deal with all the actions you may have to implement?

Commitment

This is at the heart of this stage.

- To what extent are you prepared to set challenging goals and targets for yourself?
- Will you keep these at the front of your mind throughout the process?
- How determined are you to succeed? Are you prepared to put the work in? Perhaps sacrificing things in the short-term to get to your goal? You may need to prioritize this over nicer things to do to get things done?
- Will you be honest with yourself and monitor yourself against your goals and targets?

Challenge?

This is at the heart of the process of which this is the first stage.

- Does the process and the challenge that goes with it interest and excite you? Or does it already feel overwhelming?
- How do you feel about the prospect of developing skills and qualities that you presently may not have but which will be needed in the future?
- Is there anything that concerns you about the process and the goals you are setting.
- How good is your planning? Have you set milestones for the bigger goals?

Confidence

This is about your readiness to deal with setbacks and challenge and ridicule from others.

- Are you prepared to deal with those who don't agree with what you are doing?
- How will you deal with things that go wrong?

> *What shall I attend to to ensure that I am in the right frame of mind to set SMARTER goals?*

R – Reality

Have you got a realistic and objective picture of your current skills, knowledge and preferred behaviour? What has been others' assessment of you at this point? If you have used psychometric tests what have they indicated? Then answer the following questions in the space below:

> *What is happening right now? (What, when, where, how much?) Have you carried out a SWOT analysis on your current situation?*
>
> *Who is involved with you at the present time who helps you to shape things? Are they all helpful? Who do you need to involve?*
>
> *What are the consequences of your current situation? What happens if you do nothing?*
>
> *What will help you move forward/What will constrain you? How did you get here? Have you carried out a Force Field analysis on your plan as it stands?*
>
> *How do you feel right now about your challenge (scale 1-10)? What could increase this rating?*

Reality – and Mental Toughness

The components of Mental Toughness that are relevant for this stage include:

Control

- To what extent do you feel in control of your life and your emotions? Is it enough to achieve your objectives?

- What has felt out of your control until now? How can you extend your circle of influence and bring some of this under your control?
- Some of your situation will remain out of your control? How will you deal with that?
- Are you minded to understand that success will be down to you?

Commitment

- To what extent have you set goals and targets for yourself? How have you done?
- How easily do you give up?
- What can you do to approach this more positively?

Challenge?

- How have you responded to challenges like this before?
- What usually gets in the way of success? What typically helps you?
- What generally gets you interested and excited?
- What is it about these goals and opportunities that you have identified that is likely to get you 'buzzing'? Why?

Confidence

- To what extent are you confident in your ability to succeed? What needs to be done to bolster that?
- How do you deal with those who aren't convinced by what you are doing?
- When things have gone wrong how has that felt?
- How do you pick yourself up when things go wrong?

> *To what shall I attend to ensure that I am in the right frame of mind to create a reality where I am more likely to succeed?*

Life is like a game of golf. Good golfers play the ball where it lies, not where they would like it to be.

O – Options

Reflect on your aspirations and then answer the questions in the space below to help you consider the range of options you may have. Keep open to new possibilities rather than limiting yourself to the obvious ones. The world is full of opportunity and creating awareness of this is both important and valuable. Changing your environment might help – go for a walk, play some music and let the responses emerge.

> What could I do? What are the options for me? Might I have to do something first that is less appealing to get to where I want to go?
> What have others done in similar situations? Can I think of role models and looked at what they have done – either achieving what they set out to achieve or shown flexibility and achieved something else entirely.
> What have I tried so far? How did it work? What did I learn from that? How might someone else tackle this?
> Is what I would like to do dependent upon resource – time/money/people, etc?
> What are the costs and benefits of taking action or of not taking action?

W – (The) Way Forward

Having taken some time to reflect on the reality and options of the situation, you now need to consider the next steps in the process and the action plan that will keep you motivated. Answer the following questions in the space below:

> What option or combination of options will work best for you?
> What action will you take and when will you take it?
> What obstacles might you meet and how will you overcome them?
> What support do you need and where will you get it?
> On a scale of 1–10 how likely are you to take this action? What needs to happen to make it a 10?
> How will you feel when you have taken this action?

Coaching for Employability and Enterprise

Options and the Way Forward – and Mental Toughness

The components of Mental Toughness that are relevant for this stage include:

Control

- To what extent are you happy to consider options? Or are you fixed on one thing
- What can you bring into your control to ensure that you will succeed with your chosen path?
- How do others do what you have found hard until now?
- What remains out of your control? How will you deal with that?

Commitment

- To what extent have you set goals and targets for yourself? How have you done?
- Are you content that you explored and evaluated all options and you have selected the best one for your purpose? Are you hesitant in any way?
- To what extent does your plan feel like a picture of success for you?
- What factors will drive you forward to succeed.
- What can go wrong and how will you deal with these?
- Are you prepared to do what it takes to succeed? Is it important enough for you?

Challenge?

- To what extent does this represent an opportunity to improve your life, your work, everything?
- Can you visualize a better person emerging from this process?
- Did any other options promise the same?
- Are some of the options riskier than others? Does that affect what you will do?
- There will be setbacks? To what extent are you prepared for those?

Confidence

- Have you selected the best option?
- How will you deal with setbacks? Is there support you can turn to?

- Are you able to describe what you are going to do confidently to others.... and argue if they challenge you?
- Will you be able to persuade and convince others to help you and to support you?

> To what shall I attend to ensure that I am in the right frame of mind to succeed?

A case study in coaching using MTQ48

X had been a successful student throughout his school life. He had achieved good grades in his examinations and had achieved good enough A level grades to get onto a university course that had been identified as a good choice for him. His A level results were all in the sciences and he had enjoyed the learning that went with achieving those good grades. His teacher had been interesting – even inspiring – and had shown interest in him and his potential.

His family was supportive and they were pleased with his development. Both parents were scientists who worked for a large multinational organization and had done so for many years. They valued the stability and had impressed upon him the importance of getting a good job with a big employer where there was lots of opportunity to develop and grow.

X however was uneasy about this although he didn't say anything about it to his parents or his teachers. He felt, given all the support they had provided, that they had his best interests at heart and that their advice and guidance was well intentioned and probably sound. He understood his parents' advice, they were content with their lives and had provided an environment where he could prosper.

One problem was that he couldn't envisage what he would actually do or what he wanted to do once he had completed his degree at university. In one sense that wasn't odd. Most of his friends didn't seem to have those kind of goals, believing that this would sort itself out in time.

Another factor was that he really enjoyed being with his grandfather and with his uncle. Both were different to his parents. Both worked for themselves. His grandfather had a shop which was very successful. He worked hard and sometimes couldn't come to family events at weekends but he really enjoyed his work. His uncle had developed a portfolio of property which he rented out to a local hospital which trained nurses. He also worked hard and was extremely successful.

X would often work for both to earn some pocket money. He really enjoyed that and found he seemed to learn a lot without it being such an effort to do so. In particular he liked contact with people; In his science studies a great deal of that had meant working on his own.

X's parents became aware of his unease and his concerns. Having firstly spoken to the school whose pastoral care services were rudimentary (operating on a volunteer basis by the teaching staff who were largely untrained), they decided to engage a coach for a few sessions to work with X.

The coach used a structured approach, based on the GROW model. This started with setting goals for the coaching sessions then looking at an analysis of the current situation, identifying preferred outcomes and finally enabling action plans to emerge.

It was agreed at the outset that the most important outcome would be that X would be happy with the outcome from the process, whether this was continuing with the present plan or changing it in some way.

Session One

The self reflection process used a form of SWOT analysis to identify what he liked and what he disliked from his work experience this far and what he understood about the world of work. A proactive individual, he had worked part-time in a number of organizations simply to earn some money.

X concluded:

- First, he wasn't really enthusiastic about his current plan and found it hard to be really committed to it.
- Second, he became clearer about what career or job he would need to have for him to really enjoy it. This included contact with people; opportunity for flexibility; immediacy – the opportunity for results in shorter time frames than say a major research activity.
- He was prepared to work hard and, if needed, to take measured risks such as working for little pay to get established.
- He was attracted to enterprise.

The SWOT analysis helped to crystallize his thinking and enabled him to look at the current situation rationally. The next step was to check how realistic all of this was given his limited experience of the world of work.

One thing that the coach had introduced was some description of the range of opportunities that could lie ahead. He had never heard of many of them.

Session Two – focused on his mindset

First, he observed that his confidence had been diminished because he was no longer looking forward to what lay ahead. His sense of control had been affected by his seeming inability to influence the decisions about his future. He felt these had been made for him – although he recognized that people thought they were doing what was best.

This became an area for attention. He needed to feel more involved in decisions about his life and to feel that this was sensible.

The coach showed him how to reflect on the skills and knowledge that he already possessed and how these might be useful in the future.

Problem-solving was a key issue in most sciences. He realized that he was reasonably adept at this and that this was probably easily transferable to most applications.

His work experience was mainly in dealing with customers and in working in small teams. He enjoyed this and was apparently good at it. Again, a great many careers need good interpersonal skills.

The gap that seemed to emerge was around his motivation. Although conscientious he recognized that he lacked direction and didn't appear to be particularly aspirational. This was something to which he now knew he had to attend. Particularly thinking about what skills and knowledge he might need in the future and how he might acquire these.

Session Three – focused on identifying options for the future and evaluating these to create an action plan.

What became apparent was that he liked business and business activity. Sciences could provide that but he wanted to feel less restrained and be able to examine all opportunities that came his way.

His conclusion was that he wanted to do something around business studies, marketing or economics. He hadn't even been aware of economics at the outset but realized that some elements were not unlike some of the sciences he had studied thus far.

This case study concludes with X deciding not to go to university initially but to work and study part-time. After two years he enrolled on a degree course in economics and now runs his own business – retailing specialist fast food which he hopes to franchise when he has the model right.

Summary

In this chapter we've looked at the value of coaching for developing employability and enterprise in individuals.

The coaching process (it is based on a process) appears to be highly appropriate for developing key aspects of employability and enterprise in young people. Indeed it is increasingly common for leaders in business and commerce to make use of coaches for their own development.

The facilitatory approach is also highly appropriate. Employability is a function of lifelong learning – with the accent on learning. Moreover it is often a function of experiential learning. We all experience many things in our lives and will often forget to reflect on these experiences and extract the learning. The involvement of a skilled third party – a trained coach – appears to be highly beneficial.

Where we have seen organizations include coaching in the support they provide in this area, this appears to provide excellent results. Certainly worth the investment.

Finally a word about evidence. Is there evidence for coaching and its effectiveness in developing an individual's mindset?

The investigation into the relationship between coaching and mental toughness is encouraging. Studies do indicate a relationship between coaching and the elements that constitute mental toughness: self-efficacy, cognitive hardiness, enhanced goal-striving, higher expectations about outcomes and environmental mastery (Grant 2009). A 2007 study found that coaching can increase cognitive hardiness (mental toughness) and hopefulness in high school students (Green, Grant and Rynsaardt 2007).

Coaching has also been shown to enhance goal-striving (Spence and Grant 2007), increase self-efficacy and heighten expectations about outcomes (Evers, Brouwers and Tomic 2006). We can be reasonably confident that coaching has an important role to play in supporting people to develop appropriate levels of mental toughness and through that enhance their employability.

Developing mindset and mental toughness

15

DOUG STRYCHARCZYK

What can we do about it?

Having established that mindset and mental toughness are key factors in our understanding of employability and enterprise and correspond closely with what is described casually as 'attitude', the question is 'what, if anything can we do about it?'.

The answer is 'a great deal'. Given the importance of 'attitude' in all sports, sports psychologists and sports coaches would argue that they have been looking at this for many years with significant evidence of success. Much of that is now crossing over to applications in people and organization development in just about every area where people are expected to flourish.

In fact, given that we are looking at the individual, how they think and what this means for their performance, their well-being, their feelings and their behaviour, the development of mindset, mental toughness or attitude is ideally suited to the coaching process, to training programmes that are experiential in nature, to training and developments where the learner is facilitated in his or her learning. It works well with associated processes too, such as mentoring and counselling.

Can we change or merely influence?

An important question to consider is 'are we changing someone's mental toughness or can we simply equip someone with tools and techniques that enable them to behave as a mentally tough person might behave?'.

That depends on the individual, which is why assessing individual need is important.

The answer appears to be that, where the individual or the organization wants to change or develop it is possible to change one's core mental toughness. We are not suggesting that anyone should or must develop their mental toughness; for those who see a benefit for their employability or their ability to be enterprising or entrepreneurial, there may be a good reason for doing this. There are some valuable advantages in doing this – but it also depends on what they want to achieve and how they want to live their lives.

It is also important to note here that we are not suggesting that anyone should become very mentally tough. The value of the model and the MTQ48 measure is that it can help to identify which aspects of one's mental toughness are preventing or hindering them from attaining, from achieving well-being or leading a more positive life.

This is also true for all the employability frameworks described in this book.

It is often the case, therefore, that developing an aspect of mindset or mental toughness is worthwhile. But that might mean a shift in mental toughness – not a dramatic leap to extremes. It depends on the individual and their circumstances.

What we do know is that employers, educators and clients value both a mental toughness mindset as well as its components. It's part of their employability checklist. So there is advantage is some form of development.

Moreover, mental toughness is like a lot of attributes, it needs to be maintained. The very mentally tough can sometimes dig deep and sort this out for themselves. Most will need – and value – some support to do this. Many also value the opportunity to hone and improve their mindset as they face challenge, setback or opportunity. It's one reason why it has become so popular in coaching and mentoring activity.

There is sometimes a challenge in working with those who are very mentally sensitive. Generally they have a harder time engaging with others.

A solution, which in fact can apply to everyone, involves showing mentally sensitive individuals what a mentally tough person would do and then supporting them in applying these approaches, tools and techniques. It seems to work too.

Introducing some of these techniques to some individuals as *coping* strategies can be effective. The mentally tough use the same techniques for *dealing* with stress pressure, challenge and opportunity.

How can coaches and trainers work with individuals and groups to develop mindset?

The concept of mindset and mental toughness is more effectively learned rather than taught. It's one reason why it is so suited to coaching. It fits very well with experiential learning and, like a lot of developmental activity; it is a very good illustration of the Kolb Learning Styles model usually shown as a continuous cycle:

Figure 15.1 Kolb learning styles model

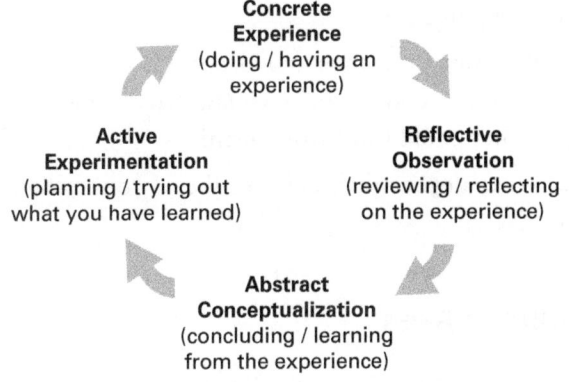

To develop mental toughness we start with self-awareness and establish a need to do something together with the commitment to act.

The learning process is usually initiated by doing something – experimenting with a new technique, tool or approach. In fact there is a plethora of exercises and activities which are suitable. It is very useful here to use interventions whose impact can be measured objectively in some way to show the effect on the individual.

Change, when it does occur, is often incremental and may at first not be detected by the individual. Having a measure of progress is both supportive and encouraging. There now Apps which have this built in.

Reflection

The next stage – reflection – is crucial. This is what rarely happens effectively if left to the individual: it's where the coach, counsellor or trainer can make the greatest impact. Typically this will mean helping the individual:

- to ask themselves the right questions
- to think about the impact on their feelings and emotions of what they have learned or done. Is it desirable? Would they enjoy feeling like this more than feeling the way they usually do?
- to consider whether they are now more effective or more efficient – even if this is marginal at this point? Could they improve on this? Was there a benefit in doing so?
- to understand why this change or development was happening. What was the individual doing now that perhaps they weren't before? Was that worth developing further?
- to evaluate the impact on their mood and their mindset. Do they feel more confident and in control, more committed and more prepared to try new things so they could learn from them?
- to consider what impact this had on others around them. Did others respond positively?

A continuous process

If the individual recognizes change and its benefits, can they capture it and make it a habit? This is something that we learn from the world of sport – the importance of purposeful practice. If something works then the individual should do it regularly and often until it becomes a habit. In the sports world, coaches will work with their charges almost daily to ensure this happens. Without this, it is comparatively easy to fall back into old habits.

And as Kolb suggests, it's a continuous process.

There are very many tools, techniques and approaches which appear to work as development activities. Almost any exercise will work although the more experiential the exercise the better.

Many trainers, coaches and managers will know of some techniques. A very common response from trainers and coaches is that they now understand better why some of their techniques and approaches work and, importantly, how to direct them more effectively.

Some techniques

Interventions and exercises can often be found under labels such as Psychology, Sports coaching, Cognitive Behavioural Therapy (CBT), Neurolinguistic Programming (NLP), Positive Psychology etc.

What we have found is that virtually all the tools and techniques can be grouped under five broad headings.

These are:

- positive thinking
- visualization
- anxiety control
- goal setting and
- attentional control.

Positive thinking

The power of positive thinking is now well understood. We can 'think ourselves into action or think ourselves out of action'. The response of two equally competent individuals can vary simply because one believes they can and the other believes they can't. It's in the head.

The underlying principle here is 'we are what we think'.

Thinking positively relies upon two interrelated ideas:

- avoiding negative or demeaning thoughts
- adopting positive language inside one's head.

Interventions then tend to fall into three groups:

Learning how to think positively

Examples here will include Self Talk and the use of Affirmations. We can learn to use positive language as much as possible. The more we use positive language the better we feel.

Self talk is one of the most successful techniques. Widely used in sports, sports coaches will encourage their charges to think in terms of achieving a personal best performance or winning and will encourage their coachees to find words which are associated with this and to use them as much as possible.

Words carry an emotional meaning in addition to their strict dictionary definition. Affirmations are statements or phrases that mean something to you. When in doubt or under pressure, using them in your head enables you to be more positive about the situation at hand.

Examples include statements such as:

- this job is perfect for me;
- I am going to really impress the interviewer;
- I have a good story to tell;
- I can be a success at running my own business;
- I can take pressure – I thrive on it;
- I like the feeling when I do something that scares me;
- I work hard;

They need to be made in the present tense, must make the person feel good when used and have a positive bent.

A particularly effective technique is *'What am I good at?'*

AQR International has developed a toolkit of around 60 for these five areas of development techniques. Set out below is an example of one of the cue cards developed for the toolkit which is for *'What am I good at?'*

Each cue card explains the technique, how and why it works, and provides guidance to the user to support reflection and learning.

What do you think I am good at?

A Positive Thinking Exercise –

Running the exercise – A highly participative group exercise which can be run comfortably as a complete session or part of a session.

1. Individuals will need a sheet of paper. They will work in small groups of three or four. Groups can be self-selecting or put together by the coach/trainer.
2. Explain that the individual will do an exercise which will help them to focus on their strengths, achievements and successes, creating a more positive mindset.
3. Explain that (model script):

    You are to think about the other people in your group. You will receive a sheet of paper with the name of each team member on the front.

You start by writing your name on the foot of a sheet and passing it to the person on your left. This means that you will receive a sheet from the person on your right.

On the sheet (in the space provided) you are to write three things that you think that your colleague is good at. This can be a skill or a quality they bring to their work or something that would impress a prospective employer. You have three or four minutes to do this.

When told to do so, fold the paper so that your comments cannot be read by the next person. Pass the sheet to the next person on your left and so on until everyone has commented about everyone else.

When you have received your sheet back, open it and read what it says.

You can provide five to ten minutes to allow people to ask each other questions.

What do you think I am good at?

Reflection

Background
This is an exercise in reflection. It picks up on what Robert Burns suggested:

'O wad some Power the giftie gie us
To see ourselves as others see us!'

Although he meant it more cynically, reflection can focus on strengths and make us self-aware about our qualities that we might take for granted.

Discussion Guides:
- How many were surprised with some of the feedback?
- What difference does this make for them? Has it improved confidence?
- Where and how can this feedback help in their work and their life?
- What do they think of the impact of their feedback on their colleagues?
- How can they help each other to build confidence?

Support Materials & Resources
Can be done with plain paper. Pre-printed A4 sheets specially designed for this with double-sided grids are available in pads of 50 from www.aqr.co.uk

▶

> **Coach/Trainer Review – Assessing Mood**
>
> Individuals rate their mood/day on a scale of 1–10.
>   Do this manually, guiding assessment as follows:
>
> 1–3   I definitely don't feel in control of my life and my work.
> 4–7   I feel in control some of the time but not all of the time.
> 8–10   I pretty much feel I am getting things done because I know I can.
>
> Group discussion: what have you learned about building confidence and the importance of giving each other recognition and feedback?

Visualization

There is a close relationship between visualization and other positive-thinking techniques.

We don't have to learn how to visualize – we do it all the time. What we have to do is learn how to harness it for our benefit. The challenge lies in the fact that often when we consider a situation in our mind we will often visualize it in a negative way. If asked to attend an interview we can imagine it going horribly wrong. We'll fluff our lines; we'll get flustered; we'll forget key points we wanted to make about ourselves; we imagine the interviewers will ask awkward questions that we fail to answer properly and so on. Similar negative things will happen when we pitch for business with a client or speak to a bank manager about a loan.

But that is all imagined; it's how we visualize something. We let our anxiety direct how we perceive events that haven't yet happened.

Visualization can be used in a positive way: you can visualize the interview differently. You can, inside your head, imagine all possible scenarios and, unlike the real thing, you can pause and reflect. You can imagine options for response. You can imagine how you might deal with that tricky moment. You can decide that it's a good idea to bring some notes with you so that you don't forget key points.

Psychologists will confirm that practising something in your head is as real to your mind as doing it in practice. The human mind doesn't discriminate between the two sets of experiences. Instead of telling yourself that you will be successful, you 'see' yourself being successful. Visualization is like watching a video of yourself.

The net effect is that you develop a positive approach to potentially challenging situations which boosts your confidence and your sense of control.

Anxiety control

Anxiety is something that affects us all no matter what age, background, sex, status or social grouping. It's natural to feel anxious when asked to do something that may be out of the ordinary or might expose us to a number of people. Actors, athletes, great orators and musicians all might appear cool, calm and collected but all will admit to anxiety.

We can't get rid of anxiety, we can learn to manage it. That's what the cool, calm and collected people do. Research at the University of Basle shows that having a mentally tough mindset enables individuals to be better able to deal with this.

In fact Cattell when he developed the Big 5 model found a correlation between anxiety and performance – it can be a driver for some.

Anxiety control techniques fall into some broad groupings. Most techniques are known to most coaches:

- Muscular relaxation
- Controlled breathing

Both work because they reverse the body's reflex to short breathing and tense muscles when anxious.

- Controlled distraction – focusing on a pleasant or alternative situation which distracts from the anxiety-causing situation
- Mindfulness – learning to be present. To inhabit the present moment.

Goal setting

In his review of education in the USA, in his book, *Goals!: How to Get Everything You Want – Faster Than You Ever Thought Possible* (2010), Brian Tracy, http://www.briantracy.com/, claims that goal setting is the most important life skill for any young individual. Yet only 3 per cent of students in the USA ever receive training in goal-setting skills. When they do – they emerge as top performers.

Goal setting, of course, is a fundamental activity in coaching processes.

Locke and Latham (2006), who carried out much of the pioneering work on goal setting, found that setting effective goals was also a significant motivator for many. They confirmed the need to set specific and difficult goals and identified three other factors which appear important in goal setting. To motivate individuals, goals must have:

1 Clarity: setting SMART goals. Clarity focuses the individual on the goal.
2 Challenge: identifying challenging goals which are perceived as difficult but achievable.
3 Commitment:

How important is the ultimate goal?

A belief in the ability to achieve the goals.

The extent to which promises are made to self and to others.

All three of these factors are captured in the Commitment element of the 4Cs model of mental toughness.

4 Feedback: this enables the sense of progress and provides the opportunity to flex or adapt.
5 Task complexity: the more complex the task the more difficult it will be to achieve. Individuals can take on too much without giving themselves a realistic chance of achieving the task.

Our experience in the full spectrum of applications suggests that there are four aspects of goal setting which are important:

- understanding what a goal is and accepting its relevance
- setting clear, realistic, achievable goals – the SMART process is a good way of achieving this.
- dealing with big goals. How do you eat an Elephant? Setting milestones. This is a major weakness for many.
- balancing goals.

Attentional control

Arguably, if there is one factor that underpins an individual's ability to be the best that they can be, whatever the situation, it is their ability to focus and control their focus of attention effectively. This means being able to focus better on what is important and to focus for longer.

It's important for almost every activity, whether it is preparing for an interview or presentation, writing a CV or a proposal.

It has been estimated that the average attention span of a young person in the UK is presently around eight minutes. That means a lot of 'stopping and starting' if carrying out an activity that should take an hour but winds up taking four hours and becomes a stressful activity.

Improving attentional control improves performance and well-being.

Nine ways to enhance your focus

1 Practise, practise, practise!
2 Use routines – reduce the cognitive load.
3 Set clear and realistic goals – you need to know what you are doing and when you have finished!
4 Minimize distractions.
5 Control technology – don't let it control you!
6 Manage stress and fatigue. If you're stressed or tired you cannot concentrate for long.
7 Work to stay fit and healthy.
8 Take a break – with a degree of physical activity.
9 Practise techniques which help to develop attentional control.

Techniques include physical activities such as the **Stork Stand**.

Find a spot away from chairs and other hazardous objects. Begin by standing and putting all your weight on one leg. Raise your arms out to the sides at shoulder level and gradually raise your free leg. Keep that leg just off the ground. Close your eyes and try to maintain your balance.

For most people this becomes easier if you 'empty your mind'. That is you don't concentrate on not falling over.

There are a number of games including Apps and Computer games which rely on concentration for success. Usefully, many also build in the ability to score performance with which you can plot your progress. They work extremely well. Like almost all exercise in this area they require reflection – 'what am I now doing that is helping me to concentrate better and how can I capture it for other situations?' and practice until it becomes a new habit.

Curiously if we ask the question about a young person's attention span differently – 'what is their attention span when playing a favourite video game?', you get a completely different answer.

Which demonstrates how attentional control can be developed and how important reflection is to enable this learning to be applied to all aspects of life – including employability and enterprise.

In summary, there is a plethora of tools and techniques available to the coach, trainer or manager to enable them to facilitate development of mindset with their client, student or employee.

Their effectiveness will rest upon:

- understanding the individual's needs;
- selecting and introducing appropriate techniques that work for them;
- capturing their commitment by helping them to be aware of the benefits and
- purposeful practice.

A full description of development activity around this theme can be found in *Developing Mental Toughness: Coaching Strategies to Improve Performance, Resilience and Wellbeing* (2015), Strycharczyk and Clough, Kogan Page.

AQR International has also developed a toolkit of 60 exercises for coaches and trainers. For more information go to: www.aqrinternational.co.uk

Global perspectives – China and the Far East

16

Entrepreneurship education in China

PETER SEWELL AND DR JIN QUAN

Background to Entrepreneurship Education issues 发展背景

The formal response by Universities in China to the concept of entrepreneurship education in Chinese Higher Education begins with the '21st Century Education Revitalization Action Plan' announced in January 1999, which was proposed by the Government of the Peoples' Republic of China to 'strengthen entrepreneurship education for teachers and students, encouraging them to start their own high-tech enterprises.' (Tang Dehai, Chang Xiaoyong, 2001)

An important social background factor for Chinese entrepreneurship education was a move from a situation of elite education to higher education popularization at the end of the 20th Century. In 1999, China's universities started to expand enrolment.

After ten years of expansion, the gross enrolment rate of Chinese universities has increased very significantly and is now taken up by more than 40 per cent of young people.

Long before that, Chinese universities tended only to think in terms of 'matching graduates to the market' and made decisions about their understanding of the market. However, with the rapid transformation of society, industry and even every enterprise in the market place, it became important to adopt an alternative strategy where 'employers make decisions in the graduate market'.

Employers had faced difficulties in the employment of university graduates, so many experts and scholars suggested that promoting entrepreneurship education would be an effective way to alleviate these difficulties.

Of course, after ten years of entrepreneurship education practices, it became generally recognized that the implementation of this type of education was not only needed to alleviate the very real problems of the current employment of university graduates, but was also needed to adapt society and individuals to the era of the knowledge economy. It was also necessary to strengthen China's higher education restructure that increasingly focused on the international competitiveness of talents.

Development of Entrepreneurship Education in China 发展历程

Gradually, it has been recognized that entrepreneurship education has had a profound impact on the reform and development of higher education. With worldwide exchanges of students and education practices as well as dissemination of the ideas behind entrepreneurship education, this branch of teaching in China's universities began to increase, both in volume and in profile.

In 1999, the Chinese Ministry of Education implemented the '21st Century Education Revitalization Action Plan' and emphasized the importance of entrepreneurship education for both teachers and students as a way to encourage them to start their own high-tech enterprises.

Tsinghua University introduced the US University Business Plan Competition to China in 1997 and one of the Student Associations in Tsinghua University SSTEA (Students Science and Technology Entrepreneurs Association) organized the first Business Plan Competition in China in May 1998.

The competition is now an important event in the development of Chinese entrepreneurship education and is considered to mark the beginning of this type of education in China (Lee Sangqun, Lan Yong, 2011).

The Chinese government attaches great importance to developing the spirit of innovation and has introduced innovative and entrepreneurial activities into the national strategy. In the National Long-term Science and Technology Development Plan (2006–2020), adopted in 2006, it clearly states that China will be developed as an innovative country and will become recognized as such by 2020.

The introduction of policies from both national and local government to encourage and support entrepreneurial activities, has led to valuing and encouraging entrepreneurship becoming a fast-growing trend in all of Chinese society. According to survey data from GEM (Global Entrepreneurship Monitor), the Chinese entrepreneurial activity index (the percentage of people, in the labour force aged from 18 to 64 who participate in entrepreneurial activities) has risen from 12.3 per cent in 2002 and 11.6 per cent in 2003 to 15.53 per cent in 2014. There are now hundreds of millions of people involved in enterprise and entrepreneurship. And China is now recognized as one of the most active entrepreneurial countries in the world (Gao Jian, 2007).

Although it is less than 20 years since entrepreneurship education emerged in China and it is not yet clear to what stage the development of Chinese entrepreneurship education has reached, according to research carried out by Liu Changsong (2009) and Liu Fan et al (2006), the development of Chinese entrepreneurship education can be divided into three stages (see Table 1), which are:

The **spontaneous exploration stage** by universities;

The **multi-exploration stage,** under the guidance of educational administrative departments and

The **comprehensively promoting stage** directed by educational administrative departments.

Although Chinese entrepreneurship education developed from spontaneous exploration by some universities, the formal and official launch of the concept of entrepreneurship education was originally under the guidance of the government and was largely in response to social requirements. The Chinese government played a very important leading role in the development of Chinese entrepreneurship education, filling the gap in the insufficient supply of this type of education prior to this.

The first Business Plan Competition staged at Tsinghua University in 1998 lasted more than five months, with 98 competitive teams participating and provided a total of 114 proposals. Students participating in the competition included undergraduate, graduate and doctoral students. These were mainly from various departments of Tsinghua University and mostly from the area of science and engineering, economics and management. The competition also attracted some students from Peking University, Renmin University and North Jiaotong University.

The first Business Plan Competition of Tsinghua University led to a number of consequences and developments. After 1999, the name of the competition

Table 16.1 Development of Chinese Entrepreneurship Education

Stage	The spontaneous exploration stage	The multi-exploration stage	The comprehensively promoting stage
Period of time	1997–2002	2002–2010	2010–now
Important Issues	1. In 1998, Tsinghua University introduced the Business Plan Competition to China by launching the first Business Plan Competition of Tsinghua. 2. Fudan University allocated one million RMB for the implementation of the students' scientific innovation and action plan and set up a venture capital fund for students. 3. Wuhan University implemented Three Innovation Education.	1. In 2002, the Chinese Ministry of Education launched innovation and entrepreneurship education pilot programmes in nine universities including Tsinghua University. 2. The Chinese Ministry of Education held a forum of entrepreneurship education pilot institutions and organized training programmes for entrepreneurship education teachers. 3. Since 2008, the Chinese Ministry of Education has set up experimental zones for innovative education modes for entrepreneurship education talent.	1. In 2010, the Chinese Ministry of Education communicated the views of the Ministry of Education about vigorously promoting innovation and entrepreneurship education and encouraging university graduates to start their own businesses. 2. The Ministry of Education and Ministry of Finance, Human Resources and Social Security and other departments jointly launched Entrepreneurship Leading Plan for university graduates. 3. In August 2012, the Ministry of Education issued the Basic Requirements of Entrepreneurship Education Teaching for Ordinary undergraduate schools (Trial Implementation). 4. The government work report of the State Council introduced widespread entrepreneurship and innovation, which led to a wide range of entrepreneurship education being offered to the whole of society. 5. In 2014, the Ministry of Education issued the Notice of dealing well with the employment and entrepreneurial activities for ordinary undergraduate schools in 2015, which allows students to start their own businesses by dropping out from universities for a period of time.

SOURCE: Xiaohua Su, Yunjun Chen, Ke Wang (2017) On the Development of Indigenous Entrepreneurship Education Ecosystem, *International Conference on Education Reform and*

was changed to The Challenge Cup National University Business Plan Competition and was jointly organized by the Central Committee of the Communist Young League, China Science and Technology Association and The All-China Students' Federation.

In fact, the significance of the competition is not just limited to entrepreneurship education, but also to providing connections amongst competition projects with the technology, corporate and capital markets. Some projects successfully entered a substantial start-up stage and, as a result, some students founded their own companies. In some sense, the Business Plan Competition for university students effectively broadens the scope of entrepreneurship education in Chinese universities.

Some Chinese universities began to explore practical models of entrepreneurship education. The Ministry of Education designed and released nine pilot units of entrepreneurship education, which were trialled in April 2002 at several universities including Tsinghua University, Beijing University of Aeronautics and Astronautics, Renmin University of China, Shanghai Jiaotong University, Nanjing University of Economics, Wuhan University, Xi'an Jiaotong University, Northwestern Polytechnical University and Heilongjiang University. This pilot project reflected a nationwide aspiration to promote university entrepreneurship education.

Employability Education and Entrepreneurship Education 就业与创业教育

The emergence and Development of Chinese Employability Education is closely related to the reorganization of the Higher Education Management System in China and also influenced by the increasingly sharp imbalance in Chinese labour supply and demand.

The *unified package system* of university students' employment policy ran from the 1950s to the 1990s. In this system, the quality and quantity of talent cultivated by universities was decided by national plans and adopted a *matching* mode. After 40 years of practice and development, this model had become the cultural norm for many Chinese universities. When government withdrew visible control and let students make free choices in the vocational and job markets, students, their parents, teachers and universities all believed that it was the universities which should take responsibility for guiding or steering the students' employment (Xi Shengyang, 2007). In the mid–1990s, because China's economy had entered into the doldrums of deflation and the baby boom of 1960–1970 led to a surge in the supply of social labour, increasing universities' enrolment had become a kind of emergency response by the government to this situation. On the one hand this strategy can start the large consumption of domestic education, while on the other hand, it can ease or postpone the threat of the coming employment issue. Meanwhile, the employment rate had also become an important indicator for judging universities on their programme design, enrolment size and quality of graduates' employability.

There are significant differences in the understanding of employability education in different universities, especially for understanding a students' employability and how to develop it. Some views connecting students' knowledge, ability and quality to specific jobs may lead to very limited opportunities for student employment choices and may consequently even decrease students' employability.

Some scholars believe that employability education and entrepreneurship education in universities are two different talent-development modes and also two different quality concepts of education.

The benefit of the former is to fill existing, obvious jobs, while the objective of the latter is to realize creative employment or create new jobs. Therefore, there is significant benefit for China's economic and social development in transferring the emphasis on employability education to one of entrepreneurship education (Tang Dehai, Chang Xiaoyong, 2001).

The challenge for universities is that, whilst entrepreneurship education will excite students' interest in business and likely help them to develop their enterprise skills, it will not explicitly deal with some of the important aspects of employability education such as understanding the structure of the world of work and knowing how to present themselves effectively during employer selection processes.

Moreover, it is also the case that only a small percentage of students engaging in entrepreneurship education actually create viable start-up companies and of those that do only a small number survive and grow beyond their first year of trading. Therefore, it is probably wise to offer both employability and entrepreneurship education as part of the university curriculum.

Education models and methods of Entrepreneurship Education 模式与途径

Chinese universities mainly use three entrepreneurship education models:

1 Combining *First Classroom* and *Second Classroom* in Enterprise Education
Renmin University is one of the universities using this mode. Renmin University believes that entrepreneurship education should focus on

training students' awareness of entrepreneurship, gaining entrepreneurial knowledge and improving their comprehensive qualities.

In the first classroom, the important elements include adjusting syllabuses and adding more elective courses in entrepreneurship education, so as to let students have more choice. Renmin University provides entrepreneurship education courses such as Entrepreneurial Spirit, Venture Capital, Entrepreneurial Management and it encourages more creative thinking, participatory teaching and the reform of examination methods.

In the second classroom, by taking part in entrepreneurship education lectures, innovative activities, entrepreneurial competitions and activities, students are encouraged to participate in a variety of creative social practice and social welfare activities.

2 Promoting entrepreneurship education by forming functional entrepreneurship education institutions.

Heilongjiang University and Beijing University of Aeronautics and Astronautics are two of the universities using this model.

In order to promote entrepreneurship education, Heilongjiang University set up a leading team for entrepreneurship education, a School of Entrepreneurship Education, an Entrepreneurship Education Centre, the Coordination Committee of Entrepreneurship Education, expert groups of entrepreneurship education and an entrepreneurship education consulting team and also identified six pilot units of entrepreneurship education at university level.

By increasing the reform of the credit system, the system of course selection, and by developing entrepreneurship education credits and the academic tutorial system, students were provided with lots of entrepreneurship teaching resources, and students were actively encourage to attend entrepreneurial practices.

This should lead to students' employability and entrepreneurship being enhanced significantly.

3 Innovation-based comprehensive entrepreneurship education

The comprehensive entrepreneurship education is based on innovation education, focusing on cultivating students' basic qualities in the process of delivering expert knowledge, and at the same time providing students with the necessary funds for start-ups (setting up companies) and the necessary technical advice. Shanghai Jiaotong University, Fudan University and Wuhan University are some of the universities using this model.

Likely future trends 问题和趋势

The rapid development of Chinese entrepreneurship education is thanks to the gradual improvement of the entrepreneurship education environment and the accumulation of enterprise education and practical experience. After ten years of exploration and practice, entrepreneurship education has become the highlight of the reform and development of Chinese Higher Education.

However, compared with the progress of mature international entrepreneurship education, Chinese entrepreneurship education still faces fundamental strategic challenges (Li Jiahua, 2009). There is much yet to be done.

The gaps, as they are presently perceived, lie in the organizing of entrepreneurship education activities, designing of curriculums, staffing of competent teachers, evaluation of students' innovation and their entrepreneurship abilities and the expansion of platforms of this branch of education. Besides that, there are significant differences and contrasting developments amongst different universities.

With China's economy entering into a New Normality, Chinese government support for entrepreneurship and entrepreneurial education is now taken more seriously. In 2012, the Ministry of Education issued a Basic Teaching Requirements for General University Entrepreneurship Education Trial, which clearly defines the teaching objectives, principles and content of entrepreneurship education.

In 2014, The Ministry of Education issued Do Good in 2015 for National General University Graduates Employment and Entrepreneurial Work, which requires that all universities establish flexible educational systems and allow students who want to start their own business to be able to take a break from university for a period of time.

At the current time, how to deliver good entrepreneurship education and how to support and help those students wishing to be entrepreneurial, which in turn helps them to start their businesses in the correct way, is becoming a very important topic for innovation and entrepreneurship educators (Song Han, Lida Zhu, Zhongliang Hu, 2015) and has risen to the very top of the Chinese government's education agenda.

References

Song Han, Lida Zhu, Zhongliang Hu (2015) On Development of Chinese Entrepreneurship Education in New Normal State of Economics, *Education Research Monthly*, **11**, pp 3–8

Jiahua Li, Fan Liu (2009) Development, Challenges and Countermeasures of Chinese Enterprise Education, *Journal of China Youth University for Political Sciences*, **5**, pp 1–5

Shangqun Li, YongLan (2011) The Events of Entrepreneurial Education in Chinese Universities, *China Agricultural Education*, **6**, pp 1–8

Xiaohua Su, Yunjun Chen, Ke Wang (2012) On the Development of Indigenous Entrepreneurship Education Ecosystem, *International Conference on Education Reform and Management Innovation (ERMI 2012)*, p 5.

Dehai Tang, Xiaoyong Chang (2001)The Process of Employment Education to Entrepreneurship Education, *Educational Research*, **2**, pp 30–33

Zhanren Wang (2015) Analysis on the History and Scientific Statements of Chinese Entrepreneurship Education, *Journal of Northeast Normal University (Philosophy and Social Sciences)*, **4**, pp 181–186.

Shengyang Xi (2007) A Study on Theories and Practices of Entrepreneurship Education in China's Universities, D Ed Thesis, Huazhong University of Science and Technology.

Jingwei Li (2013) Research on the Influence of Entrepreneurship Education on University Students' Entrepreneurial Intentions, D BA Thesis, Nankai University.

Hongxia Zhou (2008) The Research of Undergraduate Entrepreneurship Education in China, M Ed Thesis, Shanghai Normal University.

17

Lifelong learning is the key to employability and economic vitality

An insight into the responses in the USA

STACEY GUNEY – AUSTIN COMMUNITY COLLEGE

The job market in the United States has finally recovered from the recession and there are expected to be 55 million job openings in the economy by 2020 – 24 million of those openings from newly created jobs and 31 million openings due to retirements from the post-WWII 'baby boomers.'

Education is recognized as the key to tap into these jobs as nearly two-thirds of these job openings will require some form of post-secondary education. Indeed, at the current level of secondary school production and post-secondary graduation rates, it is estimated that the United States will still fall short by five million workers.

Additionally, there is an increased focus by employers beyond technical skills to more of the so-called 'soft skills', with employers saying job candidates need to improve their written and oral communication skills, adaptability and managing multiple priorities and decision making and problem solving. The unique design of the American community colleges with their ties to workforce needs and their local communities are leading the way in innovating new programmes and adapting practices to address employability challenges in order to drive economic growth.

The 21st century economy has become a learning economy that has moved beyond the concepts of the industrial age or the information era. The economic success of individuals, institutions, regions and national economies is now based on a society that has the capability to learn and to continue that learning throughout their lifelong involvement in the workplace.

More deeply integrated

There is no longer a distinction between formal learning and entrance into the workplace. Rather, the relationship between education and learning in the workplace is becoming more deeply integrated. Training and re-retraining must be responsive and agile to meet fast-changing market needs and on-going innovation. This is changing the relationships between higher education and employers with new forms of partnership being built to embrace this new economic reality.

The United States is particularly well-positioned for this evolution because of the framework of community colleges that exists which support local employers and labour markets. However, challenges still exist in maximizing and leveraging this unique system of higher education for innovation and global competitiveness.

Community colleges are now renewing their efforts to drive success in delivering education and training to citizens which builds human capital, grows the economy, drives innovation and is critical for sustaining the global standing of the United States. Community colleges boast a lower cost than traditional universities, broad accessibility and comparative flexibility which are seen as the best hope for rapid and meaningful change required by the shifting employment market.

More than half of the college population in the United States is served through community colleges – a unique open-admission system of over 1,600 campuses that provide educational access and drive economic growth in the communities they serve. Community colleges began in the United States with a mission of educational access, four-year university transfer and workforce preparation.

Preparing an increasingly diverse workforce

These local institutions have developed strong local collaborations with business and industry, universities, high schools and other key public and private sector entities in the preparation of the skilled workers needed by current and emerging industries in a region. Community colleges also play an important role in expanding access to higher education for an increasingly diverse workforce through contract training, small-business development, local economic planning and strong university transfer programmes for the future scientists, engineers, business and technical professionals who will shape a region's economic future.

By 2020, it is expected that where the US economy will see **fifty-five million job openings**, the majority of these will require post-secondary education. Community colleges will continue to be an integral part of ensuring economic vitality.

Figure 17.1 Job openings by 2020

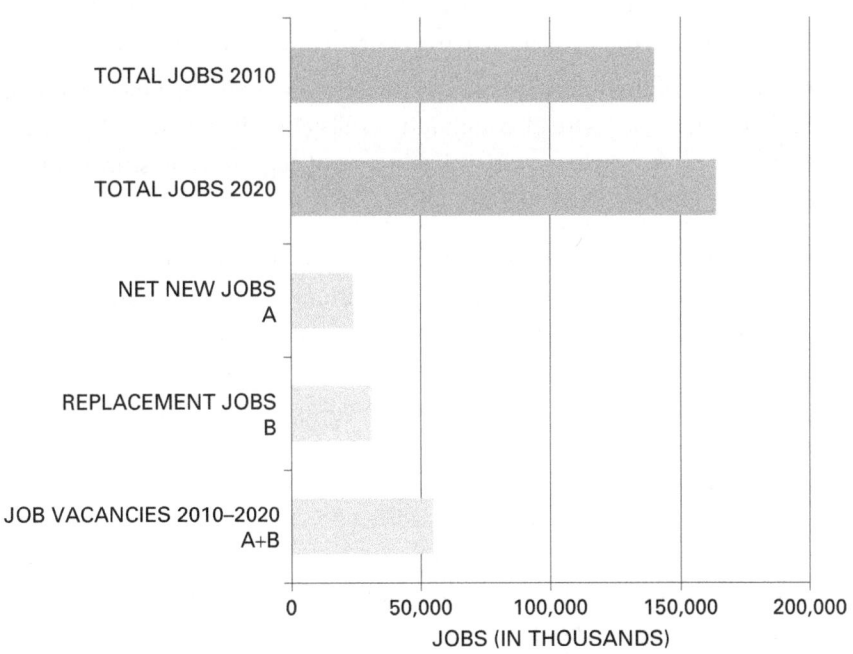

Total jobs will increase from 140 million in 2010 to 165 million in 2020. There will be 55 million job vacancies between 2010 and 2020 due to net new jobs (24 million) and retirement (31 million).

SOURCE: Center on Education and the Workforce, Georgetown University, 2013

Community colleges, originally called junior colleges, began opening in 1901 and were celebrated as 'people's colleges' as they were inexpensive and often publicly funded. These two-year schools embraced vocational education, particularly during the backdrop of the Great Depression. Dramatic growth was stimulated in the 1940s and 1950s by returning war veterans using their GI Bill benefits. This growth continued into the 1960s at the average rate of one community college opening every week as the higher education system sought to absorb and educate the Baby Boomer generation.

This community college growth also incorporated a much more diverse student body than traditional four-year institutions at the time. This diversity continues today with community colleges educating the majority of minority students, first generation in college and low-income students.

- 50 per cent of Hispanic students and 31 per cent of African American students start at a community college (compared with 28 per cent of White students).
- 38 per cent of students whose parents did not graduate from college choose community colleges as their first institution. (Compared with 20 per cent of students whose parents graduated from college.)
- 44 per cent of low-income students (those with family incomes less than $25,000 per year) attend community college as their first college after high school. (Compared with 15 per cent of high-income students that enrol in community colleges initially.)

The diversity of the student population also represents the variety of reasons that students require post-secondary education. Community colleges are able to respond with agility in the quickly changing economy and serve students through university transfer programmes, early college high schools, adult education, workforce training and employees that require new skill sets to remain in the workforce or to change jobs.

It is important that all areas of society have access to the training necessary for jobs in the United States. It has been predicted that the US economy will grow from 140 million to 165 million jobs by 2020. In addition, 65 per cent of all jobs in the economy will require post-secondary education and training beyond high school.

However, at the current production rate in post-secondary education, the United States is expected to fall short by five million workers with the required credentials for these jobs. Three of the fastest-growing occupations – STEM, healthcare professional, and community services – also have the highest demand for post-secondary education and training.

Community colleges are necessary to reach out to the communities that they serve in order to develop the resources necessary to fill the employment needs of the economy.

Figure 17.2 The need for post-secondary education

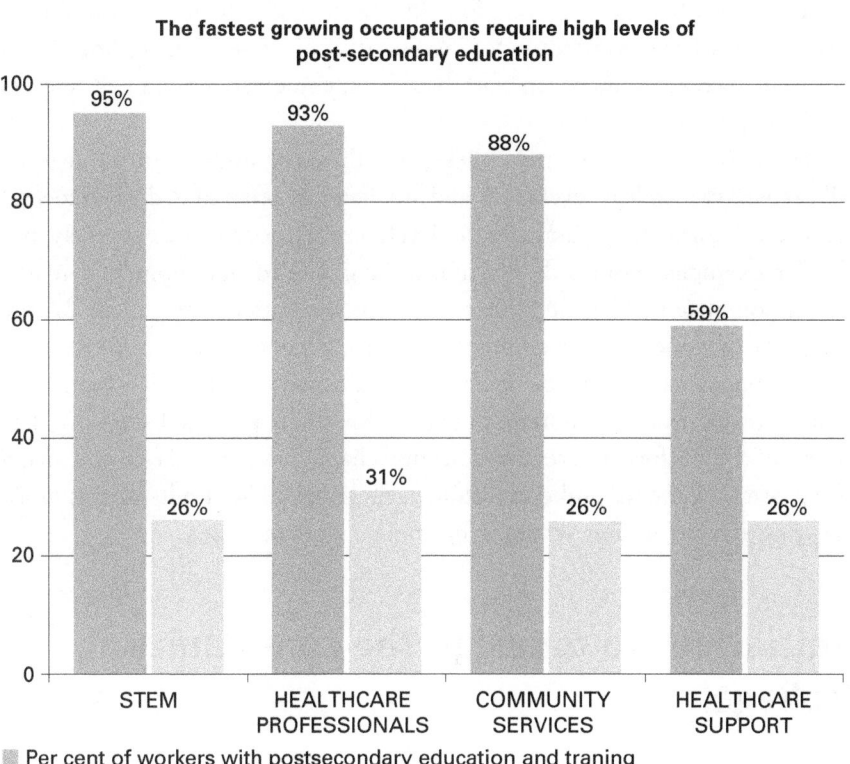

■ Per cent of workers with postsecondary education and traning
  Growth rate of occupations (2010–2020)

SOURCE: Center on Education and the Workforce, Georgetown University, 2013

Preparing students for the workforce is the central mission for community colleges and this focus is currently putting great pressure on institutions to focus on their effectiveness.

Increasing the success rates at community colleges is therefore critical for meeting national goals for college attainment and promoting upward social mobility. For students who arrive in college prepared for college-level work, college holds the key for future success.

Costly coursework and attendance

However, for an increasing number of students who arrive unprepared for college-level work, college leads to costly coursework and attendance without any credential or benefit. In the United States, college access has continued to expand over the last few decades with as many as 86 per cent of high school graduates continuing their education.

Public community colleges serve some 11 million students and 44 per cent of the US college population. In the past, the focus of community colleges has been primarily upon access and this is now being broadened with an increasing focus on data-based, outcomes-driven student success and completion.

On arriving at community college, two-thirds of students turn out to be ill-prepared for college-level work and are therefore referred to developmental courses. Unfortunately, pass rates for developmental courses are extremely low.

For example, two-thirds of students assigned to developmental maths never complete it. The gatekeeper for success in community college for the majority of students is developmental maths. Recent research and efforts to reform have focused on redesigning the traditional system of developmental education in order to improve outcomes for under-prepared students. The focus of these efforts has revolved around changes to curricula, course structure, teaching theory and curriculum realignment. The results of this work are positive but are not yet showing enough student success.

Initiatives to redesign the community college

Recently, this effort has been unified by the American Association of Community Colleges' (AACC) 21st Century Initiative which is diving into the issues and challenges of redesigning the community college through a series of initiatives:

The Pathways Project

A coalition of community colleges and seven national partner organizations aim to build capacity for a pathways approach based on models that are replicable and scalable at the national level. 'Pathways' provide students with a more structured approach with a seamless academic pathway linked to student services. These efforts are funded by a $5.2 million grant from the Bill & Melinda Gates Foundation and are favoured by research that indicates that the traditional 'cafeteria approach' (disconnected courses, academic programme, support services and employer needs) is far less effective for guiding successful community college completion for non-traditional students.

K–12 (primary/secondary school) Alignment

Each year about 50 per cent of first-year students coming directly from high schools who begin at community colleges require basic developmental courses before they can begin college-level work. AACC is promoting better alignment between K–12 school standards and first-year, credit-bearing course requirements at community colleges.

Accelerated/Redesigned Developmental Education

Developmental education has become the gatekeeper for students who wish to continue their education at community colleges. There are a variety of approaches which are being researched that will provide alternative ways to move students successfully through developmental courses into credit-bearing courses and, ultimately, onto credentials for the job market.

National Credential Framework

Currently, there are a variety of colleges, degrees, credentials and accreditations throughout the United States. Within the context of the Beta Credentials Framework, the AACC (with a $1.8 million grant from the Lumina Foundation) will work to identify methods to guide routes more effectively that students may take through college training programmes. This will also provide greater clarity for employers about what skills and knowledge various credentials represent and signal more efficiently within and among colleges the portability, compatibility and applicability of different credentials.

College Promise Campaign

This was launched by the Obama administration in the fall of 2015 to stimulate programmes and services that support tuition-free community colleges.

The ultimate goal of these initiatives is to be able to provide students with the opportunity to enter the labour market as quickly and efficiently as possible. Higher educational attainment increasingly corresponds with higher earnings and lower unemployment.

Figure 17.3 Earnings and unemployment rates

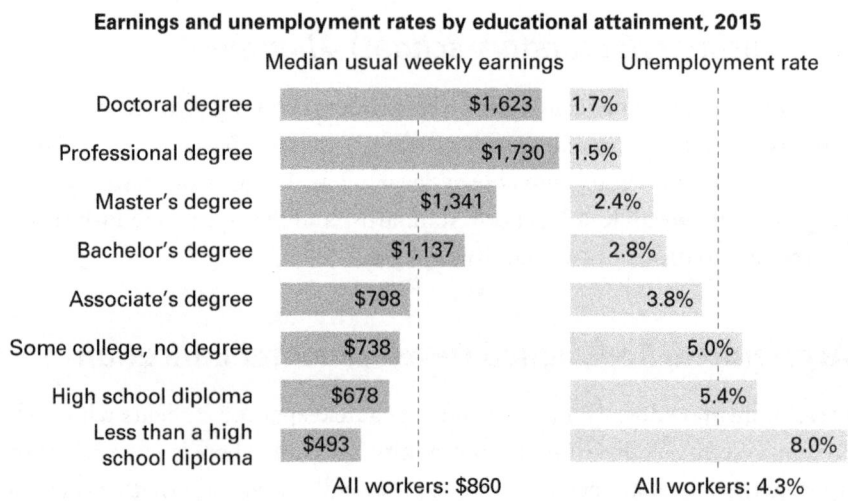

NOTE: Data are for persons age 25 and over. Earnings are for full-time wage and salary workers.
SOURCE: US Bureau of Labor Statistics, Current Population Survey

Community Colleges are providing value and also serving the unique needs of their non-traditional students. Community college tuition cost is significantly lower than that of four-year institutions. They also welcome and support everyone – students who need a second chance (like those who are coming out of jail), students who had to stop their higher education journeys because of major life events, returning veterans looking to re-enter the civilian workforce and part-time students working around complicated schedules.

The average age of a community college student is 29 years old and two-thirds of the students attend part-time. In contrast, at four-year institutions 79 per cent of students are enrolled full-time and the average age of undergraduates is 26 years old.

Figure 17.4 Student expenses

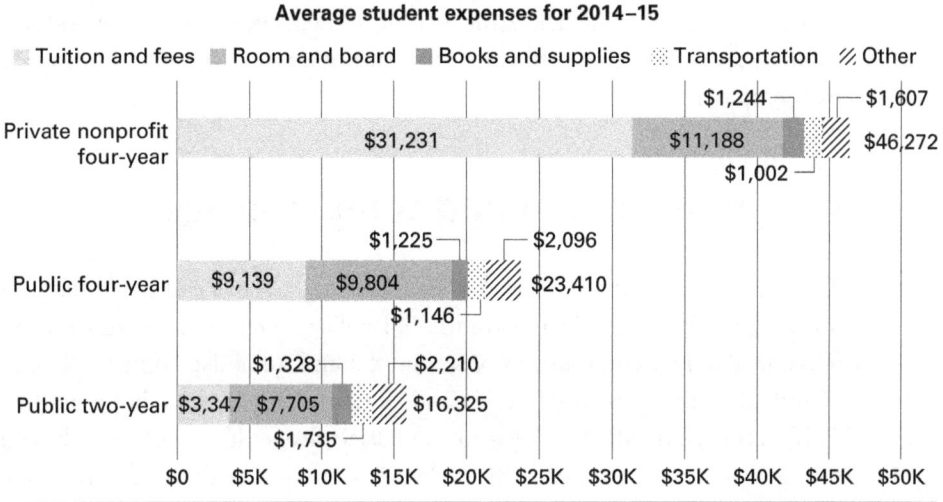

SOURCE: Trends in College Pricing 2014, The College Board, Annual Survey of Colleges (2014)

Increasingly, employers are looking to community colleges for the technical skills they offer. While there is no lack of college-educated applicants, employers are saying that those applicants don't necessarily learn skills that are applicable for their innovation-centric companies. Some employers have gone so far as to say that too often four-year colleges and universities produce degrees that have little real-world value and do not match the skills required by American employers.

Community colleges seek to provide students with the technical know-how that is often lacking in graduates from four-year liberal arts schools. Multiple high-paying jobs, like radiation therapists, dental hygienists and electronics repair, require only a two-year associate's degree for entry. Some schools partner directly with businesses. For example, Midlands Technical College in South Carolina has an apprenticeship programme that serves as a jobs pipeline to Michelin.

Community colleges also offer a wide range of continuing education (CE) courses, contract education courses that serve local industry and community-focused activities. Continuing education divisions of community colleges often offer both credit and non-credit workforce training courses and usually tailor such courses to meet the needs of local businesses. Nearly 80 per cent of CE divisions report that they have developed courses and certificate programmes in partnership with local governments over the past four years, with nearly 60 per cent having entered into such agreements with state governments. Nonetheless, the majority of financial support for workforce training courses continues to come from businesses that sponsor training for their employees.

Four most in-demand competencies

The 21st century labour market is emphasizing a variety of skills that are not necessarily taught in the traditional college environment. Judgement, decision making, communications, analysis and administration have been identified as the four most in-demand competencies in the labour market. This, in turn, has called colleges to emphasize 'deeper learning' – combining a deeper understanding of core academic content with the ability to apply that understanding to novel problems and situations – and also to help students develop a range of competencies (including people skills and self-control). In the learning age in which we live, the most important task of teaching is no longer transmitting knowledge but initiating, coaching and influencing the thinking processes that students use to learn.

A body of evidence is developing that points to the fact that developing non academic skills will also assist students with achieving their goals. In order to develop independent learning behaviour and ultimately student success, instruction should be mainly aimed at developing self-regulated learning strategies and metacognition skills.

Metacognition has been defined as a person's knowledge about the cognitive processes necessary for understanding and learning. Metacognition plays a central role in regulating student learning in higher education.

Tom Bailey of the Community College Research Center at Columbia University in *Redesigning America's Community Colleges* has advocated for a shift from a knowledge transmission model of education to a learning facilitation model that more explicitly addresses conceptual understanding, metacognition and student motivation.

The work of the Open Doors Demonstrations (supported by a consortium of foundations, the US Department of Labour, and the US Department of Education) has also examined programmes designed to improve student outcomes through integrating these types of metacognition skills at community colleges.

Kingsborough Community College's programme

One of the Opening Doors programmes consisted of a Learning Communities intervention at Kingsborough Community College in Brooklyn, New York. The Learning Communities targeted incoming freshmen, the great majority of whom required developmental English. Students in Learning Communities were placed into groups of 15–25 that took three courses together: an English course geared towards their level of proficiency; a regular college course like introductory psychology or sociology; and a student success course, taught by a college counsellor that covered effective study habits and other skills necessary to succeed in college.

Faculty who taught in the Learning Communities were expected to coordinate assignments and meet periodically to review student progress. The idea was to build social cohesion between students and faculty and to help students apply concepts and lessons across the courses.

What emerged was that students in the Learning Communities were more likely to feel integrated at school and be engaged in their courses. They also passed more courses and earned more credits during their first semester, moved more quickly through developmental English courses and were more likely to take and pass an English skills assessment test that was required for graduation.

Competency-based education

Higher Education and the US Department of Education is also moving away from the traditional model of education which emphasizes knowledge transmission through 'seat time'. A learning facilitation model favours a structure that creates flexibility, allows students to progress as they demonstrate mastery of academic content, regardless of time, place, or pace of learning. Competency-Based Education (CBE) strategies provide flexibility in the way that credit can be earned or awarded and provide students with personalized learning opportunities.

These strategies include online and blended learning, dual enrolment and early college high schools, project-based and community-based learning and credit recovery, among others. This type of learning leads to better student engagement because the content is relevant to each student and tailored to their unique needs. It also leads to better student outcomes because the pace of learning is customized to each student.

Interest in competency-based education is surging among educators, employers and students and college-level Competency-Based Education programmes are emerging across the country. Proponents see its potential to be part of an improved educational system that leads to quicker attainment of quality credentials, job placement and career success for all.

A group of community colleges (including the College at which I am based) across five states has been at the forefront in creating Competency-Based Education programmes in information technology: Broward College (Florida), Ivy Tech Community College (Ft. Wayne and Lafayette Districts, Indiana), Sinclair Community College (Ohio), Austin Community College (Texas), Lone Star College (University Park, Texas), Bellevue College (Washington), Columbia Basin College (Washington), Edmonds Community College (Washington), and Spokane Falls Community College (Washington).

The presidents of these colleges confirmed that their Competency-Based Education programmes helped them to create new partnerships. Richard Rhodes, president and CEO of Austin Community College (ACC), said his college's focus on CBE has fostered strong partnerships with businesses, which play an important role in ensuring programme effectiveness and connecting employers with highly trained graduates. ACC's programme has developed an automated process for students to create online portfolios. These are housed on the programme's website and include a personal statement, a resumé and a work product that shows competency in the field (such as a website for those in web programming). Industry partners get early access to the portfolios, which are searchable by the job description the company is seeking to fill. The ability for employers to see the exact skills that a future employee has mastered is proving to be quite enticing to them as it allows for a very specific match to employment needs.

Badges improve employability

The ability to 'badge' skills for employment began in 2011 when web browser-maker Mozilla launched openbadges.org to promote what they call 'digital badges' to anyone who can demonstrate that they've mastered a specific skill. This new model has proved to be an interesting new offering for community colleges.

In June 2015, the Colorado Community College System (CCCS) announced that they were developing a new badge designation to improve students' ability to gain employment and to meet industry demands for the manufacturing industry. CCCS sees badges as a way to allow them to work with industries to develop highly specific coursework to meet the demand they have in their companies.

For example, if a manufacturing company needs workers to have just some specific welding skills, they can work with the college to develop a badge that teaches just those skills, not an entire Welding 101 programme. The business benefits as it is now assured that the student knows exactly what is needed and expected and the badge can be specifically configured for each individual's needs. Students benefit as it takes less time and money to complete a badge and they have direct linkages to the employers for which the badge is designed. Additionally, badges may also enhance the degree or certificate a student may already have. Community colleges are poised to be central to post-secondary education as traditional credentials become unbundled.

As more young people opt out of the traditional college experience while jobs needing specific, specialized skills go unfilled, community colleges are playing an integral part in the resurgence of apprenticeship programmes and targeted training. Community colleges are proactively creating apprenticeship programmes that lead to well-paying jobs in the factories of the future, where proficiency in computer science has replaced the repetition of the assembly line.

Apprenticeship programmes

They are looking for opportunities to implement curricula with local manufacturers, many of whom have decades on the job, to train their workforce in the skills that will see them through the rest of their careers.

In 2014, the US Department of Labour announced $175 million in grant opportunities that would fund apprenticeship programmes in high-growth industries such as health care, advanced manufacturing and information technology. Community colleges and manufacturers have created a range of apprenticeship programmes:

Kellogg Community College in Battle Creek, Mich., has apprenticeship programmes that are sponsored by local companies, for which prospective students apply for an apprenticeship position. The programmes are generally four years long and consist of 8,000 hours of paid on-the-job training and a minimum of 576 hours of related classroom instruction. There are programmes in machine technology, industrial technology, electricity and electronics, among others.

Tidewater Community College in Norfolk, Va., has a unique apprentice programme with the Norfolk Naval Shipyard. Apprentices are employed with a salary range of $13.84 to $15.26 per hour and receive promotions upon successful completion of programme requirements. Students participate in a rigorous training schedule that combines academic classes at the college along with trade theory training and on-the-job experience. **Honolulu Community College** has a similar programme with Pearl Harbor Shipyard.

In Indiana, **Ivy Tech** has apprenticeship programs with the Indiana Union Construction Industry, where students receive approximately 2,000 hours of on-the-job training and a minimum of 216 hours of classroom instruction every year. First-year union apprentices earn about the same amount that most college students pay for a year's tuition. Graduates can earn up to $60,000 annually. There are programmes for boilermakers, bricklayers, carpenters and electricians. In addition, Ivy Tech works with local manufacturers such as Chrysler, ALCOA, Rolls Royce and Cummins, among others, to educate these companies' workforces.

In addition to the technical skills necessary to be successful in the workforce, a growing body of research is now focusing on the importance of the role of 'non-academic' skills required by the modern job market. Community colleges are beginning to acknowledge that there is a combination of academic skills, non-academic skills, behaviours, and personality traits that are now being required by employers.

For first generation in college students the development of these skills is even more important as they may not have had the opportunity to model these traits in their previous academic experiences or through their socio-economic background. Researchers like Carol Dweck and David Yeager are studying how student's self-perceptions about intelligence and ability to learn are associated with the levels of academic effort and achievement. Understanding the underlying student mindset and whether it is moving from 'fixed' to 'growth' is becoming important to establish the new skills required through education and training.

People with a fixed mindset believe that their basic qualities (like intelligence or an ability in a skill) are simply fixed traits. These are the types of student who spend their time documenting their intelligence or talent instead of developing it. This type of student also believes that their talent alone will create success without any accompanying effort.

Students with a growth mindset believe that their abilities can be developed through dedication and hard work because intelligence and talent are only a starting point. This perspective on learning prompts greater motivation, engagement and productivity.

Mindset interventions being developed that can shift students' mindset are proving effective and this, in turn, is showing that students are attaining greater academic success. These mindset interventions are also being coupled with academic coaching, which works with students to develop metacognition traits that they need in order to be successful students. Whether this is called grit, resilience, self-regulation, or *mental toughness* – all of these aspects are what employers are saying they require in their employees. Community colleges are beginning to incorporate this overall holistic approach to producing future workers for the modern workforce.

A changing outlook

As employers are redefining their needs in the new learning economy, there is a changing outlook that a four-year degree is a guarantee of a future job and that everyone should automatically pursue one. There is a refocus now on employability and the guided pathways necessary for students to enter employment. Students who enter post-secondary education do so for many reasons, one of the main reasons being to boost future earnings.

Over a lifetime, an associate degree holder will earn nearly $500,000 more than someone with only a high school diploma. While 86 per cent of community college students believe they are academically prepared to succeed, only 39 per cent of these students earn a degree or certificate within six years. The United States is at risk of missing out on the potential to maintain the economic vibrancy of its citizens when the majority of those who start at a community college are not completing.

By 2020, 65 per cent of the jobs in the United States economy will require post-secondary education and training beyond high school. At the current graduation rates in higher education, the United States will fall five million short of the workers with post-secondary credentials needed by 2020. Community colleges serve nearly half of the post-secondary students in the United States and this population is growing. These students represent a diverse demographic whose success in college will provide them with the tools necessary in the new global economy.

America needs a large percentage of its general population to possess the solid skills taught in community colleges in order to remain globally competitive. Community colleges will continue to lead innovative efforts to focus on the learning facilitation model of post-secondary education, thereby connecting skilled workers to employers in their communities. These are exciting and challenging times for community colleges whose mission of access and affordability still fuels the passion for serving learners who enter higher education in order to boost their employability.

President Obama has summarized the importance of community colleges in America:

> 'We don't expect anybody to be bound by the circumstances of their birth – that's the basic bargain at the heart of this country: if you work hard, you can get ahead. It shouldn't matter what your last name is, or what we look like, or what family we were born into... what matters is effort and merit. That's the promise of America and that's what community colleges are all about.'

Community colleges don't just provide the employability skills necessary for today's and tomorrow's workers, they continue to provide hope and aspiration for the future to everyone.

Employability and enterprise 18

Supporting those who may have access to fewer opportunities than most

CHRIS WRIGHT AND MILLIE SHUTER, CATCH22

The subject of this topic is sometimes described in terms of 'the disadvantaged'. Those engaged in this field of work will, with justification, challenge the use of this term. Firstly, it doesn't help to describe these individuals as disadvantaged – it implies that this is a personal characteristic. Most often it is their situation and circumstance which create a disadvantage. The individual remains someone with potential.

Catch22 is now over 200 years old. While its work has evolved massively since our creation as the Royal Philanthropic Society in 1788, our core values remain the same. Catch22 delivers services that build resilience and aspiration in people and communities. Today, this means that we don't really like to talk about 'disadvantage'. Indeed, some people are dealt a tougher hand in life but we feel it does them (or us) no good to focus primarily on this.

As an organization, everything that Catch22 does focuses on building on people's strengths and capacity. A key part of that is a strengths-based approach to getting our service users – many of whom come from deprived communities and face significant challenges – into sustainable and rewarding employment. Often we are the first organization a young person works with that helps them to see their own potential, rather than just focusing on the obstacles they must overcome.

This chapter sets out a description of Catch22's initiatives and approaches to employability, enterprise and entrepreneurship that have been successful in supporting people who would be typically considered 'disadvantaged'. This includes NEET (Not in Education, Employment or Training) young people, care leavers, ex-offenders and gang members. Their employability experiences, recounted here, span hiking in Iceland, trekking in the Sinai desert, working in Marriott hotels in Germany and even a start-up incubator in Shoreditch, London.

Its purpose is to understand the common ground between these diverse people and places. It describes the actions needed to ensure that everyone, no matter what their background, has the opportunity to thrive in the world of work. It covers the need to build the right mindset in young people, develop their mental toughness, develop strong relationships with them and set high aspirations within them. It will also shine a spotlight on the services provided by Catch22 and how these have been developed to address and deliver the above.

Building the right mindset and unearthing talent

The approach to employability is based on nurturing and providing the best talent for employers. Well-trained, talented and competent staff will help employers to improve efficiency, productivity and bring new ideas into their organizations. Talent can be found and nurtured in all people; it simply means developing the right mindset qualities for the world of work.

When discussing these themes, people often talk about 'soft skills' but this is another unhelpful term. The skills they refer to – such as honesty, commitment, teamwork, willpower, attitude and presentation – are essential core skills for the workplace. Many of the young people and adults that Catch22 supports are a long way from 'work-ready' and to prepare them for the labour market it must work hard to build these core skills, often from a very low base.

People must first be supported to develop the right mindset – the right attitude and confidence – to take the next steps into work. Some providers and charities like to put young people into boxes, calling them 'disadvantaged' – an ex-offender or a care leaver or BAME or another convenient but stigmatizing label. For Catch22 the emphasis is to look at people's assets, their potential and their talent.

For the people it supports, work is more than just a job. It is a journey. It is about personal development, being mentored and coached, practising something, getting better at it and feeling better about themselves as a result.

Initially 55 per cent of learners or young people on the work-ready programmes are found to have low self-esteem and it is through these programmes that they start to develop the resilience and aspiration that will enable their long-term employment.

Building mental toughness or 'resilience'

Success in employment cannot be determined by academic capability, intelligence or even work experience alone. Another key determining factor is too often misunderstood or overlooked.

Mental toughness, or 'grit', plays a huge part in enabling people to achieve their goals in work and more broadly. This is especially true for entrepreneurs. There is some debate about how to use the term 'mental toughness': many people use it liberally to refer to any set of positive attributes that helps a person to cope with difficult situations.

The term originated in sports and many coaches and sport commentators use the term to accurately describe the mental state of athletes who persevere through difficult sport circumstances to succeed. One sports orientated definition describes it as:

> having the natural or developed psychological edge that enables you, generally, to cope better than your opponents with the many demands (competition, training, lifestyle) that sport places on a performer; specifically, to be more consistent and better than your opponents in remaining determined, focused, confident and in control under pressure.'[1]

However, broader interpretations characterize mental toughness as a personality trait, consisting of four components: confidence, challenge, control and commitment.

For the people Catch22 works with, those facing significant barriers to employment, developing their mental toughness can be a game changer. Our service users may not be able to change their inherited intelligence, nor are they able to easily remove themselves from challenging family circumstances or the deprived communities that hold them back.

But mental toughness can be learned, developed and mobilized. Grit and perseverance can become defining traits, regardless of the talent a person is born with. While mental toughness is in some ways an abstract quality, in the real world it is tied to concrete actions.

CASE STUDY Building mental toughness, or 'resilience': Project New Horizons

Catch22 helps build mental toughness in some of our NEET (not in education, employment or training) service users through Project New Horizons. These are generally some of our most challenging young people: those with low skills, low self-esteem and low chances of making it into rewarding employment.

Delivered in partnership with the British Exploring Society, Project New Horizons is an annual expedition for selected young people who are already engaged with a Catch22 service. The programme aims to raise the aspirations of participants and equip them with the skills and opportunities to secure employment or further education.

Since 2011, 164 young people have completed expeditions and 96 per cent of those participants progressed into education, employment or training opportunities. It is Catch22's experience that the gruelling expedition builds mental toughness and resilience in a way that will transform the young people's employment opportunities and outlook for the rest of their lives.

One participant who completed the three-week expedition in Iceland, travelling to Reykjavik and then Svartarkot and up the Askja volcano, said, 'It was definitely the best experience I've had in my life. It was really challenging but I overcame my fears and pushed my physical ability to the max. I loved every bit of it – for me it was life-changing. When I came back to the UK I had a great mindset...'.

It's not a conventional team-building residential course. Participants, or adventurers as they are known, learn to be self–sufficient in the wilderness: pitching their own tents, cooking outdoors and navigating themselves on a 50-mile trip over volcanoes; stepping into the unknown, they must dig deep to find the inner strength and a perseverance that could change their lives. With an overwhelming majority of past participants on a successful future pathway, it is clear that this unique combination of intensive support and physical challenge does work.

The previous year, 33 young people completed a 15-day, 200 kilometre trek across the Sinai Peninsula from the Gulf of Aqaba to the Gulf of Suez. The adventurers were taught to navigate by the stars, work with camels and survive in the harsh desert climate with the help of the nomadic Bedouin people.

Within three months of their return, 12 young people were in employment, 13 accessed education and six were in a work placement or training. One young person explained,

'It taught me the importance of working hard to achieve something and how much more important it feels because of that hard work. It opened my eyes to a new way of life.'

It is acknowledged that this kind of experience is not accessible for everyone. It works best for small groups, takes a lot of organizing and costs around £5,400 per young person. But the life-changing outcomes it achieves makes it worth it. If those who participate go on to sustained employment, the programme has more than paid for itself.

Especially when it is known that it costs the United Kingdom Department for Work and Pensions, approximately £97,000 per NEET person over a lifetime.[2]

And it's not all about cost saving, it's also about giving people the important opportunity to flourish and thrive so that they are able to lead fulfilling independent lives and can contribute positively to their communities and wider society.

Developing strong relationships and networks

Catch22 provides alternative education to young people of all ages in schools, colleges, community centres, pupil referral units and young offender units, as well as through its own network of registered independent schools, free schools and academies. Its students in these schools are mostly there because they are unable to achieve good outcomes in their mainstream schools or are at risk of being permanently excluded.

In Catch22's schools, the focus is not on students' 'disadvantage'. Rather, their strengths, skills and interests are identified and they are provided with a supportive, nurturing, learning environment that enables them to thrive. Fundamental to this approach is a belief that, because education is a fundamental building block in transforming people's lives, every young person – regardless of the situation they find themselves in – deserves access to a high-quality education that balances both their academic and behavioural needs.

The key to success with these young people is building strong relationships. Catch22 schools have a high teacher-to-pupil ratio and hire excellent educators who understand the power of relationships and trust. The aim is to provide effective education for children and young people facing significant learning challenges (whether due to specific learning difficulties, emotional or behaviour problems or chaotic family lives) so that they can progress and succeed in sustained education or employment. High-quality teaching and learning based on effective relationships is vital for enabling the achievement of life skills and meaningful qualifications.

Often, these young people haven't had the chance to build relationships with aspirational figures – often because they haven't yet had the chance to come into contact with such figures.

It is also important to consider the issue of equality and access. A report by the UK Employment and Skills Commission (UKESC) found that more than 40 per cent of people get jobs through people they know. So what then for young people who don't know anyone who can help them? Surely everyone has a role to play in creating networks for young people who don't have them. Networking is a big factor in the workplace but when someone starts out with no connections, that foot-in-the-door is vital.

In order to level the playing field, supporting the development of relationships is important. Key to this are programmes for young people which build up networks of contacts, experience and support to ensure that all young people have an equal chance of entering the jobs market and living happy and independent lives.

Often described through the technical term 'social capital', these informal networks of people, experiences and communities, have a serious bearing on labour force outcomes for different groups.

As we have seen in this chapter, there is a great deal that can be done to level the playing field. However, without wider societal buy in, the impact and reach of these initiatives will always be limited. We need to be developing effective ways to engage communities in this agenda.

CASE STUDY Developing strong relationships and networks: Entourage

Too many people are struggling to make their way in the world without the professional and social support network they need to make a success of their lives. To tackle this, Only Connect, a London-based criminal justice charity that is now part of Catch22, developed the Entourage Project. It provides members – unemployed young people at risk of involvement in crime or ex-offenders – with those relationships: a community of Supporters (around four people) to help them grow in confidence and in connections, decide on a career path and get that career started.

At the same time, the project helps successful professionals (Supporters) to expand the limits of their own networks – introducing them to young people with different backgrounds, interests and experiences to their own.

Together, the Entourage Project makes for a more connected society.

Entourages are designed for two types of 'Star': 'Explorers', who need help with motivation and settling on a choice of career and 'Networkers', who know what they want but need help and contacts to get there.

'Explorer' Stars need help building their personal resilience and their social capital; this can happen by taking part in cultural activities or volunteering together and by Supporters making introductions to friends and colleagues in different industries and professions.

'Networker' Stars typically will want help designing a strategy for getting on the right career path, expanding their contacts and honing their skills in their chosen area.

In many ways, what makes this approach unusual is that is based on a reciprocal arrangement. Both the service user (or member) and the Supporters benefit. Rather than a 'handout' for the 'disadvantaged' youngster from the neighbouring deprived communities, this project offers a 'handshake': it creates access to social capital by introducing them to a new network of people who have the potential to help them thrive in work. At the same time it breaks down barriers between communities, encouraging understanding, mutual respect and greater cohesion.

Setting high aspirations

Why should so called 'disadvantaged' young people be expected to work menial, low-paid jobs? Why should they not be instilled with the same aspirations and high-achieving expectations as everyone else? At the same time, there are barriers that prevent these young people from entering the workforce.

For instance, Catch22 works with young people and young adults who are involved with gangs. As well as having a criminal record, the labelling and stigmatization associated with people in gangs, or who have committed crimes, plays a significant role in excluding many of them from employment.

The answer is often enterprise, entrepreneurship and self-employment. However, currently only 185,000 16–24-year-olds are registered as self-employed.

Research by RBS and UnLtd has found that accessing finance, the current economic environment and the risk involved in start-ups are the three main deterrents to young people starting their own business. In addition, studies suggest that young people are far more prone to fear of failure than the wider population.[3] The UK Government is attempting to address these barriers as part of its wider promotion of enterprise as key to revitalizing Britain's economy.

Delivering this and communicating it will also be key to encouraging young people to become entrepreneurs in the first place. After all, their principal reservation is the presumption that they may be losing out on job stability, job security and better pay. If we can support entrepreneurs effectively this does not have to be the case, especially when short-term contracts, internships and unpaid work are becoming increasingly common alternatives.

Desistance and enterprise

Research suggests that employment is the 'single most effective factor' in reducing rates of re-offending.[4] Employment provides stability, a legitimate way of making an income and creates positive and binding social ties. Recent research from the UK Ministry of Justice showed that over even a one-year period, employment could reduce re-offending rates by 10 percentage points.[5]

Despite what we know about the importance of employment for reducing re-offending, the barriers are high for ex-offenders entering the workplace. A study by the Ministry of Justice found that two years after release from custody, only 15 per cent of offenders were in employment and 47 per cent were receiving a DWP out-of-work benefit.[6]

A new report from the Centre for Entrepreneurs argues that in order to tackle recidivism the government should make specific recommendations on how to increase enterprise education and support in British prisons. They state that the current system of imprisoning offenders and keeping them entirely separate from the real world then hoping they can find a job once their sentence is finished, 'results in high rates of recidivism and great human and financial waste. In a society where freelancing and entrepreneurship are transforming the nature of work, those disadvantaged vis-à-vis conventional employment (such as ex-offenders) have the most to gain.'[7]

Gang-involved young people face multiple barriers to gaining employment. In addition to often having a criminal record, research shows that gang members are more likely to have educational disadvantages than the average youth justice entrant.[8] Gang members are more likely to have been excluded from school and have poorer school performance than young offenders in general and this is more acute for gang-involved girls than boys.[9] In the context of desistance from gang-involvement, employment is described as a pull factor, or a 'hook for change'.[10]

As a young person leaves the gang and stops seeing him or herself as a gang member, employment can play a crucial role in facilitating this process so the validation and recognition involved in becoming employed can be essential in this transition out of the gang.[11]

The Government's *Ending Gang and Youth Violence* (EGYV) report identifies employment and learning as key pathways out of gang-involvement. The EGYV report put forward the case for increased 'support for young people wanting to set up their own enterprise' as an intervention to enable young people to exit gangs.[12] Given the barriers into employment, starting a business or becoming self-employed may be the most realistic option for some young people trying to desist from gang-involvement.

There are increasing opportunities for young people to engage in enterprise. However, gang-involved young people or ex-offenders as a group bring their own specific risk factors, barriers and behavioural challenges. As a result it is likely that if we are to use enterprise as an effective gang intervention we will need to tailor the support that is offered and similarly so with ex-offenders.

Gang-involved young people are likely to have greater support needs than the average young entrepreneur. They may be dealing with mental health needs, recent trauma, educational disadvantage and chaotic family backgrounds, all of which make wrap-around support and a strong relationship with a mentor more important. While access to capital is important, for these groups in particular other forms of support are equally critical.

Many ex-offenders or gang-involved young people may have existing skills and abilities that need channelling into enterprise. However, practical business skills such as business planning, marketing, sales, raising capital, budgeting and understanding tax are essential to maximize the chance of business success for young entrepreneurs. Accessing these skills may go some way to minimizing the risk of low pay and a lack of progression that can affect young entrepreneurs.

CASE STUDY   Setting high aspirations: Launch22

Catch22 is a partner in Launch22, a business incubator that aims to promote and enable entrepreneurship amongst people from all walks of life. Launch22's innovative business model sees entrepreneurs who can pay for incubation services doing so, at subsidized rates, while those with complex needs, such as gang members or ex-offenders, are provided with scholarships to help them access support.

Launch22 provides hands-on mentoring, financial guidance and modern co-working spaces in Shoreditch, London and Liverpool in the North of England. The model has been designed to address the main problems facing start-up entrepreneurs:

- **Isolation**: Establishing a business can be lonely. Launch22 provides a physical location with quality business services which are conducive to pursuing a business idea. This enables entrepreneurs to collaborate, share ideas and network with like-minded individuals.

- **Lack of hands-on advice**: Launch22 provides a bespoke, on-site mentoring programme that centres on 'Lean Start-up' principles, enabling its members to increase their social and intellectual capital, while overcoming business setbacks. Specialist mentors (eg legal or accounting) are also available to provide expertise and advice.
- **Unaffordable Office Rents**: Launch22 offers flexible, low-cost terms in prime business locations.
- **Access to Finance**: Launch22 can provide specialist signposting to help entrepreneurs raise the finance needed for their business with the support of third parties.

Appropriate routes into work: apprenticeships

For an organization which has been around and doing this kind of work for 200 years it can sometimes be useful and interesting to look at what has gone before.

Reports on Catch22's impact dating back to the 18th century have recently been discovered. One of these reports from 1840 lists the names of the young men supported and their outcomes. Back then, the organization tackled what they called 'Juvenile Delinquency' by finding apprenticeships and employment for some of the most challenging and hard-to-reach young people.

Today, Catch22 is a leading training and apprenticeship provider[13]. Its industry experience across 15 sectors means that it understands the business requirements of employers and the training and support needs of our service users.[14] The organization supports our learners and employers to develop careers in specific occupational roles and professions and we tailor our training, work-ready and apprenticeship offers to help them become successful in their chosen careers.

Providing apprenticeships remains at the heart of how we support people into employment.

Apprenticeships are not to be confused or compounded with programmes for the unemployed or those furthest away from the labour market who have complex needs. While apprenticeships can be a valuable way to engage people with complex needs, offering an opportunity to change their lives through earning, employment and independence, Catch22's experience has shown that work readiness, mindset and mental toughness programmes are necessary in the early stages.

At the next stage, functional skills training and Level 1 and 2 apprenticeships are vitally important as entry-level opportunities and stepping stones to progress into higher skilled training and work[15]. Only with these building block skills will learners be able to meet the needs of the labour market and sustain employment.

According to UK Employment and Skills Commission (UKESC) research, the notion of an 'hour glass shaped' labour market means there will be a growing demand for people to fill entry-level jobs. That means enabling learners with apparent low skills and academic attainment to access and benefit from an apprenticeship journey as a viable route into employment.

The recruitment process, particularly with SMEs, takes time and potential applicants can drop out, particularly in areas where there is a lot of choice in the labour market. Some existing programmes and projects do not always produce the calibre of learners that would succeed on an apprenticeship programme.

And many of these learners drop out after six weeks and this can impact upon success and timely rates of the provider. There is a big job to do to better understand how to incentivize work for some young people, while recognizing the challenges they face. We should consider the barriers that prevent some young people from entering the jobs market. These can be multiple and complex and we must address them as a priority. If we don't, the social cost is potentially huge.

CASE STUDY Apprenticeships for young people in care

Less than one per cent of children in the UK are in care[16], yet almost a quarter of the adult prison population[17] and almost half of young men under 21-years-old[18] in the criminal justice system have spent time in care. Of homeless people, 25 per cent have been in care and only six per cent of care leavers move into higher education[19]. Care leavers are almost three times more likely than their peers to not be in employment, education or training at 19-years-old.

Finding work for young people who have had a difficult start in life can be very challenging but it is both possible and important.

As part of this work, Catch22 runs the National Leaving Care Benchmarking Forum (NLCBF), the largest membership forum specializing in leaving care in the UK, with an active membership of over 80 local authorities in England and Northern Ireland. The forum shares best practice and promotes the voice of care leavers through the Young People's Benchmarking Forum.

Apprenticeships case study: Care2Work

Care2Work is a flagship Catch22 service that brings together its extensive work with care leavers alongside high-quality apprenticeship and employability programmes. Launched in 2009, Care2Work creates opportunities for young people leaving the care system and raise their employment aspirations, in particular those who have expressed an interest in working within the hospitality, tourism or leisure industries.

Care2Work has successfully engaged with over 100 national and local employers to create over 11,000 opportunities. For example, in the most recent cohort (from April 2015 to January 2016), Care2Work supported 189 care leavers through Care2Work, of which 77 per cent got interviews, 50 per cent started work or an apprenticeship and 80 per cent are in full time jobs or apprenticeships.

Care2Work has also evolved to include the Willkommen Project, a unique opportunity for care leavers working with Marriott Hotels in the UK to travel to Germany to complete part of their placement. Eduard Peposhi from London is now Apprentice Concierge at London Marriott Grosvenor Square. He had been applying for 20 jobs a day and was getting no replies when he became involved with the Willkommen Project. He said it 'changed [his] life'.

The aim of the Willkommen Project was not only to enable young people to develop language skills, but to build their broader employability skills and raise their aspirations to demonstrate that being a care leaver does not prevent you from succeeding in work and life. Eduard's experience is a great example of how the project is truly transforming lives. By giving him access to good language lessons, he was able to develop conversational German which would help him on placement in Germany. He then undertook a two-week placement with London Marriott Grosvenor Square, followed by a work placement in Karlsruhe, Germany. Managers, associates and guests were able to see how dedicated he was and colleagues described him as 'the most hardworking and enthusiastic young person' the hotel has ever worked with.

Upon his return to England, Eduard was offered a concierge position.

Care leavers, like all young people, are individuals with very different needs from each other, as well as from young people who have not experienced care. Some require minimal support while others are very vulnerable with complex and varying needs. Some care leavers have often missed huge amounts of formal learning and may not have had the structure of daily routines for some months or even years. These young people usually need intensive support before they are ready to undertake training to get on the first rung of the employment ladder.

What this teaches us is that while young people with complex needs have just as much potential to grow and thrive in the workplace as their peers, they may need a bit more support to get there. When properly supported, as we have seen with Eduard, they can be great assets to their future employers.

Conclusion

Each of the examples cited here has been successful in supporting the needs of their specific cohorts. While we would broadly support the growth and expansion of any of these projects and services, it is perhaps more valuable to understand what these have in common and how these commonalities can inform a more wide-reaching approach.

This chapter has explored a number of different approaches to supporting people who could be described as 'disadvantaged' into employment or entrepreneurship.

It's not about pushing 'soft options' or making allowances. Indeed, recognizing that some people face challenges or have specific needs is important but more so, identifying and building on their strengths is what makes the difference. Confidence and self-esteem, resilience and mental toughness, are the things that enable people not just to get a job but to keep it and enjoy it.

Getting a job is not the only success measure either. We must also recognize and appreciate other routes to employment such as entrepreneurship and enterprise. As the labour market continues to evolve, these types of work will become increasingly common. If we are to ensure that our 'disadvantaged' young people can take advantage of the opportunities presented by the changing labour market, we have a responsibility to equip them with the necessary 'hard skills' and networks of people who can help them.

The vast majority of young people are fundamentally good, often willing and generally want what everyone else wants. But circumstances and situations can appear to deny that opportunity.

Whatever background they come from, whatever challenges they face, if we focus on young people's assets rather than their liabilities, we stand a much better chance of inspiring and enabling them to lift themselves out of their negative circumstances and into independence.

Notes

1 Jones, Hanton and Connaughton (2002) 'What Is This Thing Called Mental Toughness? An Investigation of Elite Sport Performers', *Journal of Applied Sport Psychology* **14** (3), p 209
2 http://www.telegraph.co.uk/news/worldnews/europe/iceland/10765615/The-Icelandic-trek-unlocking-the-potential-of-troubled-teenagers.html
3 RBS and UnLtd, RBS Enterprise Tracker (December 2013) https://unltd.org.uk/wp-content/uploads/2014/01/RBS-Youth-Enterprise-Tracker-Summary_4th-Quarter-2013-2.pdf
4 Lipsey, M (1995) 'What do we learn from 400 research studies on the effectiveness of treatment with juvenile delinquents?', in McGuire, J (Ed) *What works? Reducing reoffending*, Chichester
5 Ministry of Justice (2013) *Analysis of the impact of employment on re-offending following release from custody, using Propensity Score Matching*. MOJ, London
6 Ministry of Justice (2011a) *Offending, employment and benefits – emerging findings from the data linkage project*. Ministry of Justice, London
7 http://centreforentrepreneurs.org/from-inmates-to-entrepreneurs/
8 Khan, L, Brice, H, Saunders, A and Plumtree, A (2013) *A need to belong: what leads girls to join gangs*. Centre for Mental Health, London
9 Ibid
10 Decker, S H, Pryrooz, D C and Moule, R K (2014) 'Disengagement from gangs as role transitions'. *Journal of research on adolescence*, **24** (2), pp 268–283
11 Decker, S H, Pryrooz, D C and Moule, R K (2014) 'Disengagement from gangs as role transitions'. *Journal of research on adolescence*, **24** (2), pp 268–283
12 HM Government (2011) *Ending Gang and Youth Violence*: https://www.gov.uk/government/uploads/system/uploads/attachment_data/file/97862/gang-violence-detailreport.pdf.
13 77 per cent of Catch22 supported apprentices completed their apprenticeship in 2013/14. More than 1,000 learners and job seekers every year are supported

to find employment. 80 per cent of our employer partners are SMEs. 8 out of 10 apprentices would recommend us to others.

14 Last year we worked with 200 employers in industries that include professional and business services, leisure, early years, hospitality, ICT and non-governmental organizations.
15 In 2014/15, Catch22's functional skills success rates in Mathematics (Level 2) were 98 per cent and in English 97 per cent. Ofsted stated during their 2015 inspection that our functional skills performance was impressive. Our progression rates for all learners going on to full-time work, higher apprenticeships or university in 2014/15 were 96 per cent.
16 Care – a stepping stone to custody? (2011), Prison Reform Trust
17 Prisoners' childhood and family backgrounds (March 2012), Ministry of Justice
18 Care leavers' transition to adulthood (July 2015), National Audit Office
19 Care leavers' transition to adulthood (October 2015) *Fifth Report of Session 2015–16,* House of Commons Committee of Public Accounts

Employability training and coaching to clients with mental health problems

19

SERENA BRADSHAW, GODDARDS

This chapter describes a flexible approach to developing employability with those who have long-term health conditions. The approach has achieved significant success.

As with the Catch22 chapter, the important thing is often to focus on the individual's strengths and qualities and complement that with developing their mindset so it moves from 'I can't do that...' to 'I can now see the possibilities and I can go for most if not all of them'. Given that their personal challenges are to do with health and the majority also report mental health conditions, their state of mental health often requires a particular emphasis on developing mental toughness or mental resilience.

This area of activity is important. Health and well-being is a significant issue in any society – it certainly is in the UK. Many of those with physical and mental health problems are perfectly capable of being involved in work activity and of contributing to the common wealth of society. In the past the default option has often been the opposite of this.

The approach has been developed by Goddard Consultants. Established in 2007, their goal was to deliver employability training and coaching to clients with long-term health conditions. To do this they pioneered a blended approach combining:

- individual coaching;
- group sessions;
- online learning.

These methods are branded as Achieve! which incorporates a virtual learning environment providing bite-sized learning and resources and offering further opportunity for clients to embed change. The aim is to remove barriers to employment, motivate clients to adopt jobseeking behaviour and to support clients in their move into employment.

Goddard's approach is developmental and is evidence-based. They routinely gather a broad range of quantitative and qualitative data which they review and analyse to refine and improve their work:

- individual learning plans;
- initial assessments;
- registration forms;
- MTQ48 Psychometric test data;
- self-assessment of 4Cs (where undertaken);
- an analysis of our coaching conversations with customers.

This method reflects Goddards' approach to service design and delivery, which is grounded in the research – both the literature and our own continuous evaluation and action/insider research

The chapter also provides an insight into the experiences and perspectives of those jobseekers who took part in the programme.

Barriers to employability for those with ongoing mental health conditions

Despite many initiatives over the last two decades, a satisfactory response to the increasing gap in employment between those with and without long-term health conditions – especially mental health conditions – has not emerged.

The UK Department for Work and Pensions has been central to government policy in this area. In 2004 the Department acknowledged that their understanding of the landscape had still a fair way to go: 'The factors that

Employability Training and Coaching to Clients with Mental Health Problems

affect entry into employment and return to work for people with health conditions and/or impairments are still not fully understood'. And some 12 years later the government acknowledges that 'the **employment rate for adults** with mental health problems remains unacceptably low: 43 per cent of all people with mental health problems are in employment, compared with 74 per cent of the general population and 65 per cent of people with other health conditions'.

Goddard's own findings and experience bear this out. The 2013 Department for Work and Pensions and Ipsos MORI 'Survey of disabled working-age people benefit claimants' (Department for Work and Pensions, 2013, p14) findings, suggest there may be a combination of reasons why people don't return to work:

- lack of job opportunities;
- transport;
- employer attitudes;
- lack of qualifications/experience/skills;
- out-of-date equipment;
- lack of confidence or motivation;
- the impact of their health condition;

The table below illustrates the reasons Goddard's clients stated they cannot find work:

Figure 19.1 Barriers to employment

Employability, illness and mental toughness

Various authors have concluded that the way we behave when we're ill is determined by our culture – it's not simply about 'disease'. Some have stated that socio-economic factors can also determine how we perceive illness. Clearly the type of behaviour we adopt when we're ill can also be an obstacle to recovery or return to work. The Department of Work and Pensions (DWP) has also suggested that after two years out of work people do not always recognize improvements in their medical condition. (DWP, 2006)

Because we construct illness in different ways, regardless of 'severity', it's important to understand how individuals construe their illness. And this is where we find the mental toughness approach useful.

Achieve! is underpinned by a Mental Toughness approach designed to change the mindset of customers. This is because our beliefs shape the way we perceive our problems, our potential for recovery and indeed the type of treatment we receive. This relationship between *beliefs and illness behaviour is illustrated in these* responses to our programme:

Fear of being perceived as 'fit for work'

'I was worried about catching the bus, I thought it was to catch you out – "If you can get on a bus you must be fit for work".'

Illness that impedes activity

'I was aware of my health... was really concerned about travelling'

Desperate for help to return to work

'Been out of work for so long that I would have gone anywhere'

Inertia until in receipt of a diagnosis

'Not ready at all. I was awaiting a diagnosis.'

Helping clients to manage both their condition and their perceptions becomes a recurrent theme in the Goddard programme. Examples have included:

- encouraging customers to ask for referrals eg for counselling;
- helping customers to self-refer for counselling;
- teaching chair-based exercise;
- mindfulness, meditation and guided imagery.

A Mental Toughness-based approach changes mental illness behaviour

Given an understanding that our response depends on our social (including material) circumstances, it is entirely appropriate that an approach to improving jobseeking behaviours could involve strengthening the individual's mental toughness.

Mental toughness and its components, the 4Cs, is described in some detail in Chapter 3.

The ability to drill down to the 4Cs – Control, Commitment, Challenge and Confidence – and their subscales provides a great deal of analytical power to understand each individual client.

In reality the 4 Cs overlap – and combine uniquely for each individual. For some it may require confidence in abilities to stick to tasks; for others it may be more a question of commitment – such as setting realistic SMART objectives. Some clients may need to learn to handle unexpected challenges on the way to achieving their goals and still others may have to recognize that they need to let go of past abilities and set goals that reflect new opportunities.

The 4 Cs that measure mental toughness

Confidence – in abilities and in interpersonal skills

Control – of life and emotions

Challenge – how we respond to change

Commitment – to achieving goals

Changing ambivalence towards work

Much of the work in this area involves helping clients to understand and overcome their ambivalence towards jobseeking. When clients participated in their initial workshop on their programme, Goddard's assessed their needs and mindset using an Individual Learning Plan (ILP). This was based on a series of questions – one of which asks the clients if they want to work. At this stage they will tick the box saying 'Yes – I want to work'; yet later on the same day they will also tick the box saying 'I do not want to apply for jobs right now.'

Developing Employability and Enterprise

This apparent ambivalence highlights the need to change mind-set – to move customers from a state of learned helplessness to mental toughness, whereby they can overcome all the reasons why they cannot start applying for jobs and can begin to take steps towards seeking employment.

Figure 19.2 Wanting to work

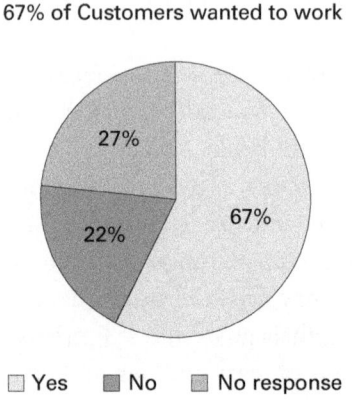

The client's belief that their condition is not managed.

Goddard's found that half of their clients told them that their health condition was not managed. And of the 25 clients who didn't respond to this question five cited fluctuations in health, ill health or mental health as a barrier to employment.

Figure 19.3 Is your health conditioned managed?

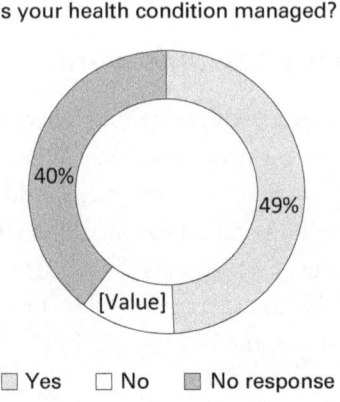

Clients address barriers through the mental toughness framework

The aims of this programme are to improve well-being and the jobseeking behaviours of our customers. Goddards describe and define jobseeking behaviours as taking steps towards employment such as engaging in:

- training and further learning activities;
- voluntary work;
- work experience;
- evidence of active job search.

Clients ask their coaches to help them address barriers such as:

- health issues – either directly within the multidisciplinary team or through referral to the NHS;
- family crises;
- debt – through referral to appropriate agencies;
- housing.

Goddards describe and define well-being through the use of the World Health Organization definition:

> 'Mental health is defined as a state of well-being in which every individual realizes his or her own potential, can cope with the normal stresses of life, can work productively and fruitfully and is able to make a contribution to her or his community.'

Clients adopt job-seeking behaviour.

'I feel a lot more positive now, I felt alone before, but now I'm a lot more confident. We reviewed my CV and I feel more confident with the content and feel more confident about myself since we changed it to a more functional style of CV. I have been doing voluntary work and I am learning from this how to build up my confidence.'

'Inside I feel better... it's a feeling I can't explain. The course has been excellent. I am looking forward to the future. I am going to enrol on two courses, English and IT'

> Teaching and coaching conversations have included:
>
> **Commitment**
> Goal setting
> Motivation
>
> **Challenge**
> Motivation
>
> **Confidence**
> Transferable skills
> Positive thinking

Clients change their illness behaviour

'Focusing on the present has enabled me to realize that my health is improving... I cannot let my past govern my present... I am beginning this year thinking about the person I am today, not used to be'

'My Coach has helped me manage my condition, eat healthily. She talked a lot about the 4Cs and taught me to look at myself in the third person and by positive talk stopping me from the worst of the panic attacks'.

> Teaching and coaching conversations have included
>
> **Control of emotions**
> Teaching mindfulness
> Guided imagery
>
> **Control of life**
> Assertiveness (eg to access NHS services such as pain clinic, counselling)

Clients develop confidence in relationships

'(Coach review) Your Dad who shows you no respect... he still makes you angry. Your guided meditations help with your stress levels.'

(Coach review) '... you have used techniques discussed to improve the situation. You have become more aware of how you can change interactions and you no longer 'stick to your guns' like you used to and are learning new patterns of behaviour, to improve your health.'

> Teaching and coaching conversations have included
>
> **Life control**
> Promoting independence
>
> **Control of emotions**
> Meditation
> Saying no to children

Clients change their perceptions of themselves

'The coach helped me think about my skills and qualities I suppose that when he talked to me about the 4 C's it did make me think differently. It gave me food for thought.'

'I feel much better and so much more positive about my future. I was in a hole when I came on the programme; I'd lost confidence in my abilities and never thought I'd have the confidence to set up my own business'

> Teaching and coaching conversations have included:
>
> **Life control**
> Promoting the benefit of work
>
> **Confidence in abilities**
> Visioning
> SWOT analysis

Assessing mental toughness through the MTQ48

Goddards assess the mental toughness of clients at induction to their programmes.

Mental toughness scores are normally distributed in general populations. However, as the graph below illustrates, 60 per cent of clients recorded

STENS ranging from 1–3. If the scores were normally distributed we would not expect this figure to exceed 16 per cent.

This indicates a correlation between mental toughness and mental health.

Figure 19.4 STEN score distribution

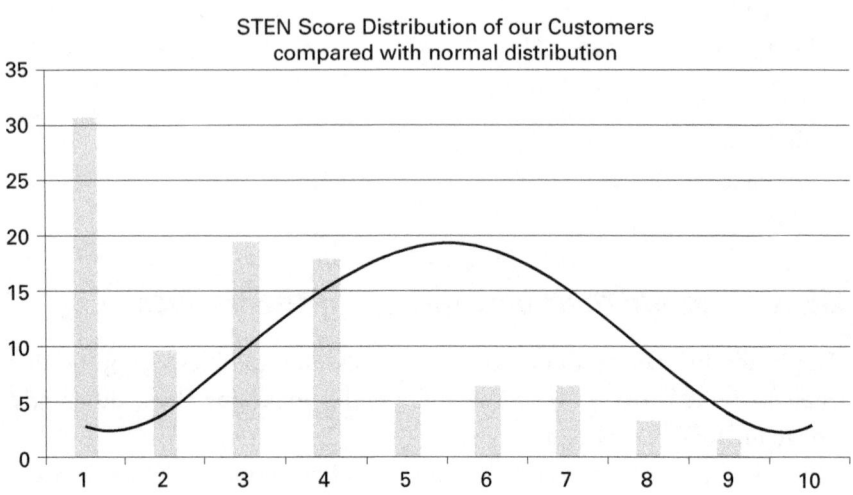

Other benefits to this approach included:

- The observation that long-term illness, mental health conditions or disabilities undoubtedly contribute to the low STENS is significant.
- The exercises and support required to improve mental toughness are easily learned by clients.
- The psychometric test acts as an initial assessment tool and can measure distance travelled.
- The concept of Mental Toughness and the 4 Cs are easy to understand. This is important because so many psychometric assessments are beyond the grasp of our clients.

Finally, it is worth noting that nearly 55 per cent disclosed their main health condition or disability as a mental health problem. Many stated that their own health care professionals judged their problems as 'severe.'

Coaching conversations

The coaches built on the Mental Toughness model and used a range of tools to address health, work and well-being. These included: motivational interviewing; a CBT approach and coaching models such as GROW and STEPPA. The coaches work in a multidisciplinary team of vocational rehabilitation specialists, employability coaches, counsellors, occupational therapists and psychologists. This means that any issue can be tackled from sleep, hygiene and nutrition, through to exercise and CVs.

In a person-centred approach the type of support offered is wide and varied. As expected, the most common type of support emerged as development of mental toughness – this is the crosscutting theme for all programmes.

Through analysis of customer logs, Goddards confirmed that most coaching conversations actually concerned mental toughness.

The table below shows coaching topics in rank order:

1 Mental toughness
2 Cv and application
3 Sourced courses
4 Sourced volunteering
5 Access to NHS or health care
6 Job search
7 Other
8 Self employment.

Client Profile

What type of clients does Goddard work with?
Most have mild to moderate mental health conditions.

Figure 19.5 Declared health conditions

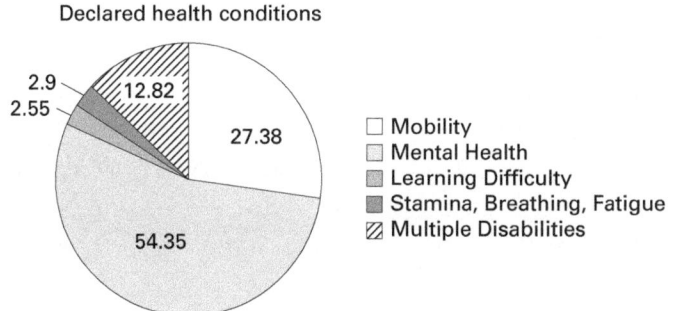

More males than females

Figure 19.6 Gender

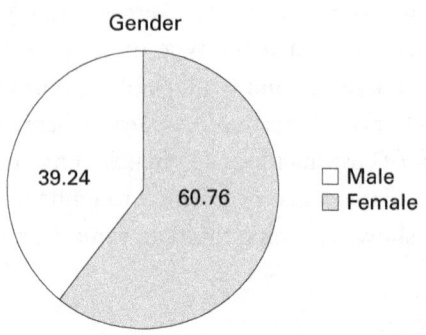

The results

Sixty-four per cent of participants on the first two programmes improved jobseeking behaviour. Ninety-nine significant gains were recorded (some participants achieved in more than one area).

Figure 19.7 Jobseeking behaviour and well-being

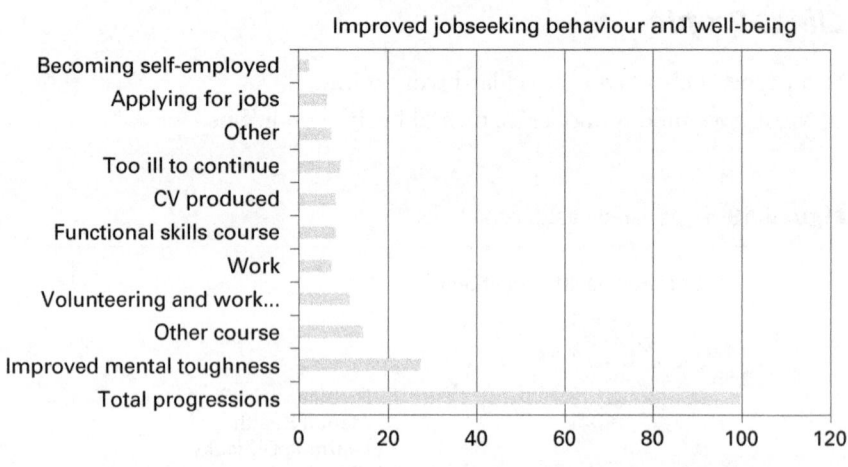

The 'Other' progressions included:

- One client began working with Pain Management and Health Psychology.
- One customer began physio and was seeing an occupational therapist.
- Four clients have begun further counselling to assist them with their conditions.

Mental Toughness – over 90 per cent of customers responding to the Service evaluation increased their self-assessment scores on the 4Cs.

Figure 19.8 Self-assessment scores

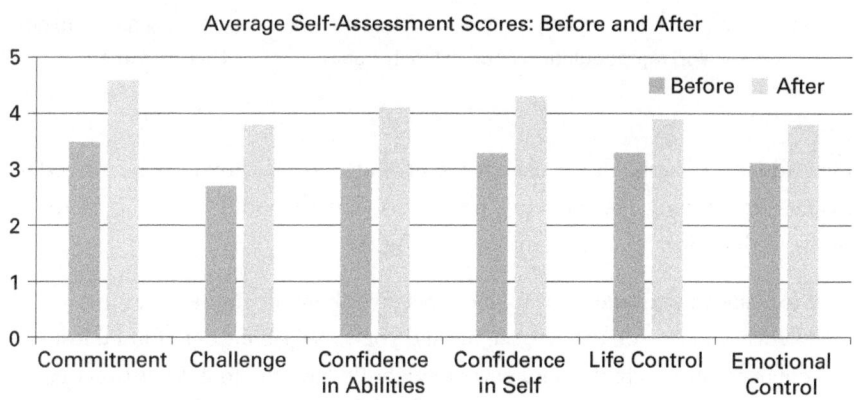

Making a difference in terms of numbers and outcomes is important. It is also important to assess the effectiveness and efficiency of what is achieved. At time of writing that analysis is underway and the projected outcomes appear very positive. These people remain individuals and the impact on the individual can be neatly summed up in these case studies:

Out of a Black Hole

Recent acute illness affected this client's confidence in their ability and interpersonal confidence.

This client described himself as 'in a black hole' when he met us.

As a direct result of the coaching and mentoring programme, he has now signed up for a New Enterprise course with a view to establishing his own business and has attended another course to update skills for the new business.

Figure 19.9 Out of a black hole

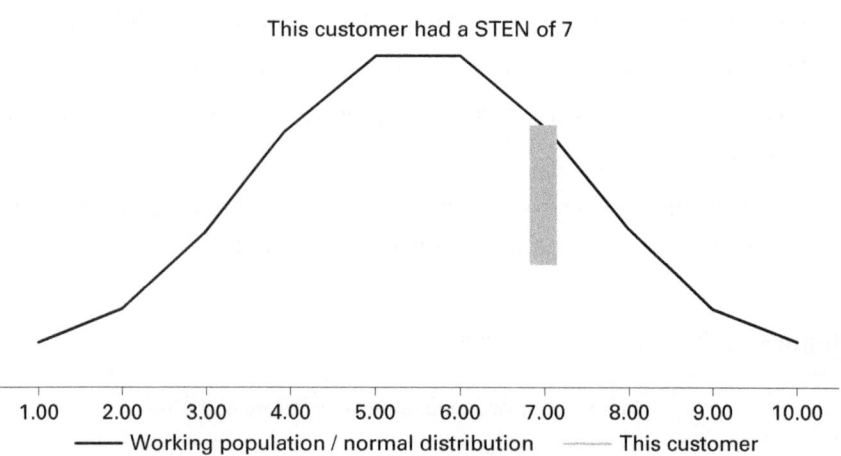

He had a small setback for urgent medical attention – however he agreed to discussions during his recovery period so that he could continue to make plans with a view to a start in the New Year.

> 'I feel much better and so much more positive about my future. I was in a hole when I came on the programme and you've helped me out of it. I'd lost confidence in my abilities and never thought I'd have the confidence to set up my own business'.

Debilitating anxiety.

The main focus in the five sessions with this client was to support him with his anxiety and to improve his self-confidence. Through coaching he:

- Gained a sense of perspective and acceptance – for example about feeling unwell.
- Began writing lists instead of keeping things in his head – which can cause stress.
- Became more assertive – not allowing friends to impose upon him and practising useful ways to say 'No'.

Employability Training and Coaching to Clients with Mental Health Problems

Figure 19.10 Low STEN score

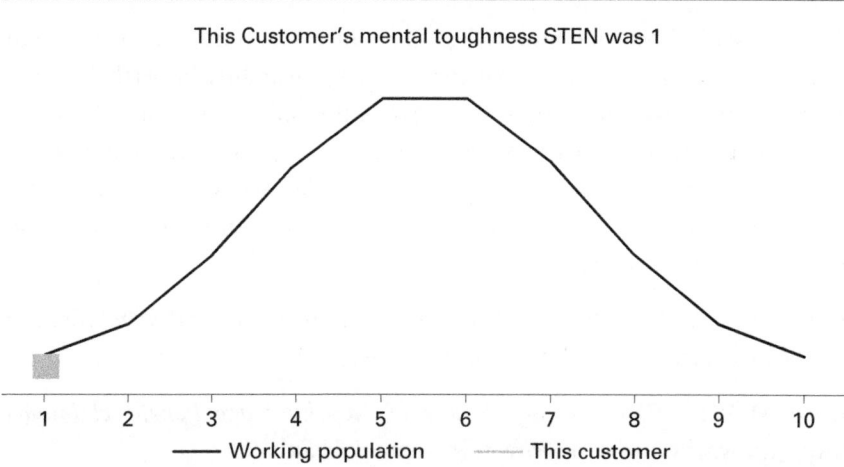

By the end of the programme his scores on the 4Cs (commitment, confidence, control and challenge) when compared with those when he first started the course were higher, particularly on commitment to achieving goals and confidence in relation to people.

The customer told us that 'In just a short space of time, I found that talking to my tutor has been very constructive, and has helped me to reclaim a good deal of self-belief. I have been given a lot of food for thought.'

Figure 19.11 Before and after

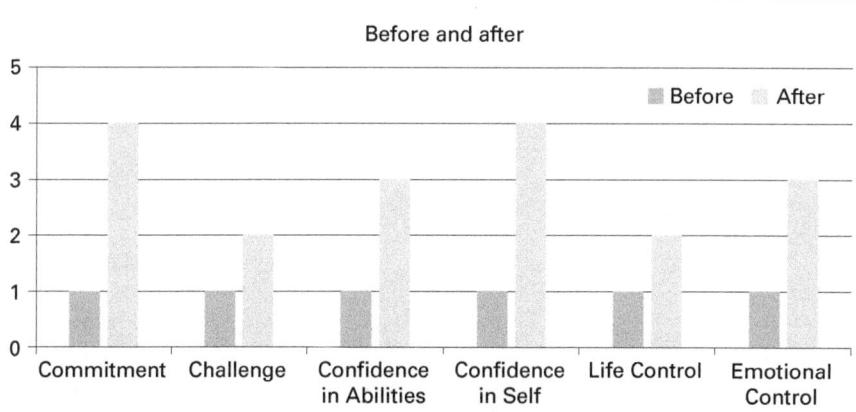

Summary

Working with those who endure health problems, and in particular mental health, is one of the bigger challenges in employability. Nevertheless, the core issue remains consistent, irrespective of the person concerned. Whether it's a graduate who has earned a good degree or a person who has suffered from mental health issues, the challenge is similar and so are the interventions. Changing 'what I think I can't do' to 'what can I do and what do I need to do to get there?'.

Building Capacity for Work: A UK Framework for Vocational Rehabilitation (2004), Department for Work and Pensions, p 10.

Ipsos MORI (2013) *Survey of disabled working age benefit claimants* http://www.who.int/features/factfiles/mental_health/en/

'The five year forward view for Mental Health' (February 2016), *A report from the independent Mental Health Taskforce to the NHS in England*

The role of sport in developing life skills, employability and enterprise

DR JOHN PERRY

A metaphor for life

Sport has a special place in the development of individuals – especially for young people.

Firstly, most sports are capable of acting as a metaphor for life. We'll examine that shortly in more detail. People who participate in sports do so with a degree of motivation even if they lack many of the skills needed to be competent at that sport.

Participation in sport is an excellent ways to learn many essential life qualities – preparing to play against a better team and having the self-belief that you could 'do it', understanding the process of improving by always seeking to achieve one's personal best, coping with defeat and learning from that and building confidence in one's abilities to be 'the best that you can be'. It is said that participation in sports in schools is dropping. If so, a reversal should be encouraged.

Secondly, most people engage in some way with sport. Either as a participant or as a spectator. Sports of all types form a large part of the leisure interest for many. With that interest they will often become knowledgeable about that sport to the point that they can understand and learn from events in sport – even if it isn't happening to them.

Accessible role models

Thirdly, sport provides readily accessible role models and champions. This is especially important for young people in their teens and twenties. Their role models are often from the world of sport, music or the dramatic arts. Their associations are often with either athletes/players or in organized sport, the clubs they play for.

So when these athletes behave badly and are reprimanded or succeed because they have trained hard, their followers can recognize those lessons. Similarly if sports clubs begin openly and publicly to be involved in wider developing activities, they will sit up and pay attention to that in a way that they might not do if their parents or teachers were involved.

This is especially true in the modern era when vast sums of money are poured into the word of sport – especially in soccer, rugby, American football, tennis, etc. Participation in a variety of sports the world over is enormous and growing. Sport England's recent Active people survey estimates that during the year up to October 2015, 15.74 million people aged 16 years and over in England played sport at least once a week. That represents roughly one in three people and an increase of 1.65 million since the survey was first conducted in 2005/6.

In the United States, approximately 45 million children participate in sport and this is growing (Merkel, 2013). Clearly, the vast majority of people who play do so at a recreational level. Apart from enjoyment and health benefits, why do they gain from this participation?

Character building

It has long been said that sport builds character. This is true and indeed, there is a lot of evidence for this. It would be naïve, however, to assume that all aspects of character that can be developed in youth sport are positive. Rather, sport participation has been occasionally associated with aggression, rule-breaking and disrespect (Bredemeier & Shields, 2006). Overwhelmingly though, evidence points towards more positive character-development gained through sport.

The Role of Sport in Developing Life Skills, Employability and Enterprise

Consider for a moment, some of the life, employability and enterprise skills considered in this book. Mental toughness is inextricably positively associated with sport. Indeed, the 4Cs construct of mental toughness (Clough et al, 2002) was established using sport performers. An enormous array of what we know about motivation stems from research in sport.

It is in sport environments that we learn most about motivational climates, which reflect task mastery and self-referenced systems to be most successful (Treasure, 2001). This means that an environment where individuals make judgements on their performance and subsequent enhancements, use their earlier selves as a reference point, rather than comparing themselves with others. In sport, intrinsic motivation is king. Rivalry within teams is old hat and supportive environments where people put the overall good of the team above personal goals is now taught.

Continuous improvement

Training is conscientious, with attention to minor details and a willingness to continue to practise until a skill is mastered being required. Communication is at the heart of a squad and all relationships. Striving for continuous improvement is the nature of sport. This is why mediocre golfers play at 5.30am at the weekend in the rain to improve their handicap from a rubbish one to a slightly less rubbish one. For a sports performer, aspiring to improve all skills is engrained – why wouldn't you?

There is also the cruel nature of sport itself. It is intentionally stress-inducing to make it harder for the individual to achieve the goals they value the most. Rules, opponents, and league structures are deliberately distorted to slightly skew the odds against success each time. This means that uncertainty, which creates stress, is rife, and failure is regular.

I once worked with a football club where the Manager's favourite phrase after defeat was 'we've lost the game, let's not lose the lessons'. The belief that failure is informative and useful is vital to ensure it is not wasted. It is skills such as this that means sport is a tremendous vehicle for personal growth.

Finally, an interesting observation about the evolution of the idea of sport brought to our attention by John Eades, Operations Director at Manchester United Foundation.

Today's definition of sport is stimulating compared with, say, 10 years ago. A decade back we would simply describe sport as a physical exertion/effort/activity with an element of agony and competition.

Sport today now includes mind games such as chess. The Olympic Council of Asia, for example, includes chess in their Indoor Games event.

They also have billiards and snooker on the programme. Also, we are seeing more and more the word sport being used to describe digital games and other online activities as there are now related competitions.

To see how sport can be used to promote important life, employability and enterprise skills, we now present two case studies.

The first is from the **Manchester United Foundation**, which has an excellent community engagement programme, as do most soccer clubs in the UK. This provides a first-class example of how, possibly the biggest name in world soccer, uses its name, its image and its expertise both in people development and in footballer character-building to deliver progressive programmes into the community. Many of those programmes are explicitly employability development programmes.

Soccer Club Foundations are a key vehicle in the UK for tackling barriers to social and educational attainment for young people and for adults. This is mirrored by equivalent work in sporting institutions all over the world.

Much of the focus by these foundations has been to support individuals to achieve their potential and develop their skills through a range of activities and programmes. It was observed that Mental Toughness (and resilience) had often been both an enabling factor and sometimes a desired outcome. But this was poorly evidenced.

In 2015, Football Foundations across England, funded in part by the Premier League Community Fund (PLCF), were invited to take part in a national pilot to access MTQ48 through the PLCF. The aim was to support, enhance and gather evidence on some of their programmes and to look at the impact Foundations had on the individuals they engaged with.

Six clubs were identified for the pilot (including Manchester United Foundation) and trained by AQR to deliver and integrate the mental toughness measure and its model into PLCF-funded programmes such as the Works and Kicks programmes.

The second case study is from **London Youth Rowing**, who use their sport very specifically as the vehicle through which they engage with and develop individuals. Using a combination of wet and dry rowing as well as the involvement of elite athletes including Olympic medallists, they can capture the imagination of young people. *Breaking Barriers* is a mentored employability programme which embodies all the principles identified in Chapter 1 of this book. Their programmes are holistic, well thought-out; they develop the individual before developing their knowledge and skills and, above all, are monitored and measured. This is not only to assess success but to consider ways of improving what is already a successful programme.

The Role of Sport in Developing Life Skills, Employability and Enterprise

CASE STUDY 1 Manchester United Foundation

Working in communities to develop aspirations, employability and enterprise

Philippa Harrison, MU Foundation

For many people football is so much more than a game. Its power and inspiration goes beyond the 90 minutes. One of the game's greatest ever players sums this up perfectly:

> In the sweep of its appeal, its ability to touch every corner of humanity, football is the only game that needed to be invented.
>
> Sir Bobby Charlton CBE

Manchester United Foundation was formed in 2007 to celebrate 50 years of the club playing in Europe and as a way of continuing Sir Matt Busby's legacy of supporting youth.

Greater Manchester currently ranks number five out of 326 local authorities in England for overall deprivation and number 53 for employment deprivation. These statistics alone show the need for greater focus on providing the practical, social and psychological building blocks for young people in Manchester to be able to access the opportunities that are available to them.

In the 2014/2015 season alone, the Foundation engaged with 17,920 young people, across 16 separate projects, from education and social inclusion activities to sport participation and health. A total of 587 recognized qualifications were gained and 2,215 hours were volunteered by participants across multiple projects to enhance this academic attainment.

Many non-sporting organizations and people at large often wonder why the Foundation, as the charitable arm of a football club, is in a position to achieve more than just identifying and developing talent into professional and international-class footballers. This is what has traditionally been assumed what football clubs and other sports organizations were doing in their communities: a talent identification mission.

However sporting bodies know more than most that sport is simply the vehicle through which to engage and then facilitate personal development both on and off the pitch.

Underpinning the educational programmes is the development of capabilities such as attitude, aptitude and behaviour. All of which are essential competencies developed with and through the Foundation's core activities.

Developing Employability and Enterprise

The Foundation has a focus on four main areas, in each of which the young person is central, and informs how to strategize and operate:

1 Foundation mission

2 Foundation programmes and projects

3 Staff

4 Quality assurance.

Figure 20.1 Engage, inspire, unite

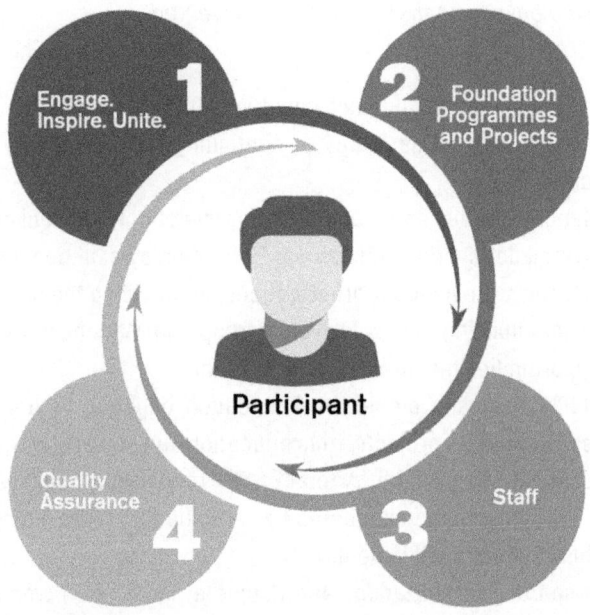

Foundation Mission: Engage. Inspire. Unite.

Manchester United Foundation uses football to engage and inspire young people to build a better life for themselves and unite the communities in which they live. Dedicated, experienced and qualified staff deliver football coaching, educational programmes and personal development, providing young people with opportunities to change their lives for the better.

The Foundation's strapline is to Engage, Inspire and Unite.

Engage

Using the power of the Manchester United brand as a way of engaging with young people, the Foundation provides additional and bespoke learning through individual projects and programmes.

It's important to understand that not all of the Foundation's work is focused on those with a passion for football or who play the game: it goes beyond the ball. The Foundation is able to make use of many of the club's assets and departments to support what it is offering. As well as the traditional football areas of the club, expertise is available from the catering, finance, HR, hospitality, communications and media departments.

The knowledge and experience from these divisions provides essential support to young people involved in all Foundation projects, turning the disengaged into the engaged.

Inspire

Using the inspiration of the club, its history and its many legacies, the Foundation creates programmes which encourage learning. This, for example, is achieved with the help of players, past and present, either in person, at player days, on school visits or as imagery on materials such as workbooks and creative media.

Examples of the club's achievements are often featured, using the expertise of staff and departments in case studies and references. The Foundation also suggests key characteristics that will promote and support participants' personal development, focusing on areas such as motivation, resilience, confidence, participation, responsibility and passion.

Unite

A primary objective for Manchester United Foundation is to create continuing support networks and relationships, so that the young participants continually develop leadership, personal and interpersonal skills that they can take back to their communities. Many young people do this through volunteering their time helping with projects being run in their own schools and communities.

Foundation programmes and projects

Manchester United Foundation provides opportunities for participants to practise the skills they have learned out in the real world, away from the theoretical concepts, with staff there to challenge them and help them to develop the right mindset.. This is done through a series of programmes from enterprise and leadership to NLP and physical literacy as well as volunteering and mentoring projects. All of these have the same thread woven throughout – to help young people to develop and believe that success for them is possible, tangible and within their capabilities.

Once they realise that they can develop themselves, and they are not defined or restricted by their current situation, the idea that 'anything is possible' opens up. Once they believe it is possible they will engage and work towards achieving it through the programmes provided.

Manchester United Foundation has three main pillars of activity:

1 **Hub of the Community** – One of the longest standing projects the Foundation has to offer is the hub model, which places a full-time Hub Development Officer (HDO) into certain high schools to create a permanent physical presence and constant familiar point of contact for staff, pupils and their families.

   The Foundation currently has 18 partner schools and works directly in the high school and the surrounding primary schools. The HDO has set KPIs that they work towards, which are dependent on the school's objectives; for example parental engagement, year 7 intake, attendance, etc. The HDO will deliver a range of Foundation programmes alongside additional support and mentoring in the school.

2 **Community Cohesion** – Running 48 weeks of the year in the evenings, and at 12 sites, the Street Reds project forms part of the community-cohesion strategy and uses the power of football to give young people an opportunity to pursue their interest in playing, leading and coaching football.

   Based on the ENGAGE part of the strategy, Foundation coaches encourage further personal development by running pitch-side workshops covering the areas of discrimination, money skills, healthy living, drugs and alcohol, employability and crime in the community, all of which have subsidiary workshops running for around 10 to 20 minutes.

3 **Girls' Development** – Forming part of a wider strategy to involve girls, female inclusion is a core element of the Foundation's mission. Despite Physical Education being compulsory in school, one in five girls does no physical activity in a week and stubborn barriers to increasing this figure still exist, despite taking part in sport having many benefits for individuals' physical and mental health and well-being.

The Foundation has a threefold role in reducing the barriers to growth and pursuing this mission:

- Support retention in the game through high level competition: Regional Talent Club.

The Role of Sport in Developing Life Skills, Employability and Enterprise

- Support ongoing participation: Funding and strategic advice to South Manchester Girls' League
- Support engagement in the game: Girls-only programmes within the partner hub schools and their feeder primary schools.

Staff

Manchester United Foundation is able to engage with its participants through non-traditional methods, not only through the connection with the club and the brand, but also through its approach to delivery and the specialized skill set and approaches adopted by the staff. It is essential that staff work within the Foundation's values and philosophy and are selected specifically for the projects they run.

Although the Foundation takes pride in employing staff with a wide range of experience and expertise, it also makes sure that the staff recruited have the right skills for a current project and its users. The Street Reds football project employs both a football specialist and a youth engagement officer, which allows the scheme to provide the best level of both technical and psychological support for participants.

Quality assurance

In order for Manchester United Foundation to be able to provide the best service to key stakeholders (participants) and funders it has to be accountable for all areas of operation and the reasons why decisions are made.

Staff continuously monitor and evaluate performance and inform best practice through youth voice consultations, focus groups and systematic reporting, as well as using tools such as baseline questionnaires and psychometrics (MTQ48), which provide the organization and its participants with a platform from which to work.

The Foundation also uses a social monitoring tool to track engagement levels, contact time and outcomes, which gives a wider picture of which projects are successful and why, and which areas could be developed. Both the programmes and the staff are continuously evaluated and monitored so that the organization can be sure that it is adapting and changing to the needs of our young people.

CASE STUDY 2   London Youth Rowing

Breaking barriers

Ben Cox and Layal Marten, London Youth Rowing

Organized sport can play an important role in the development of the whole child. It is a forum in which mental toughness can be tested and developed. It helps create a 'mental map' and provides a vital tool with which young people can build their own futures. This can be reflected in – and measured by – educational attainment, employability and inter-generational economic mobility.

At London 2012, the seven per cent of privately educated citizens in this country made up 50 per cent of Great Britain's Olympic team. That is an arresting statistic. Such a disproportionate impact at the highest level does prompt a question as to whether investment in school sport, including a willingness to fully exploit its educational capacity, is possible within the state sector.

Many independent school Head Teachers feel sport is a crucial area which helps create their 'competitive advantage' – both in terms of the product they supply – and the life chances of their graduates. But what of the other 93 per cent of young people in this country, particularly those from more deprived communities?

Conceived on the banks of Henley Royal Regatta and based on the notion that the developmental benefits of sport could be better shared throughout the capital, London Youth Rowing (LYR) was established in 2004. For the past 12 years, we have sought to show that through sport in general, and rowing in particular, such positive activity can become a vehicle for personal development in those young people considered 'hard to reach'.

Through its Sport England-funded Satellite Hubs and Clubs model, London Youth Rowing has brought the sport of rowing to tens of thousands of new participants. Whilst this has been successful in terms of creating open access to a traditionally exclusive sport, our most exciting results have been through targeted and intensive programmes of activity. The most effective initiative has been our Rowing Academies programme where full-time professional coaches are seconded into participating state schools.

Based on the success of this framework, and seeking to build a systematic link between sport and employability, London Youth Rowing's life skills programme, 'Breaking Barriers' was introduced in 2014. We feel that each training session, mentoring conversation and every race needs to be understood and exploited for its educational value. In doing so we hope to engender the non-cognitive traits which will promote progression into further education, employment and training.

The Role of Sport in Developing Life Skills, Employability and Enterprise

From its inception, LYR recognized the importance of efficient monitoring and evaluation to demonstrate success, to gain actionable insights, and of course to apply for future funding. Our preference for market-based accountability – and therefore our insistence upon a recognized impact assessment tool for Breaking Barriers – led us to AQR.

We became aware of AQR during the launch of Alan Milburn's Social Mobility Whitepaper in 2013 and came to understand that AQR shared a commitment to the issues which drive London Youth Rowing's work. Before formalizing our partnership with AQR, we explored a variety of tools and options. We made the decision to proceed with AQR for two main reasons. Firstly, AQR's 4Cs model was a good framework and the MTQ48 is a well-respected measurement tool for the seemingly intangible outcomes we sought. Equally important, however, AQR showed a genuine enthusiasm to partner with London Youth Rowing to support us and gain insights into the application of the MTQ48 test across our programmes.

Breaking Barriers

Figure 20.2 Breaking barriers

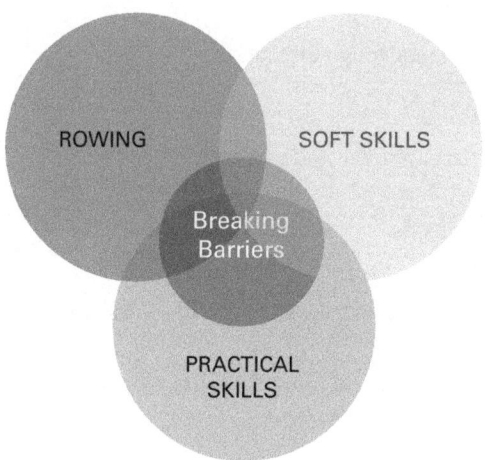

In September 2014, London Youth Rowing launched the Breaking Barriers pilot. Run alongside London Youth Rowing's participation and performance rowing programmes, this initiative links a rowing programme with corporate mentoring, skills sessions and providing project management. This helps students consciously to link the attributes they take from sport (and other disciplines) to the non-cognitive skills which will lead them into further positive outcomes in education and the workplace.

For a school to take part in Breaking Barriers the percentage of its students on Free School Meals (FSM) has to exceed the London average of 25 per cent.

To qualify for free school meals, the combined household income threshold is £16,190 per annum.

Students remain part of the programme for two years to ensure that they have the long-term support they need. The core objectives of the programme are as follows:

1 To develop the life skills of young people through a structured programme of rowing and mentoring.
2 To broaden the future aspirations of young people as to what is available after school.
3 To provide future pathways for young people into further education, training or employment.

The programme

The programme itself is highly structured. Year One focuses on providing participants with key skills, knowledge and behaviours that are applicable and useful both within school and outside school. The 4Cs mental toughness model is a constant theme throughout the session in year one. A key gaol is to build self efficacy – confidence and a sense of 'can do'.

Figure 20.3 4Cs mental toughness model

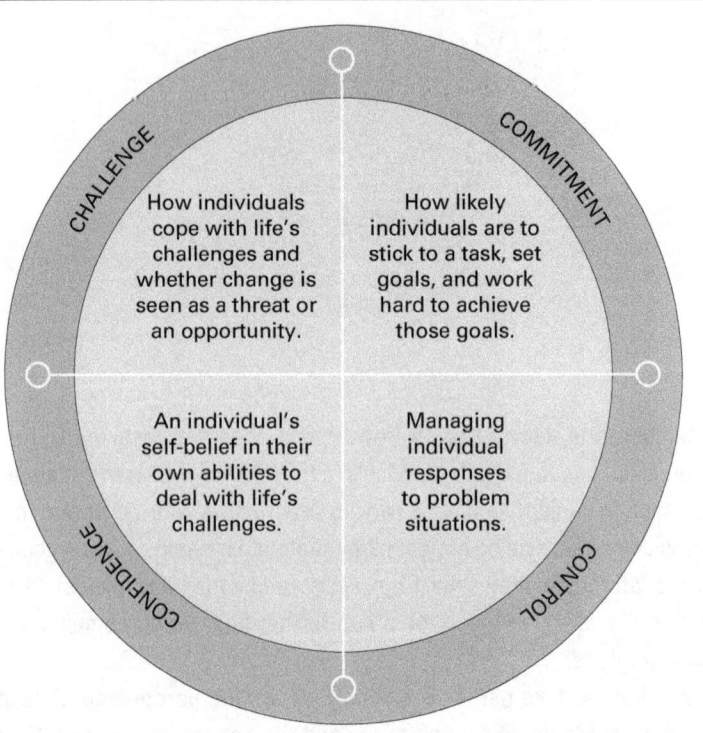

Year One Sessions embrace:

- time management;
- an introduction to project management;
- communications skills;
- goal setting;
- team working;
- defining a project team;
- presentation skills;
- pitching an idea;
- problem solving;
- overcoming project challenges;
- decision making;
- changing project briefs;
- networking.

The coaching and mentoring element encourages reflection and learning through participation.

Year Two Sessions

This builds on Year one. Now the focus of attention is to encourage participants to be involved in the development of the next cohort, supporting their learning. To which are added sessions which are now more directly focused on employability.

Year Two Sessions include:

- networking with year one students;
- branding and personal branding;
- career day session with mentors;
- CVs and personal statements;
- writing CVs
- interview techniques;
- mock interviews;

- leadership skills;
- coaching and mentoring skills;
- leadership and coaching in action.

Monitoring and measurement

Participants are tested at three intervals throughout to assess the impact of the programme using the MTQ48 test. The chart below shows improvements made (red bars) by the pilot cohort vs. a control group, and then progress so far this year by the 2015/16 cohort.

Figure 20.4 Monitoring and measurement

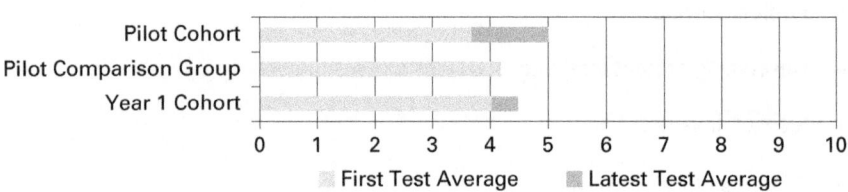

Interestingly, all participants have claimed to really enjoy the testing and particularly liked seeing their early development reports compared with those at the end of the process. The mentors found the coaching reports very useful and, for London Youth Rowing, it allowed us to match mentors with mentees based on the skill sets we thought would be most useful to each candidate.

Responses from participants and Mentors

Testimonials

Importantly, the feedback from corporate partners has been very encouraging. The senior partner at PricewaterhouseCooper (PwC), responsible for the establishment of the programme during its pilot phase, spoke of the benefits to his firm:

> As an employer it gives us a great opportunity to spot and nurture talent; it also – and I'm sure all the PwC and LYR participants will agree – gives us as individuals the chance to be part of something truly meaningful. For LYR I hope it's helped in the realization of their mission. But most importantly I hope and believe it has shown [these] fantastic young adults that despite clear challenges, social disadvantage can be overcome and should not be a barrier to achieving potential.

The Role of Sport in Developing Life Skills, Employability and Enterprise

Mentors, coaches and teachers all recognized the progress made by the students:

Following several skills sessions held between PwC and LYR, there was a notable difference in the way that the participants engaged in activities. Those who had less confidence were now confident enough to speak their opinions to the group.

Mentor

It's clear that their confidence has grown throughout the programme from the mentoring sessions. At first they were too self-conscious to ask many questions, but as the sessions have continued, so has their ability to analyse and evaluate their own performance. The feedback they receive is not so much one way – they really ask to understand what is being asked of them and apply this in a practical sense in their rowing.

Coach

Comparing the students now to how they were back in January, there is a real difference. Confidence, enthusiasm, motivation and a hard work attitude are now synonymous with our students.

Teacher

Not only have the young people on the programme made measurable progress in terms of their results on the MTQ48 test, now they are able to articulate that progress in more challenging environments and in more sophisticated terms.

I now know it is more important to get yourself in the right mindset, and I'm really proud of speaking to a room full of business people at the event that we helped to organise with PwC. I also won my first medal! My goals are more organised, to push myself, and to practice as much as I can by using the skills I have learnt on Breaking Barriers

Another participant writes:

Before starting Breaking Barriers I wasn't very confident, especially in situations where new people were involved as I felt shy. The past six months on the programme have taught me not to be afraid and to do new things.

Looking Forward

As Breaking Barriers matures we are aiming to further incorporate the insights, structures and resources that AQR offers.

In a bid to drive retention on the programme we will now seek to begin with more informal engagements in Key Stage 3 and progress gradually to the more formal learning environment of the Key Stage 4 mentoring sessions.

By introducing participants to rowing earlier in Key Stage 3 we will aim to establish social groups sooner and engender an enthusiasm for the sport ahead of the more structured mentoring in Year One. It is critical that participants are not to be shielded from experiencing the disappointment that inevitably sometimes comes with competition. While we acknowledge the importance of developing mental toughness through exposure to disappointment, at this transitional age, the focus will be mainly on enjoyment and in learning to win and lose as part of a team.

We will look to promote a sense of esprit de corps and introduce consistent messaging around key themes. In allowing a more informal introduction to the programme at a slightly more formative stage of the students' development, we hope that the later step into more sophisticated and conscious adjustments to mindset will feel more natural and therefore be more enduring and effective.

Beyond this, we will be looking at evolving our mentoring programme to incorporate Key Stage 5 wherein we will train the sixth formers to be mentors and coaches to their younger peers. We are keen that students identify more as leaders than performance athletes and will aim to weave this language into our programmes in the future. This important distinction will allow students to demonstrate leadership qualities in a number of ways, but importantly, always by example.

AQR is a very important and valued partner for LYR. As Breaking Barriers grows and improves, we see AQR as a key contributor in helping to refine and improve our model. The ongoing support we receive and the exciting new resources being developed will all be vital components in allowing LYR to develop the programmes which are so important to us and hopefully to the young people we exist to support.

Summary

These two case studies are excellent examples of how sport can be an extremely useful vehicle for the development of life, employability and enterprise skills. The good news is that there are many more examples in existence and even more instances where there are opportunities to begin something like this. Although the impact in both cases has been positive, it is worth noting that success in such environments is in part due to the relationships established by the deliverer. As noted by Holt Tamminen, Tink and Black (2009) p160, following an interpretative analysis of 40 interviews:

> 'sport can provide an educational context for acquiring life skills but highlight that interactions with key social agents (peers, parents and coaches) are crucial components of how people learn life skills through their involvement in sport. In particular, peer interactions appeared to be the most meaningful aspects of youth sport participation'.

In terms of employability, sport itself is a valuable economic resource. Sport England figures show that in 2010, sport and sport-related activity contributed £20.3 billion to the English economy – 1.9 per cent of the English total. Moreover, the contribution of sport to employment is vast. It is estimated to support over 400,000 full-time equivalent jobs, 2.3 per cent of all jobs in England. The same report on economic costs values healthcare savings (even after sport-related injuries) to be between £1,750 and £6,900 per person.

These are direct economic outcomes of sport participation. When we consider the indirect outcomes as a result of learning invaluable life skills and growing in confidence through sport participation, as the case studies in this chapter exemplify, the employment impact of sport is overwhelmingly positive and important.

References

Bredemeier, B J and Shields, D L (2006) Sports and character development, *Research Digest President's Council on Physical Fitness and Sports*, 7, 1–8

Clough, P J, Earle, K and Sewell, D (2002) Mental toughness: The concept and its measurement. In I Cockerill (Ed) *Solutions in sport psychology* pp 32–43) Thomson, London

Holt, N L, Tamminen, K A, Tink, L N and Black, D E (2009) An interpretive analysis of life skills associated with sport participation. *Qualitative Research in Sport and Exercise*, 1, 160–175

Merkel, D L (2013) Youth sport: Positive and negative impact on young athletes, *Open Access Journal of Sports Medicine*, 4, 151–160

Sport England (2015) *Active people survey*. Available at: https://www.sportengland.org/research

Treasure, D C (2001) Enhancing young people's motivation in youth sport: An achievement goal approach. In G C Roberts (Ed), *Advances in motivation in sport and exercise*, pp 79–100, Human Kinetics, Champaign, IL

INDEX

4Cs model of mental toughness 43–54, 253, 261, 261
  challenge 45, 49, 51
  commitment 45, 48, 51
  confidence 45, 50, 51
  control 45, 46–47, 51

abilities 39–40
ability tests 133
academic qualifications 83
Access to Higher Education Diplomas 126
achieving potential 36
action plan, considering the way forward 169, 174–76
Affirmations 185
Alternative Education setting 94
altruism 37
ambition 36, 37
anxiety control 189
apprenticeships 67, 85, 103–04
  advanced apprenticeships 141
  at Further Education Colleges 142
  Catch22 organization 228–31
  programmes in the USA 215–17
  with employers 141
AQR International Ltd 15, 24, 33, 43, 186–88, 196, 261, 266
aspirations, and mental toughness 44
assertiveness 37, 42, 51
assessment centres 131–33
  ability tests 133
  personality tests 133
  preparation for the day 132
attentional control 190–92
attitude 9, 32, 181
  and mental toughness 45
  as reason for new recruit failure 68
  to work 81
Aviva 15

BAE Systems and the Outward Bound Trust case study 103
Bailey, Tom 212
Barclays Apprenticeship Programme 85
Barclays Bank 15
  recruitment 84–85
Big 5 model (Cattell) 189
Bradford Pathways initiative 85–87, 90
brain drains 2

Branson, Richard 93, 100
Breaking Barriers 254, 260–66
Bridges Ventures 15
Busby, Sir Matt 255
Business Class Girls into Technology event 84
Business in the Community 90, 107

Capita 15
Care2Work case study 230–31
Career and Technical Education (CTE) model 86
career change, employability advice 127–29
  acquiring new skills and qualifications 127
  investigating the prospective job 127–28
  providing accurate information in applications 128
  use of social media 128–29
Career Connect 11, 13, 14–15, 33, 72–80
career guidance
  adapting to changes in society 1–2
  early access to good guidance 12–14
Career WorkOut 87–90
  developing confidence and resilience 89
  STEPS employability skills 88
CareerEDGE model of graduate employability 55–62
  advantages 58–59
  applications 58–59
  career development learning 56
  degree subject knowledge 55, 56
  emotional intelligence 58
  Employability Development Profile 59–62
  generic skills 57
  life experience 56
  skills and understanding 55, 56
  University of Central Lancashire case study 62
  University of Lancaster case study 61
  work experience 56–57
Careers and Enterprise Company 12, 14, 120
Careers Lab 83–84
careers
  access to information about options 83–90
  making the best choices 109–18

Index

CARRUS measure   40–41
CARRUS model   9, 33–42
   abilities   39–40
   dealing with problems   34–35
   development process   33–34
   interpersonal skills   37–39, 40
   motivations and drivers   36–37, 40
CARRUS profile   41
Catch22 organization   13, 219–32
   apprenticeships   228–31
   appropriate routes into work   228–32
   building mental toughness or 'resilience'   221–23
   building the right mindset   220–21
   Care2Work case study   230–31
   developing strong relationships and networks   223–28
   Entourage case study   224–27
   history of   219
   Launch22 case study   227–28
   Project New Horizons case study   222–23
   supporting 'disadvantaged' people   219–32
   unearthing talent   220–21
challenge   45, 49, 51
character   44
Charlton, Sir Bobby   255
Chichester College case study   160–63
China
   background to entrepreneurship education issues   193–94
   development of entrepreneurship education   194–97
   education models and methods   198–99
   employability education   197–98
   entrepreneurship education   197–98
   likely future trends   200
   methods of entrepreneurship education   198–99
Cineworld   37–38
client satisfaction view of employability   32
Clough, Peter   43, 44, 73
coaching for employability and enterprise   167–79
   case study using MTQ48   176–78
   clients with mental health problems   235–50
   GROW coaching model   169–76
Cognitive Behavioural Therapy (CBT)   185
commitment   45, 47–48, 51
community colleges in the USA   203–18
completion of commitments   48, 51
confidence   45, 50, 51
   definition   50
   in own abilities   50, 51
   interpersonal   50, 51

conscientiousness   36
continuous improvement   35
continuous personal development   36, 37
Continuous Professional Development   13
control   45, 46–47, 51
coping strategies   183–83
creative industries, skills shortages   67
Creighton, Ted   104
Cusdin, Alan   89
customer service, emphasis on   8
CV preparation   127

decision learning   56
deeper learning concept   212
delivering employability programmes   98–100
desire to do things right   36
digital industries, skills shortages   67
digital natives   4–5
Digital Passport   122
digital visitors   4
disadvantage
   environmental and socio-economic factors   3
   see also   Catch22 organization; mental health problems
doing things right and doing things better   35
DOTS model   56
drive and motivation   36–37, 40
Dweck, Carol   43, 216

Eades, John   253
education
   about enterprise and entrepreneurship   155–56
   as the bedrock of sustainable growth   24–25
   choice of subjects and qualifications   83
   higher education participation rates by area   3
   improving employability of young people   10–11
   influence on mobility   2–3
   millennials in higher education   2
   vocational and academic qualifications   83
   see also   schools
emotional control   47, 51
emotional intelligence   37
   and professional success   101–103
emotional management   51
employability
   as a transferable skill   7
   challenges to overcome   12–15
   defining   7–12, 31–21
   effects of social change   1–2

Index

employer's perspective   8–12
growing importance of   17–30
individual perspective   7–8
lifetime perspective   8
link to enterprise and
  entrepreneurship   29
mechanisms to improve   4
older people   15
employability advice
  for young people   117–23
  second chance education   125–27
  those seeking a career change   127–29
employability development, delivery sources   16
Employability Development Profile (EDP)   59–62
employability measurement tools   59–62
employability programmes
  approach to delivery   98–100
  for 'pushed-out' children   93–100
  funding for   14–15
employees
  empowerment   37–39
  engagement   37–39
employers
  assessing employee development needs   11–12
  perspective on employability   8–12
  valued behaviours   3–4
  websites of   82
employment environment, ongoing changes   82
empowerment of employees   37–39
enterprise   28
  barriers to   155
  education about   155–56
  link with employability   29
  NACUE case studies   158–66
  NACUE programme   156–58
Entourage case study   224–27
entrepreneurial mindset   155–56, 157
entrepreneurs, distinction from business owners   29–30
entrepreneurship   28–29
  barriers to   155
  education about   155–56
  link with employability   29
  NACUE case studies   158–66
  NACUE programme   156–58

Facework   93, 96, 98–100
first impressions   83
Football Foundations   254
Force Field analysis   115, 172
Four Branch Model (Mayer and Salovey)   58

Gatsby Foundation   14
gender differences, entry into higher education   2
Generation Y   1, 5
Generation Z   1, 5
global perspectives   *see*   China; United States
goal orientation   48, 51
goal setting   51, 189–90
goals   169, 170–72
Goddard Consultants, helping clients with mental health problems   235–50
Goleman, Daniel   58
Gordon, Kieran   15
graduate employability
  defining   55
  measurement tools   59–62
  see also   CareerEDGE model
graduate internships
  applying for   143–44
  commitment to   145
  feedback   145–46
  follow-up afterwards   145–46
  potential route to a job offer   144
  references from   145
grit   43, 221
GROW coaching model   169–76
  Goals   169, 170–72
  Reality   169, 172–73
  Options   169, 174, 175–76
  Way forward   169, 174–76
  preparing the coachee for the coaching experience   170
growing capability   36
Güney, Stacey   8, 15

Hudson, Dr Maria   158
Hult International Business School   12

illness beliefs and behaviour   238–43
in-tray exercises   134
individual perspective on employability   7–8
influencing others   37
internships
  applying for   143–44
  commitment to   145
  feedback   145–46
  follow-up afterwards   145–46
  how to optimize their impact   147–52
  potential route to a job offer   144
  references from   145
interpersonal skills   37–39, 40
  development   101–102
  development case studies   102–07

Index

interviews 133–40
  arriving in good time 135–36
  asking questions 139
  be ready for unusual questions 138
  body language 138
  dress code 136
  drinking water 139
  feedback if unsuccessful 140
  follow-up afterwards 139–40
  in-tray exercises 134
  planning and preparing for 82–83
  presentations 135
  reflection after the interview 139
  research beforehand 134
  shaking hands 138–39
  smiling 136–37
  think about questions and answers beforehand 136–37
  what employers look for 133–34

Jenkins, Anthony 85
job action plan 115–17
job shadowing 152
Jobcentres 124
jobs
  changing over time 110
  churn in types of jobs 110
  extent of the choice 110
  investigating the options 110–18
  making the best choices 109–18
  RACPAC investigation process 110–18
Jones, Dr Steven 150–51

Klaus, Peggy 95
Kolb Learning Styles model 183

labour market
  massive change in 69–72
  preparing to enter 82–90
Launch22 case study 227–28
Le Gallais, Tricia 151
learned helplessness 44, 124
learned optimism 44
learning from experience 51
life control 47, 51
Life Skill qualifications 126
life skills 68–69
lifelong learning, responses in the USA 202–18
lifetime perspective on employability 8
LinkedIn 128–29
London Youth Rowing 11, 13
  case study 260–66
Luminary Bakery 12, 13
  case study 104–07

Manchester Metropolitan University case study 56
Manchester United Foundation 13
Marantz, Professor 7
mechanical reasoning 40
mental health problems 235–50
  Achieve! initiative 238
  assessing mental toughness through MTQ48 243–44
  barriers to employability 236–37
  beliefs and illness behaviour 238–43
  client profiles 245–49
  coaching conversations 244–45
  coaching tools 244–45
  Goddard Consultants employability coaching 235–50
  mental toughness-based approach 238, 239–43
mental skills, acquiring and developing skills 70–71
mental toughness
  and aspirations 44
  and employability 46
  and goals 170–72
  and mental health 243–44
  and performance 44
  and positive behaviour 44
  and wellbeing 44
  approach for clients with mental health problems 238, 239–43
  appropriate level of 182–83
  assessing options 175–76
  building 221–23
  coaching 183–84
  considering the way forward 175–76
  coping strategies 182–83
  definition 44
  developing 181–92
  key employability competencies 51
  Manchester Metropolitan University case study 54
  realistic perspective 172–73
  relationship with enterprise and employability 50–53
  role of reflection 184–85
  role of sport 253
  tools and techniques to develop 185–92
  what we can do about it 181–83
Mental Toughness model 43–54, 73–80, 261, 262
  4Cs framework 43–54
  challenge 45, 49, 51
  commitment 45, 47–48, 51
  confidence 45, 50, 51
  control 45, 46–47, 51
  mental toughness scale 45–54

Index

metacognition skills 212
Micro-Tyco 156
millennial generation 1–2
   access to better information 5
   characteristics of 5–7
   digital natives 4–5
   views on work 5
mindset 9, 43
   and mental toughness 45
   coaching 183–84
   coping strategies 182–83
   developing 181–92
   role of reflection 184–85
   tools and techniques to develop 185–92
   what we can do about it 181–83
mobility of well-educated people 2
models of employability 31–62
   CareerEDGE model 55–62
   CARRUS model 33–42
   DOTS model 56
   Four Branch Model 58
   Mental Toughness model 43–54, 73–80, 261, 262
   USEM employability model 32
motivation and drive 36–37, 40
MTQ48 psychometric tool 45, 46, 73–80, 261, 263, 265
   coaching case study 176–78
   mental toughness and mental health 243–44
My Vocational Situation Diagnostic Form (MVSDF) 59

NACUE (National Association of College and University Entrepreneurs)
   case studies 158–66
   programme 156–58
National Enterprise Challenge 156
NEET (not in education, employment or training) 88, 223
Nelson, Tony 89
Neurolinguistic Programming (NLP) 185
neuroscience, developments in 69–71
New Horizons programme 73–80
   positive impact 76–80
   return on investment 80–76
Newcastle under Lyme College case study 163–65
Next Steps Evening (Titus Salt School) 87
non-cognitive skills, importance of 3–4
non-verbal ability 40
Northbrook College case study 158–59
numerical ability 39

O*NET database of occupational information 111–12

Obama, President Barack 218
OCR Employability and Life & Living accreditation 96
OCR's Project Approach case study 102
offenders
   importance of employability development 25–28
   wider benefits of learning 27–28
Open Awards 126
open mindedness 51
opportunity awareness 56
options, assessing 169, 174, 175–76
organization of the individual 35
Outward Bound Trust case studies 103

Pedagogy for Employability Group generic skills list 57
performance, and mental toughness 44
personal competence 102
personality
   developments in understanding 69–71
   tests 133
positive attitude 49, 51
positive behaviour, and mental toughness 44
positive thinking 185–88
Premier League Community Fund (PLCF) 254
preparedness to stretch oneself 49
prison service 12
   developing employability of offenders 25–28
   wider benefits of learning 27–28
proactive approach 37
problems
   active problem solving 35
   dealing with 34–35
Project New Horizons case study 222–23
psychometric testing 11, 69–70, 133
   see also MTQ48

qualifications
   requirements in addition to 67–69
   skills shortages 67–68

RACPAC process 110–18
   Research all the facts and options 110–13
   Analyse to consider alternatives 114–15
   Consider the consequences 115
   Plan of action 115–17
   Action to implement the plan 117
   Check your decision 117
   Change your mind or confirm your decision 117–18
realistic perspective 169, 172–73

Index

recruitment
    attributes employers look for   8–9
    better evaluation of desired skills   11–12
    failure rate of new recruits   68
    problem areas for employers   9–10
    skills that managers want most   10–11
Reflex youth charity   105, 106, 107
resilience   44, 72, 221–23
    skills to improve   71
Rhodes, Richard   214
risk taking   51
Robinson, Ken   98

Saturday jobs   94
schools   17–25
    change in focus   19–22
    development across three areas   22–24
    funding for innovation   18–19
    importance of soft skills development   17–18
    see also education
Schumpeter, Joseph   4
second chance education   125–25
    Life Skill qualifications   126
    preparing a CV   127
    types of qualifications   125–26
    volunteering as valuable experience   126
    ways to gain qualifications   125–26
self-awareness   56
self-belief   51
self-confidence   58, 72
    development   101–102
    development case studies   102–07
self-efficacy   51, 58
self-employment   6, 8   *see also* enterprise; entrepreneurship
self-esteem   58
self-presentation to potential employers   83
Self Talk   185–88
Siegel, Daniel   70
skills
    importance of non-cognitive skills   3–4
    new approaches to evaluation   11–12
    that managers want most   10–11
    see also soft skills
Skills for Learning and Employment   126
skills shortages   4, 67–68, 84
    in the USA   206–07
SMART goals   170, 190
SMARTER goals   172
Soccer Club Foundations   254
social competence   102
Social Impact Bonds   14–15, 74
social media use and employability   128–29
social mobility

    and social and emotional skills   17
    decline of   67
    factors influencing life chances   67
socio-emotional skills   3–4
soft skills   9, 68–69, 94, 95
    demystifying   95–100
    development in schools   17–18
sport
    accessible role models   252
    and mental toughness   253
    as a metaphor for life   251–54
    benefits of   252–53
    character building   252–53
    continuous improvement approach   253
    dealing with failure   253
    economic benefits   267
    London Youth Rowing case study   260–66
    looking forward   266–67
    Manchester United Foundation case study   255–59
    role in developing employability   251–67
    role in developing life skills   251–67
standards, concern for   36
STEM areas, skills shortages   67, 84
STEPS (self-management, team work, enterprise awareness, problem solving, speaking and listening) employability skills   88, 96–97
Stork Stand technique   191
Student Engine case study   165–66
study, making the best choices   109 18
SWOT analysis   172 177

TalentSmart   102
team working   37
tenacity   51
The Measure of Guidance Impact tool   59
Tracy, Brian   189
transferable skills   156
transition learning   56
Triodos Ethical Bank   15
trust between employers and employees   37–39
Twitter   128–29

unemployment
    effects of   15
    environmental and socio-economic factors   3
    supporting successful transition to work   72–80
United States
    apprenticeship programmes   215–17
    badges to designate skills   214–15

changing outlook on employability skills 217–18
competency-based education 213–17
employers' focus on soft skills 203
four most in-demand competencies 212
initiatives to redesign the community college 208–12
integration of education and workplace learning 204
job market 203
Kingsborough Community College's programme 213
lifelong learning 203–18
preparing for an increasingly diverse workforce 205–07
preparing students for college-level work 208
role of the community colleges 203–18
skills shortages 206–07
University of Central Lancashire case study 62
University of Lancaster case study 61
university work placements 142–43
USEM employability model 32
Uxbridge College case study 160

verbal ability 39–40
visualization 188–89
vocational education 3, 8
   for older people 15
vocational qualifications 83, 101, 155–56
Volkswagen Group UK and the Outward Bound Trust case study 103
volunteering as valuable experience 126

Webster, Kate 89
well-being
   and mental toughness 44
   skills to improve 71
Westminster Kingsway College case study 159
women, entry into higher education 2
work, changes in the nature of 4
work experience
   finding a placement 94
   lack of 81–82, 94
   value for young people 94
   see also internships
work experience effectiveness 147–52
   age to undertake it 148
   challenges for schools 152
   how to do it 151
   job shadowing 152

relevance for different courses 149–51
sourcing work experience 151
timing in the school year 148–49
what to do 149
who takes part in work experience 149–51
work placements
   university work placements 142–43
   see also graduate internships; internships
workforce
   digital natives 4–5
   patterns of change 2–4
working with others 37
workplace, massive change in 69–72
Worktree 88–90

Yeager, David 216
Yorke, Professor Mantz 31, 32, 55
young people
   access to information about options 83–90
   connecting with employers 95
   creating links with the world of work 93–100
   employability advice 119–25
      accept all help offered 124–25
      advice applies to all ages 124
      applying without the necessary qualifications 123–24
      awards and achievements 121–22
      building a portfolio 122
      career direction and subject choices 120
      Digital Passport 122
      early guidance on subject choices 119–20
      lateral thinking for job and career options 121
      learning about the job-hunting process 121
      membership of clubs and groups 120–21
      ways to gain work experience 120
      what employers actually want 123
      work experience follow-up 122–23
   failure rate of new recruits 68
   preparation for working life 68–69
   preparing to enter the labour market 82–90
youth offending service 12
youth unemployment, supporting successful transition to work 72–80